# GOD IN CAPTIVITY

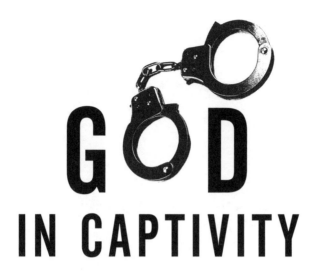

# GOD
# IN CAPTIVITY

### THE RISE OF FAITH-BASED
### PRISON MINISTRIES
### *IN THE AGE OF*
### MASS INCARCERATION

## TANYA ERZEN

Beacon Press
Boston

BEACON PRESS
Boston, Massachusetts
www.beacon.org

Beacon Press books
are published under the auspices of
the Unitarian Universalist Association of Congregations.

20 19 18 17    8 7 6 5 4 3 2 1

This book is printed on acid-free paper that meets the uncoated paper
ANSI/NISO specifications for permanence as revised in 1992.

Text design by and composition by Kim Arney

Many names and other identifying characteristics of prisoners mentioned
in this work have been changed to protect their identities.

*Library of Congress Cataloging-in-Publication Data*

Names: Erzen, Tanya, author.
Title: God in captivity : the rise of faith-based prison ministries in the
    age of mass incarceration / Tanya Erzen.
Description: Boston, Massachusetts : Beacon Press, [2017] | Includes
    bibliographical references and index.
Identifiers: LCCN 2016034638 (print) | LCCN 2016038621 (ebook) |
    ISBN 9780807089989 (hardcover : alk. paper) | ISBN 9780807089996 (e-book)
Subjects: LCSH: Church work with prisoners—United States. |
    Prisoners—Religious life. | Religious work with prisoners—United States.
Classification: LCC BV4340 .E745 2017 (print) | LCC BV4340 (ebook) | DDC
    259/.50973—dc23
LC record available at https://lccn.loc.gov/2016034638

*To the*
*FEPPS students*
*at WCCW*

# CONTENTS

# REDEMPTION AND PUNISHMENT

IT'S HARD TO FOCUS ON ANYTHING, much less the Book of Jeremiah, when the air presses against your skin like steam, and it's not even 9 a.m. In Louisiana, a May morning like this portends a truly oppressive day, and for prisoners, one without the reprieve of shade, air-conditioning, or privacy. For the three women missing from the college class, sent to disciplinary segregation for violating one rule or another, the small room each is confined to twenty-three of twenty-four hours a day is a sweltering prison within a prison. The chapel classroom is an alternative to the "hole," even with the cinder-block monotony of its walls disrupted only by a map of Jerusalem in the time of Jesus. Monica renews her focus. She has a final exam next week, and this is the professor's review session. What are the symbolic acts in Jeremiah, the professor asks. Monica, scrutinizing her Bible on the battered table, must describe the meaning of the basket of figs and which prophet saved Jeremiah, if she is going to pass.

In the Louisiana Correctional Institute for Women (LCIW), her home for fifteen years, Monica is one of twelve hundred women. Here in class, she is one of only twenty. The defining facts of her existence are numerical: forty-six years old, eight children and three grandchildren, Louisiana Department of Correction number 405636, a forty-seven-year sentence, a one-in-a-thousand chance of a pardon in a state where pardons are rarer than snow. Monica is also a student working on her college degree in

Christian ministry. She's sassy and weary. Others listen when she speaks in class. With her sharp cheekbones accentuated by hair piled high on her head, she exudes a flair that defies the drabness of her prison-issued blue shirt.

As Monica and others listen, the professor, Dr. Kristi Miller, drills them on potential final exam questions: "How long were they in captivity in chapter 25?" The class answers automatically, "Seventy-five years." There are a lot of murmurs and sighs. Class discussion veers suddenly from exam prep into existential territory. Jeremiah is a book about being oppressed by a foreign power (the Babylonians) but also about how faith in God freed the Israelites. "God does not play with those who oppress others for their own gain. God takes seriously those who abuse their position of power," Miller explained. The discussion becomes more animated, and theology suddenly seems sharply relevant. "Is the book of Jeremiah implying that punishment and suffering are necessary before freedom?" Monica asks. Captivity, according to this interpretation, is an inevitable prelude to freedom, and captivity is meaningful as long as one has faith. The chilling lesson resonates in this maximum-security prison where most students are lifers without even the possibility of parole, and freedom, in the absence of any real hope of release, can only be a state of mind.

Monica is grateful to be in school. There is no other way to obtain an associate's degree or four-year bachelor's degree in a Louisiana prison except through the Baptist seminary. For the past five years, I have directed a secular college program, almost weekly, in a maximum-security women's prison. I visited the Louisiana program and other prisons to understand how faith-based groups are shaping the religious life of prison and as someone engaged in the field of higher education and incarceration. My dual role as a professor, writer, and program director enabled me to gain access to many prison programs that might otherwise have been closed to me.

Prison is about time, relentless and banal, and Monica has the relative privilege of spending her days in the chapel, in class, and in the computer lab or library. Monica and her classmates are a sea of pink, yellow, gray, and blue T-shirts and prison denim, as each woman quietly defies the prison garb regulations. For a moment, it seems they could be in an adult education class anywhere. Three women are assigned to each of the coveted laptop computers, and tensions surface over who gets to use them. Like harried college students, they fret about their papers, due in a few days. Monica is nonplussed. She's been in prison for many years and has already graduated from culinary arts, tutored other women preparing to take the General Educational Development or GED test, and worked in the hospice program and infirmary. How difficult could it be to understand the symbolic acts of the book of Jeremiah?

When Monica completes her bachelor's degree in Christian ministry as part of the New Orleans Baptist Theological Seminary's (NOBTS) first graduating class, she won't return to the free world. She and her classmates will be sent forth to spread the word of God and, the seminary hopes, reduce violence throughout the vast state prison system. Monica also studies English composition, math, and world history, but the college degree is secondary to NOBTS's ultimate purpose: widespread conversion. Monica and others will become emissaries of moral rehabilitation and, according to the seminary's statement of purpose, will "evangelize their peers within all areas of the prison and other institutions of the Louisiana Department of Corrections." The seminary's mission is to win unbelievers to Jesus, and the prison system hopes to find a way to manage the vast numbers of people who fill its cells: the state of Louisiana has a higher incarceration rate than any country in the world.[1] The prison system has placed its faith in Christian prisoners who will, it is hoped, spread moral reform and produce an acquiescence to their own captivity.

Today, all over the United States, with federal assistance and private volunteerist zeal, a quiet faith-based revolution is taking place in fits and starts in state and federal prisons from minimum to maximum security. Christian prison ministries, religious volunteers, policymakers, conservative politicians, fiscal conservatives, private contractors, and evangelical and nondenominational Christians all attest to the power of faith to transform people in prison. Whereas prison authorities and outsiders have long viewed prisoners' claims to religious conversion and transformation a ruse, a way of convincing others that they were reformed, supporters of ministry tout faith-based interventions in prison as the most effective form of rehabilitation. Once derided and trivialized by skeptical prison authorities, prison ministry is now a legitimate rehabilitative program.

The prison ministry or faith-based group and the prison dovetail neatly because they attend to both the spiritual and material aspects of life in prison. Pat Nolan is a longtime champion of prison ministry and leader of Prison Fellowship, one of the largest Christian prison ministries in the world. Nolan, who first convinced politicians like Newt Gingrich and Grover Norquist to champion prison reform, says that Prison Fellowship will "help bring volunteers inside prisons to do the work the state just cannot afford to do on its own. And these volunteers will provide something that government employees cannot: love."[2]

The intervention of faith-based groups is based on the expectation that men and women in prison will become religiously redeemed, rather than simply rehabilitated subjects, by becoming conversant in or strengthening an already existing religious identity. Spiritually, faith-based groups argue that men and women in prison are not incorrigible criminals. Instead, prison ministries view people in prison as beings who always have the potential to be reformed. They operate on the principle that incarceration requires spiritual, not just political or economic, solutions. Their message is that, ultimately, God, Jesus, or the Holy Spirit transforms the hearts of prisoners, and that such transformation requires unwavering faith in God's power. The phrase "heart change" exemplifies the faith-based idea that religious belief will alter someone from the inside out. A transformed heart is a transformed prisoner who, in the view of prison ministries, will not return to prison. Thus, state and prison authorities desperate for a way to manage overcrowded prisons now support and sanction heart change.

"Faith," at first glance, appears to be an innocuous or neutral term, but in prison ministry, it most often stands for a Protestant form of Christianity. In many states, nondenominational Protestant Christians make up more than 85 percent of the volunteers who enter the prison. These statistics include the vast numbers of religious volunteers, working under the supervision of primarily Christian chaplains, who, throughout the day, regularly conduct worship services, Bible studies, AA and addiction groups, trauma counseling, GED programs, anger management programs, and mental health assessments in prison chapels.[3] But many groups and ministries call themselves faith-based or spiritual to avoid violating the establishment clause of the First Amendment, which prohibits government from favoring one religion over another.

The Baptist seminary in LCIW, where Monica resides, isn't exceptional. There are prison seminary programs in Louisiana, Texas, California, Georgia, Illinois, Michigan, Mississippi, New Mexico, Tennessee, and West Virginia. According to the Office of Justice Programs, almost all US prison systems offer faith-based worship services, and 93 percent also offer prayer groups.[4] In Florida, the state has created eleven "faith and character" or faith- and character-based institutions (FCBIs), entire prisons where religious volunteers administer classes, study groups, and educational programming. Evangelical groups like Prison Fellowship have over twenty thousand volunteers and oversee evangelical programs in 334 US prisons, jails, and detention centers. Prison Fellowship also operates a twenty-four-hour evangelical program in entire wings of state prisons.[5] In the Federal Bureau of Prisons, 41 percent of prisons operate or are developing faith-based residential programs where prisoners sleep, work, and study in an area of the prison dedicated to adherence to religious ideals. Kairos Prison Ministry and Horizon Prison Initiative, two other evangelical prison ministries that have been active since the 1970s, run faith-based dorms and retreats in federal and state prisons. In Texas, Georgia, Louisiana, Illinois, West Virginia, and Mississippi, people in prison can receive a degree in Christian ministry from Baptist seminaries and are then sent out as missionaries to other prisons. Mainline or progressive Protestants rarely hold services or studies in prisons today. Conservative Protestants have the monopoly on prison ministry.

In a prison system that no longer offers even the pretense of rehabilitation, faith-based programs allow massive numbers of Christians to enter and proselytize to those desperate for a lifeline. To some extent, religious volunteers also reflect the religious landscape of the areas where prisons are located, and often the chaplain of the prison, another product of America's intertwined history of prisons and faith, can forbid groups to meet if an outside volunteer cannot be found to run the group. Mujahid Farid, a former Muslim prisoner and activist who advocates for the release of aging men and women in prison, explained that a wide range of people are excluded from redemption. If you don't profess to being a born-again Christian, you don't receive help or consideration. In LCIW, for example, the chaplain knows of no self-identified Muslim prisoners. And when two Buddhist women, both from Vietnam, sought a faith-based group, they converted to Christianity.

The geographic reach of evangelicals in prison is a phenomenon of the past several decades, when mainly conservative churches began to view prisons as both a problem and a mission field. In many ways, the faith-based presence in the American prison system is a religious movement spurred by the belief that the conversion and salvation of the individual is also the salvation of the prison system itself. After 1970, the prison population skyrocketed 700 percent due to mandatory sentencing laws and drug legislation. At the same time, educational, vocational, and other programs were stripped from the system because of escalating costs. Just as prison terms across the country lengthened, most rehabilitative programs disappeared.

In the aftermath of this profound shift, legal scholar Jonathan Simon labels US prisons a mere "waste management system" for the poor and socially marginalized.[6] Social geographer Ruth Wilson Gilmore writes that mass incarceration is inextricable from the dismantling of systems of mass access to education, health care, social services, and jobs. The construction of prisons for mass incarceration resolved problems associated with surplus populations, surplus capital, and surplus state power. To explain this final point, Gilmore argues that, since the 1970s, "the state built itself by building prisons fashioned from surpluses that the newly developing political economy had not absorbed in other ways."[7]

The rise of post-1970s mass incarceration is not therefore merely about prisons per se, but more broadly about a transformation in the systems that define and distribute human value, including what precisely humans deserve, and who is accountable to provide this for them. Programs in prison are part of this equation. Several incarcerated women at Bedford Hills Correctional Facility for Women in New York evaluated the effects of a college program there, writing in a coauthored article, "Rehabilitation looks like radical language now that punishment is the explicit project of incarceration."[8] New York and other states withdrew funding from prisons, while consigning astronomical numbers of people to exist inside them.

Today, the US incarceration rate of about seven hundred per one hundred thousand is the highest in the world and rivals the estimated rate for the Soviet Union at the height of the gulags in the 1950s. The United States has 5 percent of the world's population and 25 percent of the world's prisoners.[9] According to the Sentencing Project, the foremost think tank on incarceration in the United States, one of nine people serving time in prisons, including those convicted as juveniles, are serving a life sentence. The racial gulfs are glaring: "Black Americans are incarcerated five times more than whites, and Latinos are nearly twice as likely to be incarcerated as whites."[10] The United States also spends more than $80 billion on prisons each year.[11] These figures don't take into account the cost, economic and personal, to the children and family members of those in prison, and how they are trapped in an ongoing cycle of generational absence and pain. Black children today are less likely to be raised by two parents than they were in slavery because of the high imprisonment rate of African American men and women.

Faith-based volunteers and ministries provide something that has always been the bottom line of the punishment industry in the United States: they save money. Faith-based programs have grown as a result of policy initiatives—particularly during George W. Bush's presidency—but economic constraint helped to solidify the programs' hold as a solution for prisons.[12] With the evisceration of social services outside the prison, and the subsequent dismantling of mental health care and college education in the prison, the corps of free labor drawn from conservative, nondenominational, faith-based groups has filled the void created by budget cuts, stepping in to do the work of the state. As access to educational, vocational, and recreational programming that is secular, non-Christian, or even mainline Protestant has diminished, Christian ministries like Prison Fellowship, Kairos, and Horizons have flourished within American prisons. Most jails and state prisons now commonly support religious classes and groups as alternatives and replacements for traditional programs like job training and education. In the prison where boredom and lethargy reign, faith-based groups provide some of the only available programs. They frequently administer everything from trauma counseling to Bible studies, GED preparation, and mental health services in cash-strapped prisons.

Prisoners whose families can't or won't visit sometimes spend years without contact from outside, what men in Louisiana State Penitentiary, or Angola, refer to as "free people." They find solace in religious volunteers who show up every week, in services and in the certitude of belief.

There is the love that someone like Pat Nolan professes religious volunteers bring and, then, there is money. Individual redemption and financial austerity have melded together at a time when even the president of the United States heralds reforming the prison system as a key priority. In prison, the evangelical belief that personal transformation is the cornerstone of change melds with social theories that emphasize individual freedom and personal responsibility. In free-market evangelicalism, transformation resides in the individual, not in the social body.[13] Heart change and fiscal austerity have underpinned the bipartisan efforts at prison reform, such as the unlikely alliances between the American Civil Liberties Union (ACLU), the Koch Institute, funded by the conservative billionaires Charles and David Koch, and groups like Right on Crime, whose signatories hail from the upper echelon of the conservative wing of the Republican Party.

The faith-based ministries flock to prisons to convert, pray, teach, and proselytize, but they tend to neglect why people end up there in the first place. In the prison where I direct a college program, there are few wealthy people with college degrees. Whereas at the elite liberal arts school where I am a professor, my students come from primarily middle- and upper-class families. My prison students, 90 percent of whom report childhood abuse and sexual and domestic violence, do not have parents who went to college; they mainly grew up poor and contend daily with addictions and mental illness. Women represent the fastest-growing segment of the prison population in the United States. The United States has one-third of the world's female prisoners. Initially, the War on Drugs disproportionately affected African American women. In recent years, the number of white and Latina women imprisoned for violent offenses and property offenses has increased substantially. The rising rates of low-income white women having contact with the criminal justice system are likely a consequence of the recent sharp deterioration in their health and social conditions.[14]

When Monica, the NOBTS student, graduated from high school in Shreveport, Louisiana, she was smoking marijuana and within a few years became addicted to crack. "The only time I was clean was in jail," she says. "And, the longest I stayed clean was six months. Idle time is the devil's workshop. Same cycle, same cycle." During these years, she gave birth to her first five children and struggled constantly to feed and care for them. On one occasion, she stole two pairs of jeans from JCPenney and was arrested for shoplifting. There were other shoplifting charges for clothing and food. She continued to have more children as she moved in and out of jail. In spring 2004, Monica and a friend drove to a Kroger grocery store in an old Chrysler with license plates pilfered from another car. Monica had a fake ID doctored to match the name on a stolen checkbook. She loaded up her shopping cart with four cans of Similac baby formula, two giant packages of diapers, T-shirts, and a purse for herself. When she realized the sympathetic cashier to whom she hoped to pass the bad check wasn't working that day, she rolled the overflowing cart out the door. A Kroger employee chased her through the exit; she abandoned the cart and sprinted for the car, where her friend was waiting in the driver's seat.

Accounts of what happened next vary. Monica says she plunged into the driver's side and tussled with her friend behind the steering wheel. With the door ajar, the car jerked forward. Danny Maguire, a seventy-four-year-old Kroger employee, was stacking grocery carts. The Chrysler knocked him down, ran over both his legs, and kept zigzagging down the street. Employees followed and retrieved the plate number. At the hospital, doctors treated Maguire for a broken leg and various contusions, but that night he died of cardiorespiratory failure. He had a history of heart disease that was exacerbated by the collision, but the doctor listed Maguire's death as homicide. Police found Monica within days. The courts deemed her a habitual offender and sentenced her to forty-seven years in prison because they took her juvenile crimes into account. (Louisiana is one of only two states that uses juvenile records as evidence that someone is a habitual offender and therefore deserves a life sentence.) Monica maintains she was not driving, despite conflicting witness testimony. The value of the merchandise in the abandoned cart was $270.

Should Monica be punished indefinitely? What does it mean if she says she has been redeemed? Are forty-seven years enough time, and enough time for what? As I discuss in chapter 2, the rationale for prison has morphed and overlapped through the centuries: to punish, to redeem, to avenge, to warehouse, to extract profit, and to reform. Prison officials, the public, reformers, and prisoners themselves have put forth conflicting ideas about the purpose of prisons.

Captivity has long been a resonant theme in American life. Caleb Smith, in his book on prisons in the American imagination, argues that the captivity narrative in which Native Americans held white English colonists in bondage can be understood as the first distinctly American genre and may have been an ideological source for the creation of the penitentiary.[15] The famous account from the colonial era of Mary Rowlandson, who, while held captive by Indians, took solace in her Christian faith, is one of the most well-known examples.[16] Captivity invoked its inverse—liberty and freedom. As Toni Morrison writes in *Playing in the Dark*, the liberated American self emerged in contrast to an enslaved other.[17] These zones of captivity are also present in contemporary war prisons and detention centers, where redemption is forgotten and endless incapacitation and captivity are the norm. Thus, captivity saturates the ideas of who is human, what is sovereignty, and whether the condition of unfreedom is permanent or contingent.

Evangelical Christians, Quakers, and Methodists built the first American penitentiaries in the late 1700s as alternatives to hanging people or confining them in stockades. These Christian reformers fervently believed that prisons were places where people would do penance for their crimes, and that prayer, solitude, and labor were the avenue to a reformed self. The architects of the prisons called them "penitentiaries" because they were convinced that prisons spurred individual penitence that might reshape prisoners' inner lives. Therefore, from the very first American prisons, religious redemption has been uneasily but inextricably bound to punishment. A prison chaplain in the early 1800s noted gloomily, "Preaching a religion of brotherly love to convicts while you are treating them upon a basis of hatred is a discouraging performance."[18] How a person preaches love and solidarity within a hateful institution is the ongoing paradox of mass incarceration. Early reformers of the penitentiary considered themselves humanitarians and defined their institutions as a contrast to the horror of slave plantations. They represented the penitentiary as a space that prepared the prisoner for freedom, even if it was provoked by the lash and solitude.

Today, although they exist throughout the United States, faith-based prison programs are notably flourishing in the most notorious prisons in Louisiana, Texas, Mississippi, Georgia, Florida, and Kentucky. These states are the world leaders in imprisonment, with more than eleven hundred per one hundred thousand residents in prison or jail.[19] Most of the prisons with Baptist seminaries or a significant faith-based presence are on the site of former slave plantations or convict-leasing farms, where bodies were once measured solely in profit and loss. The faith-based resurgence is strongest in these former sites of slavery and forced labor with the most violent histories of enslavement and white supremacy. In these places, the subjugation of black men and women reigned as a rationale. Penitence and redemption were immaterial.

Despite intermittent cycles of reform, the purpose of a prison has always been control; the ministries serve as agents of surveillance and authority and make it easier to maintain order in a prison, a subject I discuss in chapters 1 and 3 in relation to the seminaries in Louisiana State Penitentiary (Angola) and LCIW. Prison ministries have become carceral churches that enable prison administrators to monitor vast numbers of men and women in overcrowded situations. For many faith-based volunteers, God is akin to a warden who works through the prison to reform individuals. Jonathan Burnside, a criminologist who has written about faith-based units, reflects on the premise that faith-based ministries bolster the prison. "By making prisons more human and punishment more humane, faith-based units promote ethicality and legitimacy," he writes. "Faith-based units can be of great value—to keep faith in prison."[20] Burnside's quote reflects the argument that prisons have a just purpose, that punishment is meaningful in some way, and that ministries work to legitimate the prison itself.

As prisons have become increasingly overcrowded, understaffed, and underfunded, faith-based groups perform an essential service in maintaining control and authority. The ministries embody the benefits of privatization for fiscal conservatives who argue that allowing faith-based groups free rein inside prison is fiscally efficient. If the state has jettisoned any financial commitment to rehabilitation and reform, prison ministries can fill the gap. Wilbert Rideau, an author and editor who spent forty-four years in Angola prison, told me, "Faith-based groups have been invented and foisted on the public by authorities so they appear to be doing something rather than just warehousing people. It's window-dressing."

In her book on women in prison, *Partial Justice*, Nicole Hahn Rafter writes, "All records pertaining to prisons have to be approached with mistrust."[21] Prisons have elaborate, capricious sets of rules and may restrict access to outsiders or prohibit those who go inside from writing about them. To outsiders, the lives, religious or otherwise, of prisoners are often intentionally made inaccessible by those who run the prison; even when one spends some time inside, they remain so.

As the director of a college-in-prison program, I spend most of my days with people who are in prison and the few that have been released. When I'm inside prisons, I go to the chapel, the library, and the classrooms, and I talk to people as we pass between jobs and classes. I've witnessed men and women graduate from Baptist seminaries, preach in crowds, converse in small, heated discussions and had them explain how to fashion a pair of cowboy boots from the finest leather, ask me to read their novels, and expound on the mystery of finding God. I have spent hours with students discussing the meaning of utopia, but I have rarely been to their cells and units where they sleep and live. I've spent time in prisons in Louisiana, Texas, California, Florida, Washington State, New York, Georgia, and Ohio, where I interviewed men and women, observed and participated in their classes and religious services, corresponded with them through letter and e-mail, and sat in chapels and study halls. Inside and outside, I've accompanied ministry volunteers and leaders. But I do not have to endure what they endure: the monotony of days and years, the total lack of autonomy, the idea that all they have can be ripped away and their cells dismantled. One woman I knew in prison was particularly distraught one day. In a blanket search for contraband, officers had confiscated all her belongings, books, photos, and mementos, and overturned the six-by-nine cell where she had lived for a decade.

In prison, life is contingent. Given that precariousness, the question of what a woman or man in prison turns to at the height of desolation is central to understanding why I wrote this book. When I was growing up, my aunt was in prison, and I can see more clearly from the vantage of adulthood how the arc of her life returned over and over to her experience inside. She gave birth to a child in prison who was adopted by someone else. No matter how many years passed after her release, that time haunted her. My aunt often said that everyone gets religion in prison. For her, it was simple: If you only have the option of endless and pointless captivity or religious redemption, who wouldn't choose the latter? When redemption is presented as only possible through religious faith, few would turn away.

I first taught in a women's prison in New York City in 2003, just after finishing my PhD, and I was struck that, aside from families and loved ones, the only visitors I saw were religious volunteers. For many men and women, to believe in and identify themselves as part of a religious group enables self-cultivation and a way to redefine themselves in spaces of neglect. There are tangible material and ephemeral spiritual benefits to participation in religion in prison, just as there are limitations and restrictions, which I explore throughout the book. These benefits are why the president of the United States, the prison warden, and the woman or man inside prison have embraced faith-based groups.

The reasons for that embrace vary according to place and whether you're talking to a warden, a minister, or a prisoner, but sometimes they overlap. For a woman facing life without the possibility of freedom or a long or even a short sentence, faith-based ministries can be a resource, a practice, a belief system, a sense of authority, and a space of belonging. Participation in a ministry provides the rituals and shape of daily life: Bible reading and prayer in the morning, tending to the chapel, visiting those in hospice or segregation, classes, studying, prayer groups, and a return to the unit. In many prisons, a person's adherence to Christian beliefs may mean being able to live in air-conditioned rooms in the safest and cleanest part of the prison or having access to coveted work-release assignments. Participation in religious services is a chance to interact with outsiders, especially when someone hasn't received a visitor in years. Others join a faith-based group for protection or because it is the only way to obtain a college degree. The group can be a lifeline in a space of despair. Calvin Duncan, who left Louisiana State Penitentiary, also known as Angola, after twenty-eight years, told me that his advice to men in prison is "get with the faith-based groups. They are the only possibility of any help once you are released in Louisiana." In the chaos and uncertainty of prison, being part of a prison ministry provides certainty about the world and one's place in it. People in prison have eloquently described to me their experiences of redemption, rebirth, enlightenment, reconciliation, and love for the divine, oneself, or others. They talk about transcending suffering and shame for a while, enveloped in the love of God.

For a woman or man separated from children and families for years, the fellowship in religion recreates familial and kinship bonds. Monica's children are cared for by her mother and sisters. "When I was on the street, I gave everything to the devil doing his work. I can put forth even greater effort for my good and for the Lord," she says. Raised primarily by her Baptist aunt, Monica only truly became a Christian after she was imprisoned. She explains, "I didn't grasp the full concept of what Jesus did for me until I was in jail." In a service during her first years there, she finally understood what she'd been hearing from pulpits since she was a child: "I was in church one night. You do a lot of hollering. But one night I listened and I was taught the word rather than preached the word." The God she believes in is forgiving and, unlike anyone else in her life, does not resent, judge, or blame her. She cannot watch her children grow up or care for her ailing mother, but in the limited world of prison, participation in the seminary offers a rationale for existence.

Many churches and faith-based groups have chosen not to ignore mass incarceration and the massive suffering inside prisons. They've created a theology that includes the prisoner, spurred by the Bible verse in Matthew 25:36, "I was in prison and you visited me." Yet, for the volunteers, ministries, and churches that go inside, the prison contains a captive population, ripe for proselytization. Norris Henderson, a criminal justice reform leader who spent twenty-eight years in Angola prison, told me to ask faith-based groups a simple question: "Why are you here?" Faith-based ministries are often concerned with salvaging individual souls, rather than asking why they are there in the first place.

Some of the key questions I explore throughout *God in Captivity* are how faith-based ministries and the people who live in prison grapple with the meaning of punishment and redemption, and how their daily lives reflect Norris's question of why the ministry is there and why the prison is there—to punish indefinitely or to reform? How faith-based ministries conceive of punishment and forgiveness as inextricable thus remains a central concern of the book. Another urgent question that emerges is around the legal and ethical issue of predominantly conservative evangelical Christians as the main force inside prisons, and the implications for prisoners of other religions, particularly Muslims. I explore how Muslim prisoners survive inside the Christian faith-based ministries in chapter 4.

Theologian Timothy Gorringe writes that, for too long, Christian thinking about justice and punishment has also been dominated by notions of retribution.[22] "Western criminal justice systems have inherited a retributivist theory of punishment. . . . That degenerates into pure revenge in the absence of a convincing mode of punishment; and a prison system, based on a mishmash of incoherent and unbelievable principles that in reality does little more than warehouse the problem," he says.[23] The majority of faith-based ministries in prison do not share Gorringe's skepticism about the Christian emphasis on vengeance as necessary to redemption, but in chapter 5, I look at examples of ministries and their volunteers grappling with the concept of forgiveness. As the state no longer funds many rehabilitative functions in prisons, faith-based ministries have stepped in, which has a particular impact on women, who experience high rates of sexual violence and trauma. In chapter 6, I examine how women negotiate faith-based groups based on fundamentalist Christian principles of submission, and the differing expectations ministries have for fathers and mothers. The final chapter analyzes how faith-based ministries were central to the emergence of conservative support for prison reform, and how faith-based ideas of transformation intersect with a fiscally conservative agenda to make prisons safer and more cost effective.

The predominance of faith-based groups in prisons raises the same questions about whether the prison's aim is to redeem or to punish those remaindered to it, and what part faith in God plays in carrying out this mission. Faith-based ministries promise redemption through a relationship to God, but it is a partial freedom. The seminary's idea of freedom for a prisoner is to find Jesus and convert others, without ever leaving prison. Thus, we are back to where we began, to the discussion of Jeremiah. Dr. Kristi Miller told the students that those who retain their faith, even in captivity, will eventually be freed. But freedom generally implies self-autonomy and the ability to make your own decisions about your life. This is impossible in prison. The ministries promise a personal redemption, but freedom remains elusive. Monica gave birth to three of her children while in jail or prison. One of her daughters just graduated from high school. In another thirty-seven years, when Monica's sentence is up, she will be eighty-three years old. She doesn't have a life sentence, but she may as well. Monica says her mother prays every day that God will let her take Monica's place. In the meantime, Monica teeters between tentative hope and resignation. "They don't believe in second chances. It's always the nature of the offense. That's never going to change. That's always going to be before me," she says. "But when are you going to forgive me for it?"

# CHAPTER 1

# THE CONVERT'S HEART

## *The Quiet Stasis of Faith*

PATRICIA HAS BEEN DOWN ELEVEN YEARS. "Down" means she's eleven years into a life sentence, and in Louisiana that means life without the possibility of parole. It is one of the few states that still practice this form of hopeless sentencing. According to the Prison Policy Initiative, Louisiana has the highest incarceration rate in the United States and the world, with 868 of every 100,000 of its citizens in prison.

For years, Patricia's home was the Banshee Motorcycle Club of Louisiana, but now she's an avowed Christian involved in dozens of ministries and activities in prison: Toastmasters, the prisoners' magazine, the lifers' group, Kairos Prison Ministry, the college program in Christian ministry, and culinary arts. Lately, she's been reading the Bible in segregation, where women are locked down twenty-three out of twenty-four hours a day. At the Louisiana Correctional Institute for Women (LCIW), ministry is a higher calling. Some women counsel the elderly, hold prayer circles, and even run an ex-gay ministry for lesbians. "I'm so busy," Patricia smiles at me ruefully. "I'd like to just put my bed in the chapel and not go back to the dorm."

LCIW is a grim collection of one-story buildings amid the agricultural fields south of Baton Rouge. A few of the concrete paths that weave between prison buildings have decorative wooden arches over them that do little to shield anyone from the sun or rain. The prison starkly reflects the dueling tension of warehousing and efficiency. There are some women like Patricia, too busy to sleep, but everywhere I notice clusters of women sitting on the sparse grass, vying for a patch of shade. They pluck idly at the ground, and at first it seems a reflex as they talk. However, LCIW is so overcrowded, straining with twelve hundred women when it was built to hold nine hundred, that the administration sends hundreds of them to pick grass, simply to give women something to do. They call it "goose-picking": labor for the sake of labor. The women are corralled into using their hands to pull up grass already shorn to a half inch or less.

There is little redemption to be found in goose-picking, so Patricia seeks it in the chapel, which is to her a Christian haven from the rest of the prison. While grass picking is a way to temporarily occupy people until they are churned out or come back to the prison, faith is a way of doing time within a framework and structure. It gives an endless string of days a shape and a rationale, especially when confronting the possibilities of dying in prison. The boredom and routine of prison life may be punctuated by moments of crisis and drama, but time is still the enemy. The question is, How do you make something of your time instead of, as Patricia and others say, "letting the time do you"?

Faith-based groups emphasize self-transformation for people like Patricia. They promulgate a hybrid message in which participation in faith-based programs serves the age-old Christian purpose of "rebirthing" the self. The premise that a person can become something new while in prison mounts a challenge to the logic of incorrigibility that has defined mass incarceration in the past three decades. Yet, the state of Louisiana has little interest in redemption of the individual, unless it takes place in prison. Many faith-based ministries support imprisonment itself because they operate under the assumption that grace and transformation are possible because punishment is ordained by God and manifested in incarceration. Punishment in prison makes sense for Patricia because God is there to forgive her. Her faith and participation in ministry grants Patricia a measure of peace and relief from despondency. At the same time, the faith-based idea of redemption promises personal liberation and transformation through religion, but only as part of being in prison.

Patricia believes that her heart has changed. She frequently quotes Ezekiel 36:26: "A new heart also will I give you, and a new spirit will I put within you: and I will take away the stony heart out of your flesh, and I will give you a heart of flesh." Christians in prison ministry and people in prison talk of having a "heart for God," "a prayerful heart," or a "heart for helping." There are suggestions to guard your heart and to open your heart. You can, as one Christian minister promises, have a "makeover" of the heart. Belief in the idea of a heart change that is a total metamorphosis in a person's life motivates a range of faith-based prison ministries and programs throughout the United States. Their message is that God, Jesus, or the Holy Spirit ultimately transforms hearts and that such transformation requires unwavering faith in God's power.

These programs profess that a person in prison is irrevocably made anew and less likely to return to prison because of his or her altered heart. Prison Fellowship claims in its mission statement that it "reform(s) the hearts of offenders, and, in doing that, restores peace to communities."[1] According to the Christian program Weekend of Champions, "In order to have the most effective impact, one must seek to change the hearts of criminals."[2] Southwestern Baptist Theological Seminary's Christian bachelor's degree program in Darrington Unit, a prison in Texas, exhorts its students to let their studies result in heart change.

This sentiment of a heart transformed is echoed by prisoners, religious volunteers, and prominent supporters of faith-based ministry. Change in a prisoner's heart means that something authentic, core, inherent, and biological has shifted within. A Christian volunteer tells me that giving your life to God instigates a total transformation akin to a caterpillar and butterfly: "The same organism completely changes and the brain is different, the respiratory system is different; you want to go somewhere else. You do not want to go where you used to go; you do not want to eat what you used to eat. Everything changes, it is dead and gone."

Heart change is an inner revolution that faith-based groups claim is more powerful and long-lasting than any secular program. One warden of a Florida prison, citing his years of experience working in prison, explained to me that education and drug treatment alone are unsuccessful. What are job skills, he said, when what a person needs are "heart skills," a thorough change from the inside that allows a prisoner to remain impervious to external circumstances: "Prisons aren't going to stop the crime problem, no matter how tough you get, because crime is the result of a breakdown of moral values. It springs from the human heart. We can replace a person's sin-infected moral choices with Godly, biblical values."[3]

Patricia says she no longer wants to do what she used to—drinking, doing drugs, going to wild parties, and being a biker's girlfriend—because her heart has changed. As a child, her family moved around Louisiana and Texas because of her father's military job. They were Catholic, but the rigidity of her Catholic church reminded her of the military world surrounding her, and she wanted to distance herself from both worlds. At eighteen, she left home and avoided churches altogether. Biker clubs with their rituals and insignias of outlaw affiliation became her community and lifeline. These were people whose vows of loyalty meant they would die for one another. They socialized, traveled around the country in a roaring pack, and often lived together. They had long-standing rivalries with other biker groups. Patricia disdained anything related to religion. She told me, "I remember going to a biker rally, and we were camped near the Christian biker group. I kept thinking, How can you be a Christian biker? I told them, 'You don't want to be near us because we aren't doing Christian things,' but they were kind and said they would be fine."

Eventually, Patricia married a man who wasn't a biker and valiantly attempted to settle down in a rural parish near the Texas border and renounce the biker lifestyle. While she raised their three children, her husband drove trucks long distances. She seemed to have found some semblance of normalcy, but as she tells it, when she realized he was cheating on her, her sense of self-worth was damaged and she rejoined the bikers, those she'd always felt she belonged with. "It destroyed me. I went back to biker life. I felt safer there than trying to do the right thing," she said. Her new boyfriend, Larry, went by the moniker "Lost Larry." A biker in the Banshee Motorcycle Club, he worked offshore on the oil rigs of Louisiana. Just like her previous husband, he was gone for weeks and then back again for a few days. When he was there, they spent time with other Banshees.

They lived well on his salary and shared the biker lifestyle, although Patricia was never able to join the club. Only men could be members.[4] She was merely Larry's girlfriend, known as "Lost Bitch." Like most of the women affiliated with the Banshees, Patricia was an appendage of Larry, only welcomed as an extension of him. The Banshees are "one-percenters," an outlaw club not affiliated with the more respectable American Motorcycle Association. They consider themselves, along with their enemies, the Hells Angels or Outlaws, the 1 percent of non-law-abiding motorcycle riders. Many of the one-percenter clubs function as criminal organizations, selling or moving drugs.[5] Patricia and Lost Larry owned two houses but were living what she recalls as an "alternate lifestyle," dressing in the leather regalia of bikers, socializing only with other bikers, drinking and partying. She is vague about whatever illegal activities she may have known about or participated in.

Patricia swears her association with reviled and little understood bikers "got me found guilty" for murder. She confesses to excessive drinking and drugs before prison, but she declares her innocence. Accepting the God she rejected as a young adult into her life has provided her with the framework she needs to understand why she is in prison. Without God in her life, she was a "lost bitch," and now she has found purpose, even though it took a life sentence in prison to jolt her toward this realization. She believes that, in retrospect, God had been trying to reach her for years. "Now looking back," she observes, "I can see all the times in our lives that God was trying to get our attention." One clue she ignored but sees now was how her aunt prayed and prayed that Patricia would meet Jesus; Patricia was too high or drunk to notice or care. Her aunt's son is a Baptist preacher who also prayed that God would put somebody in Patricia's life whom she would hear, but she wasn't open to hearing God's voice at the time. She now believes that God was tapping her on the shoulder when she and Lost Larry met the Christian bikers at the national rally, but again, neither of them would listen.

Patricia's story of her heart change and hearing God after a shattering crisis is deeply evangelical. One undergoes a conversion and becomes a new creation through an intimate and accountable relationship with God.[6]

After reaching a nadir in one's life, faith initiates a heart change, softens the inner worlds of the most hardened, incorrigible criminal in order for the redeemed person to blossom. Patricia's idea of faith means that she may stumble or falter, her faith may even waver, but if she recommits to God, she will be forgiven and ultimately reformed. Her favorite scripture is 2 Corinthians 5:17, which reads: "Therefore, if anyone is in Christ, he is a new creation. The old has passed away; behold, the new has come." This narrative of change is inseparable from the prison's model of punishment. To the parole or clemency board, prisoners must express remorse for their crimes and prove that they have become newly restored people through their prison sentences. Patricia's preacher cousin says that two of his relatives (Patricia's niece is in the same prison as Patricia) are doing what God would want. It just took prison to make it happen.

A person's testimony of heart change becomes the narrative vehicle for potential freedom. The way one's heart changes is to renounce sin or "criminal thinking and actions," and repudiate the person she was when she committed criminal acts. As James Bielo, a scholar of evangelicalism, writes, "A great deal of energy is devoted to explaining who you are not in an effort to state who you are."[7]

Evangelicalism is a broad rubric, but in the simple meaning of the word itself, "evangelical" refers to the good news that Jesus died for us, and that salvation is possible solely in knowing that God is concerned with your personal life, so long as you maintain faith. Within evangelicalism, some churches and denominations understand the Bible as infallible, true, and literal in contrast to a liberal Protestant view that considers the Bible a product of human history. Historically, evangelicalism's main tenets— that each person can be transformed through conversion, that people have free moral agency, and that inequality is not divinely mandated—altered the ways marginal people in the United States viewed themselves and their social circumstances during the eighteenth and nineteenth centuries. Evangelicalism and democracy have always been bound up with each other. Conversions and revivals had an impact outside religious life and ultimately represented new forms of democratization in which women, African Americans, and working people achieved greater access to the public realm and social power. Evangelicals led the nineteenth-century temperance, abolition, and women's rights movements as part of what one historian calls the "democratization of American Christianity."[8] But this history of democratization through religion is not necessarily present in the prisons, where evangelicals are the dominant religious groups. Instead, many modern evangelicals understand their mandate as spreading this good news and winning souls for Jesus by testifying to their own life-changing experiences. This is an individualistic mandate, concerned with the soul of the person, rather than the social structures of prison or a country.

Theologically, evangelicalism refers to a belief system that includes the necessity of personal salvation and commitment to Jesus Christ in an intimate relationship. It enables a person like Patricia to place herself and her present circumstances within a sacred and cosmic order in which she hears and internalizes God's voice. Patricia equates her born-again experience with a belief in the death and resurrection of Jesus. Her story of self-transformation connects her with a sacred reality and imparts to listeners the experience of being filled with the word of God. In that sense, it provides a contour to her life and a reality beyond that of the prison walls, however intangible it might be. Women in prison often talk about being "stated-down" or "state-raised" to describe growing up in the prison system. They see themselves in the terminology of the state and the prison, which is the language of punishment. In the faith-based groups or the seminary at the women's prison, they speak of themselves as "in God's hands" or "walking with Jesus." When one has put one's life in Jesus's hands, one is no longer subject to a state narrative of guilt, punishment, and retribution. In this sense, religion for Patricia is liberating because she is no longer merely the property of the state, DOC number 421245. Faith enables her to reject her own brutalization and the anonymity of prison to become someone figuratively held and cherished by God.

Patricia was far from saved when a young couple in the Banshees— Susanna and her boyfriend, Jim, along with their beloved dog—moved in with Patricia and Lost Larry for a while. Susanna and Jim were more restless and unsettled than Patricia. There may have been a police warrant out for them, which is disputed in the legal documents pertaining to Patricia's case.[9] After a few months, Patricia claims she grew fed up with the younger couple because they lazed around her house without offering to clean up or cook. Susanna's dog was messy, destructive, and fiercely attached to Susanna. Lost Larry was often offshore. Tensions grew between the couples, and eventually Susanna and Jim moved out. Patricia claims there was no lasting ill will between them. After all, they were all Banshees; it was simply too claustrophobic living in such close quarters.

Patricia and Lost Larry helped their friends move by loading their possessions into a truck, placing items in boxes and storage bins, and closing them with duct tape. Not too long after, a boy fishing on Bayou Cocodrie, the meandering canals of water that radiate in snakelike funnels and twists from the coast of Louisiana to the interior of the state, noticed a plastic storage box, sealed with duct tape, drifting and bobbing in the water.[10] A body with the legs severed from the torso was crammed inside the box. Another box containing a dismembered body appeared in the bayou a few weeks later. Nearby the police discovered Susanna's dog with a bullet through its head. Lost Larry was arrested for the murders, and the police caught Patricia in Texas a few weeks later. She was a wearing a jacket that read "Property of Lost Larry."

Patricia acknowledges that many people in prison claim innocence, but nonetheless she swears she is an exception: "Everyone in prison says they're not guilty. That's not true. They are quick to say what they did. Our trial proved our innocence. He was offshore. They were looking to close the case." In the trial transcripts and subsequent appeals, it is unclear whether or not Larry was offshore during the murders. Patricia believes that Susanna and her husband were informants for the FBI, and that they had enabled the police to shut down the methamphetamine labs of a rival gang. Patricia thinks the murders were vengeance for their testimony to law enforcement. Nevertheless, Patricia and Lost Larry are both now serving life sentences in Louisiana.

The idea of grace is central to Patricia's sense of being a Christian because it grants her a forgiveness that the state will never bestow. In her worldview, God grants forgiveness to all people, regardless of their sins. Purity is rather subversive in the prison context because it grants innocence to those whom society deems most intractable and irredeemable.

Patricia's idea of redemption through a heart change means that a person is essentially born unscathed, but circumstances intervened. This concept is central to the appeal and ubiquity of prison ministries. Through participation in the seminary or faith-based groups, people like Patricia have a conceptual framework in which their inner selves are pure and can be forgiven. As they are reborn, the guilt of sin disappears, and an inward process of renewal or sanctification takes place. Patricia has ceased to be the sinner and now exists in a state of grace because of her place in an evangelical theological world.

Narcissism is inherent in the evangelical narrative of heart change. Change is so focused on the individual that it often overlooks the true damage a person may have done to others or even the social factors that shaped that person's existence. Having God forgive you is easier than facing the person you hurt or killed, or addressing the poverty, abuse, and lack of opportunity that drives incarceration. In evangelicalism, Jesus extends grace to all people, as long as they vow to stay with the ministry and maintain their faith. Patricia recovers what she once was within this narrative of change and accepts the grace bestowed by a God of forgiveness in order to start anew. Patricia and others use the narrative of heart change to show how they were initially born in God's image but were deformed by the corrupt world around them. Thus, when God transforms her heart, she will encounter her unblemished earlier self. This reformed person is a composite of the self created in God's image and the one who slogged through a lifetime of sin and emerged on the other side with a cleansed heart.

Patricia was very forthcoming with me, someone she did not know well or for long, because of the nature of a testified life. Little of a personal nature is off-limits for discussion, as confession is mandatory. Public confession transforms what is only an individual process into something communal and makes Patricia accountable to others and to God. Even as Patricia attests to change, her former degenerate self is useful to her narrative. The experience of the biker chick or "lost bitch" can illuminate the depths to which a person might fall before reemerging whole and pure. Patricia isn't amputating her former self but transforming the negative into something renewed and superior. Her story is like so many stories of the women in the seminary program, and of the men and women in faith-based programs around the country who renounced a criminal self and became renewed and saved selves. Conversion is, in part, a process of acquiring a specific religious language or dialect that other Christians recognize.

Out of her suffering and through heart change, Patricia has some self-efficacy, even if it is within the prison. The divine is a way to grant herself agency when she has no control over the actual time she will spend in prison. Through participation in evangelical groups, a person internalizes the structure of a testimony that, in the telling, becomes a retrospective narrative shaped by evangelicalism. According to Robyn R. Warhol and Helena Michie, Alcoholics Anonymous has a similar master narrative for recovery groups: "The master narrative functions mnemonically to provide the speaker with a structure for shaping the individual story's details."[11] The testimonies reinterpret the teller's past life in the language of sin and salvation and in the light of a new evangelical Christian identity. Patricia's redemptive testimony about her life as a biker, with drinking and sin, and now as a committed Christian, is an evangelical born-again narrative of transformation. Shadd Maruna, a sociologist of religion and a criminologist, defines these narratives as redemption scripts, a way a person can rewrite a shameful past into a necessary prelude to a productive and worthy life.[12] The person begins with a traumatic story about past lives of drug use, sex, and illegality, then reaches her lowest point and finds herself either calling out to God or hearing God for the first time. A born-again experience and the discovery of God follow, and she finishes by becoming a Christian. The idea of grace means that a person may backslide, may fall into sin, may fight, may recommit a crime, but there is always the possibility of forgiveness and of heart change as long as she repents to others and to God.

In 2010, when the New Orleans Baptist Theological Seminary started a program in which women could earn a bachelor's degree in Christian ministry, Patricia was certain that God wanted this for her. There is no other way to obtain an associate degree or four-year bachelor's degree in

Louisiana prisons. So, the program is intensely competitive; most people end up goose-picking grass. Candidates must have at least fifteen years remaining on their sentences and a high school diploma or adequate scores on the TABE test, a standardized assessment administered in Louisiana's prisons. Disciplinary issues automatically exclude a person from the seminary. Patricia filled out an application, confident of her acceptance because she had her GED and a clean record inside. When the list was posted for the first class of students, Patricia scanned it, expecting her name to be on it. It wasn't. Undeterred, she was certain the seminary had simply made a mistake in omitting her. She approached the director, Dr. Kristi Miller, and said, "I should be here. You forgot to put me on the list." Miller, an elegantly lanky woman in her early forties with wavy auburn hair, gently explained that, no, Patricia had not been chosen. At first, Patricia was stunned and then furious. The next year when the seminary program asked for applicants, she refused to even try, but her friends signed her up. Patricia feigned disinterest in the whole endeavor until a week later when Miller asked her if she was ready to join the seminary.

All day, Patricia takes classes taught by Miller and other professors. Some classes are in English composition and world history, but the majority are specific to the degree: New Testament interpretation, marriage and family issues, Christian scriptures, biblical backgrounds, the practice of evangelism, a survey of church history. Patricia also learns public speaking, counseling, and leadership training. Unlike a regular college classroom, the seminary has a pulpit. For many of the women, this is the first time they've been treated seriously as students or challenged to learn a new language or to write English papers that are structurally and grammatically rigorous.

The seminary is theologically and socially conservative. Miller has a PhD in the Old Testament, with specializations in Hebrew and Greek from the NOBTS. Her degree is unusual because most female graduate students in the seminary are encouraged to major in church education or counseling. Her advisor had warned her that, as a woman, she would never be hired as a professor despite her academic credentials. When Miller taught Hebrew on the main seminary campus, the seminary's directory listed a man's name instead of hers; chauvinism is embedded in the seminary's culture.

When we talked during lunch together, Miller and Dr. Deborah Sharkey, who are chaplains and the seminary directors, lamented the conservatism of their own religious denomination. To become chaplains, each had to sign a paper saying that their chaplaincy would never transfer anywhere beyond the prison. For women to have so much authority was an anathema. The seminary believes in the idea of genders being complementary and defines specific roles for women and men.[13] When they tentatively asked if I had experienced sexism as a professor, I told a story about an older man whose class ended shortly before mine in a cavernous lecture hall. Each day, without fail, three times a week, he'd ask in a booming voice, "Are you really the professor? You're so young!" as my students filed in. Miller and Sharkey laughed bitterly as they described the wife of a Baptist seminary president in Texas who teaches a class called "How to Pack Your Husband's Suitcase." Miller admits that her true passion is teaching Hebrew. What is ironic is that she can empower women at LCIW to become college graduates only as an employee of an institution that consigns women like her to extremely limited roles.

The seminary's mission is to bring unbelievers to Jesus. It hopes Patricia, Monica, and others will become emissaries of moral rehabilitation and "evangelize their peers within all areas of the prison and other institutions of the Louisiana Department of Corrections." The seminary's idea of freedom is that, without ever leaving prison, a woman like Patricia will find Jesus and convert others, a welcome solution in a prison where women pick grass to keep busy. In just a few years, students like Patricia have founded dozens of ministries within the prison, and Patricia is one of the most active proponents. By day, she takes classes, but her real work is evangelism. One of her school papers was about an eight-week discipleship strategy to bring other women into the fold.

Patricia's life now has a purpose that is divinely mandated: to bring God's message of redemption through Jesus to others. Patricia is emboldened by the sense that God was always there, waiting patiently, and only catastrophe, the destruction of everything in her life, made it possible for her to hear and, more importantly, to believe. From the shell of her presumed criminality, she has become a witness to others of the persuasive power of a born-again conversion that engenders new identities. Her testimony is a public enactment that provides evidence of the power of Jesus to transform lives.[14]

The purpose of a testimony is to act as a public witness and to recruit, convince, and reconstitute its listeners; it needs an audience to fulfill itself.[15] By giving witness to her transformed self, Patricia can convince others that their only option is to disavow their previous lives of sin. The impetus behind the evangelical testimony is that the listener will hear and absorb the saved speaker's language and sacred view of the world as part of their own conversion.[16] To this end, Patricia initiated an intercessory prayer group. She and others pray for the prison, and the women who haven't found God and are convinced they can make it on their own, without God's help. The group has a wooden mailbox where people can drop in prayer requests. After the group reads them, they pray fervently on the petitioner's behalf.

Although the idea of conversion is individual, there is a communal nature to sharing testimony and in identifying as a seminary student with a select group of others within the prison. Patricia and another lifer, Sheryl—who, at age fifty-three, is serving a sixty-year sentence and will most likely die in prison—created a ministry for women in solitary. Patricia, Sheryl, and five other women go to lockdown, otherwise known as "seg" or solitary confinement, to pray and talk to women isolated in cells for all but one hour a day. The women in lockdown are the "bad kids," Patricia explains. These women get in fights, move contraband, are falsely accused, can't handle the teeming chaotic life of the prison, or haven't acclimated to doing time. Getting out of lockdown is a step-by-step process. A prisoner moves from Max 1 to Max 2 and stays there ninety days. In Max 2, she might get more time outside and less isolation.

Twice a week, Patricia and the ministers visit those in solitary and answer questions about the Bible; the aim of their ministry is to bring community into the most horrific of spaces. A member of the first seminary class, Sheryl herself was sent to solitary for three "lost months" during the semester before I met her; she described the psychological toll of isolation. "To me," she says, "it was incredibly terrible. I had grown accustomed to the freedom I have out here. I really had to physically and mentally fight myself to stay in some kind of focus. I understand now how people I love and care about have gone to lockdown and never really came back. Not the same person that they were." Eventually, the warden and professors allowed her back into the program.

Patricia recalls her terror the day she faced a young black woman in a segregation cell, wondering if she would be ignored or dismissed: "This little black girl with dreads. Why would she want to talk to an old white lady like me? She's going to think I'm crazy." Tentatively, Patricia asked, "Is there anything you want to pray about?" The girl responded, "You would pray with me? Really?" "Really," replied Patricia. Patricia describes to me how they made a connection, but that the girl in lockdown came out, stayed three weeks, and went back to solitary; she claims the girl prefers to do her time there. "Some of these girls when we were first going back there, there wasn't no chance of them getting out. Because they were getting reports," Patricia said. Despite the failure of the one woman to stay out, Patricia believes her ministry can change hearts and sees it as being in opposition to the prison, which wants the women to remain in segregation: "They make you feel like they don't want to see you do good." Within the belief system of the seminary, however, when you make a mistake as Sheryl did, you will be punished, but from that punishment, you can be born anew figuratively and brought out literally from segregation into a Christian community.

For Patricia and others, the appeal is not just their relationship with God but with each other, in a community that the prison and God sanction. Her best friends are in the program with her. That's why she'd like to sleep in the chapel. Deprived of the bonds of family, she has recreated her own family in the prison. "I have babies on the yard. God has blessed me with children in here, and they look to me as a mama," she says.

In the sociality of redemption, the ministries succeed. These women are in ministry together. They change together. They hear and internalize each other's narratives. Prisoners spoke of how this new identity alleviated the anonymity of the prison experience. "We have a family here. We call ourselves sisters in Christ. Aunties. It's a relationship, a bond. It's amazing," said Helen, another seminary student. Patricia, Sheryl, and others are unconditionally accepted within this Christian group of women. Patricia credits Miller and Sharkey with shifting the dynamic of the chapel. "Our chapel community has changed since they have been here," she says. "People see that the love is not fake. I used to think about church volunteers, that they were just here to get points. They don't love me. They don't know me. But that changed."

Most women in prison grapple daily with the loss of their families and children, low self-esteem, and past traumas like sexual violence and abuse. Affiliation with those who have undergone the same process often alleviates their burden of shame, a central experience of incarceration. Their community accepts and forgives them, as does God, an acceptance that may never come in the form of a pardon or parole.

Although the seminary provides psychological succor, bonds of kinship, and even love for the women who participate, there is a flip side for the prison authorities and the seminary. One feature of prison life is the range of close friendships, prison families, and romantic and sexual relationships women form. In women's prisons, I've encountered a great deal of frankness and openness about who is dating whom, about couples celebrating their anniversary, or a fight between friends or girlfriends.[17] One of my students was thrown into segregation because she was kissing someone in her cell. (For a variety of reasons, I never heard anything resembling these stories from men: I didn't spend as much time in men's prisons, I am a woman, and codes of masculinity in men's prisons often stigmatize same-sex relationships.)

The seminary students agreed that most conflicts are interpersonal. There are long-standing friendships, prison families, girlfriends, and people who have lived with each other. The nuances of these relationships are often lost when it comes to punishment. The seminary program will reject a student for being in a relationship with a woman, and the prison administration will punish a woman if she is hugging, kissing, or having sex with another prisoner.

The seminary and prison administration view sexuality as a chaotic force and religion as a way to manage it. Students have internalized this view as well. Patricia's niece has been in lockdown at LCIW for nine months. According to Patricia, she visits her niece because no message of love or heart change has reached her yet. Patricia explains that her niece is in "the gay lifestyle" and says, "I go visit her, and she's saying she wants to change her life."

If ministry is, in part, prisons' solution to managing the women confined there, lesbianism is another aspect they feel a need to control. Miller proudly tells me about an ex-gay ministry called Turning Point, initiated by Chandra, a former lesbian who is now a seminary student in the prison. Until a few years ago, she had been in lesbian relationships for twenty years. When we spoke, Chandra eagerly poured forth her testimony. "I didn't realize I was really in darkness until I got here," she told me. "I could see how much darkness I was living in. I was dying. I was in denial." Her story is structured by the language she has learned from her seminary studies. She equates being gay with a form of bondage, and her struggle is a battle between darkness and light. For her, being gay provides the rationalization for her crimes, her prison sentence of forty years, and her new-found Christianity: "Everything that has happened to me has happened because of my lifestyle or drinking."

Chandra feels that her sexuality doubly burdens her, and the seminary only reinforces the message that grace is for those who are heterosexual. It does not include women who are Christian and lesbian. In the seminary, Chandra felt self-disgust because her clothes and mannerisms marked her as stereotypically masculine. Therefore she places significant emphasis on alterations in her outward appearance as a sign of something changing inside. "Each day, something different is occurring with me. Something is being taken away from me that God doesn't approve," she told me. Chandra's wide smile is accentuated by a gold grill across her upper teeth. She proudly pulled out a photograph of herself to show me how much she had transformed from her formerly butch appearance, with close-cropped hair, to the equally butch-looking woman in front of me, with one-inch dreads. "I used to wear men's cologne," she explained. "I never wore makeup. Little things like that. It's freaking me out, but I feel good about myself.

I feel good to say 'I'm a woman.' I would get defensive before if someone called me a lady. God has transformed me. God is putting me in rehab right now."

Chandra's past life provides a way for her to access her idea of herself as originally pure, and purity means heterosexuality, as she's come to understand it in the seminary. "I wasn't always gay," she says. Chandra now shares her testimony with others as part of her ministry within the prison. "I think about all the filth that took place. One moment I'm embarrassed. One moment I'm OK, because I know God has delivered me. It makes me want to reach out and help others more," she explains. She says that being in lesbian relationships precipitated her attempted murder of her partner: "When I got involved with a female, it just overpowered everything. It led me to this incident right here." In prison, Chandra continued to be involved with women. She applied to the seminary program but was rejected because she had a girlfriend. When she was accepted, the second time she applied, it was on the condition that she pledge celibacy. For eight months, she avoided her girlfriend to get over it. "God, I'm tired. I no longer want this," she explains. "Please help me." In 2011, she gave her life to Christ.

Turning Point ministry gives Chandra an opportunity to evangelize to a group of women she knows well, and it supports the seminary's and prison's prohibition against any intimacy or sexual relationship inside the prison. According to Chandra, most women aren't really gay, just "gay for the stay," a phrase about women in prison I've heard used ubiquitously by administrators, prisoners, and guards. Given her past, Chandra believes she can uniquely address the dynamics of women's prison relationships. When Miller accepted Chandra's proposal for an ex-gay ministry, she posted flyers around the prison, and sixty women of all ages showed up. Chandra tells them that homosexuality is akin to addiction. She believes that it is not the worst sin, just one of many that can keep you from going to heaven. Alcohol, sex, and drugs are all just forms of bondage. Salvation is the goal. "I want the ladies to become not just heterosexual but to become holy," says Chandra. Women give testimonies of their own escape from bondage, and they have frequent one-on-one conversations with Chandra. The ministry creates a sanctioned form of intimacy that is

centered on faith and sharing personal stories that replaces the close relationships the prison and the seminary forbid.

The seminary's idea of purity enables Chandra to do penance for her
crime. Chandra preaches that God hates homosexuality or any sexual sins,
and purity of the body is central to being a transformed person. "Our body
is a temple, and when we are involved with sexual immoralities, it tears
our body down because it's not what God gave us our body to do. You
shouldn't have sex until married. And you should only have sex with your
husband," she exhorts them. I can't help but tell Chandra about a woman
I know well in a Washington State prison, who recently married her wife
(who is not incarcerated); the prison chaplain officiated. Chandra is mo-
mentarily speechless. "It's the end times. That's all I can say. It's the end
times. A lot of us are going to lose our lives for Christ and that's a good
thing," she replies.

Disavowing her sexuality, no matter how arduous or even fruitless, is
a way for a woman to give herself agency and forgiveness where she has
none. Chandra forges on: "I find myself questioning God, and then I'm,
no, God knows best. Father knows best. Is it going to be easy? Nah, but
God is going to give me the strength to be able to endure. This is my final
chance here. This is my final chance." Chandra's description of her life and
calling sounds like atonement for harming her partner and a way to make
sense of her time inside.

Making a distinction between a convenient conversion and true heart
change is impossible to achieve and not necessarily productive. Despite the
narratives of change and remorse, there are multiple reasons that someone
gains faith. However, suspicions about devout prisoners are a particular
irritant for Patricia and others. "I hate that word 'jailhouse religion.' Because it's not about that," she says. Everyone, from the chaplains to seminary students, incessantly discuss "faking it." Patricia is quick to dismiss
the well-worn cliché that religion is merely another ruse among many
manipulations inside a prison.

A chaplain in a Florida prison once said to me, "When they ask how
many are faking it on the inside, I tell them, no more than those faking
it on the outside." There is no hiding flaws or mistakes when women and
men sleep, shower, eat, and go to the bathroom together, with almost

no privacy. Most prisons have open dormitories stacked with bunk beds. Bathrooms lack doors. People keep their possessions in a locker, and if they are in a cell, they can be moved anytime. When choosing to become prison missionaries, the men and women I met in prison told me that they will be scrutinized mercilessly by other prisoners. Is she acting superior? Does his behavior align with what he says? According to the women in seminary, these questions are the true test of the missionary's success and sincerity.

Seminary students talk about women who may comport themselves like Christians in the presence of the professors or the chaplain but act otherwise in the dorms. Patricia explains, "You see how they are in church, and then you go live with them. We see them 24/7. It makes it hard." She scorned the women who profess to be Christians while in prison but discard their Bibles in the laundry room once they are released. "They leave God at the gate, and then they come back." She implied that only maintaining faith will enable someone to become truly free. Miller has a slightly less rigid view of the role of the seminary and insists that any person might be reached by God. She doesn't mind if women join the program for the education, not for their Christian convictions. "Who is to say that even if someone is in something for the wrong reasons that a seed won't plant?" Miller comments.

I ask Patricia what one thing she wants others to know about her life in the prison and the seminary. It's an unfair question, but she answers immediately: "I would tell them that it's not jailhouse religion. And God is not only on the other side of the fence. And that more people on the outside are more locked up than we are on the inside." Patricia claims that she possesses an inner freedom from heart change. She belongs somewhere, and her life has purpose and value to others, despite the length of her sentence and the state's verdict that she is a murderer. She has found a way to justify her existence, not just to others but to herself. Patricia swears fervently she is where she is meant to be. Despite the prospect of a life behind bars, Patricia protests that becoming a Christian and finding God liberated her: "You're not free until you have Christ in you. And I'm more free than I have ever been in my life." On the outside, she wouldn't have been a missionary, college student, counselor, mother to many, and leader.

She was merely Larry's property in a motorcycle club, where she wasn't even valued enough to be a member. "To know now if I could change that, I don't think I would. I'm in prison and I'm getting a theological education," she says. "I would never have went to college. I'm in college, girl. I'm in university, and I can do it."

A prisoner's heart may change, and she may be a new person or Christian, but the freedom and transformation are built inside walls. Despite protestations of redemption, this is still very much at the forefront of everything in Patricia's life. Patricia is a member of the lifer's club. It has grown to 150 women since 2005, and this doesn't include the women serving forty, fifty, or sixty years, a life sentence in all but name. Patricia knows all the elderly women in the prison. I visited one in the infirmary, Mary, a bank robber who is now eighty years old with snow-white hair, who is dying because she has refused to quit smoking for the past thirty years. Mischievously, she explains that the prison put her in the infirmary so she couldn't smoke at all. She is a talented artist whose murals decorate the walls of the infirmary and chapel prison. She's also written and illustrated a book about Jesus in the manger and hands me a copy. Mary explains that some of the older lifers had been imprisoned for defending themselves against abusive men. About the older lifers, Patricia asks, "They're not going to hurt nobody. Why not let them go home?"

Patricia's redemption is predicated on and promised by a life in service to others, the sociality of the seminary, and her relationship to God. She says she is doing what she wants: "So whether or not I go home isn't an issue. I can still do what I want from right here. And that's minister to other people." Patricia claims she is free, loved by God and her sisters in the ministry, even in a space of punishment. She feels, then, that her mind is outside the punishment regime of the prison, while her body is still captured inside it. She makes her own time, even if she is denied the space and place of freedom. She finds comfort in her sense of certainty, in a closed belief system in which doubt appears to play no part. But eventually doubt seeps in: "I thank God every day that I came to prison. Do I still want to come home? Yes."

Patricia's case is still in the courts. She rants about Louisiana's lack of eligibility through parole, the crooked courts, and the bigoted town where she was tried. She knows the intricacies of her appeal in the same way she does the book of Jeremiah. Then she veers to the idea that it is God who will break the prison walls. God forgives, bestows redemption, and loves her. Perhaps this faith will free her in a real sense. "God gives us a second chance and third chance and a fourth chance," she says. "It doesn't matter if you find God in prison or if you find him in a church on the outside. I think he is building an army inside here. And these walls are going to fall down. And that army is going to go out."

# CHAPTER 2

# THE PENITENTIARY AND THE FARM

*A History of Redemption and Control*

AS A PREACHER READ the Bible before a mass of prisoners in a Philadelphia jail, a deputy stood guard beside him with a lighted torch and loaded cannon. Should anyone move, the head jailer had ordered the deputy to fire upon the audience of prisoners.[1] Almost 250 years later, a retired Southwestern Baptist seminary professor and minister stood at a lectern using the Bible to explain how to win others to Christ. "Assume good motives of those around you," he explained to a room of thirty men at a maximum-security prison in Texas. As he spoke, a cockroach scuttled by his foot. No one seemed to care or notice. Quickly, numerous students raised their hand. One man, Keith, with a round face and small eyes, says, "I'm listening to these questions and I'm thinking of it in a prison context. You said the words, 'assume good motives.' Well, that just set off an entire alarm system. Here you always assume evil motives. You always approach the actions or the words or the input of others from a very critical stand-point." Citing 1 Corinthians 13, Dr. Bob Overton responds that it means they have to approach people discerningly. A person's bad motive could be an index or way to reach them or convert them. Leroy Youngblood, at sixty-seven the oldest man in the class, mutters, "This isn't as boring as I thought." He wears a self-constructed name tag with the words "Washed in the Blood" hand-lettered on it.

The contemporary Christian class was in Darrington Unit, a maximum-security prison in Texas. As part of a prison program, the men can receive a bachelor's degree in Christian ministry from Southwestern Baptist Theological Seminary in Houston. Ben Phillips, a professor at Southwestern and director of the Darrington program, which graduated its first class in 2015, escorted me. The program occupies an entire wing of the prison, with two classrooms, a library, a computer lab, conference rooms, and offices. (Its supporters are raising $2 million to convert a prison gym into a chapel and more classrooms for the seminary.) It is one of many faith-based college programs throughout the South, such as the Louisiana women's program I discussed in the previous chapter, in which women and men receive a degree in Christian ministry and then are sent to proselytize to other prisoners.

Whether preached under the threat of cannon fire or with the enticement of a college degree, the promise of redemption for prisoners is a spectral presence underpinning the rise of modern punishment, from the penitentiary to the reformatory to mass incarceration as we know it today. Redemption and punishment have maintained a tense symbiosis throughout the history of US prisons. The first models of punishment were based on warring theological ideas that the prisoner was permanently stained by sin, and that conversion and reformation of the individual was possible. Initially, the reformers of the first US prisons, the penitentiaries in New York and Pennsylvania, promised a novel form of captivity in which redemption of the individual might occur under the right moral conditions. If a person was penitent, he could be reformed. Quaker, Calvinist, and Methodist reformers constructed the first penitentiaries in the early 1800s based on the belief that confinement within walls would reawaken the divine in each criminal. Christian theologies of innate wickedness, of the possibility of grace and transformation, and of the concept of an eye for an eye shaped ideas of punishment. Reformers forged the first penitentiaries and their modes of punishment around questions of whether crime was the manifestation of an inherently corrupt nature or an act of free will. These first Northern penitentiaries had penance and penitence as their founding principles. Religious redemption was the antidote to physical punishment.

Yet, control has always been the perennial and underlying logic that persisted through various manifestations of incarceration in the United States that involve the body and soul of the prisoner. The prison requires discipline and surveillance in order to function, and religious models justified physical punishment, routinized prayer, individual isolation, and silent, congregate labor. In the first Quaker penitentiaries, prisoners were expected to labor and study in complete silence and isolation. The theological ideas of religious reformers were also directed toward molding the will of the prisoner. According to Andrew Skotnicki, a professor of religious studies, "It was believed that a methodical regimen regulating every aspect of the inmate's life could produce the conditions where revival preaching might find an open heart."[2]

Control of prisoners' bodies and souls found a more overt and harrowing form in the Southern convict lease system in the late 1800s. Men, women, and children—many former slaves—died harvesting sugarcane or rice on the sites of former slave plantations. Their labor generated profit and was the gruesome genesis of companies like Domino Sugar. Many of the convict lease farms on which prisoners toiled eventually became giant state prisons like the Mississippi State Penitentiary or Louisiana State Penitentiary. Control took the form of total subjugation without any pretense of redemption.

Vestiges of the penitentiary's emphasis on the prisoner's redemption, and of the plantation-era idea of the prisoner as dispensable laborer, remain in faith-based prisons today. In the history of religion in the American prison, a strain of logic views punishment as just, as long as it is imbued with religious principles, a logic that persists in faith-based ministries. Skotnicki, writing of the role of religion in American prisons, argues, "The history of the penitentiaries reveals, however, that it is possible to invest structures of control with meaning, as long as there is a stated moral organizational principle that is the channel through which an institution can be ordered and its inhabitants socialized. This task has been and always will be fundamentally religious in nature."[3]

Darrington Unit, the maximum-security prison in Texas, is a former plantation and farm. It is at the end of a long country road that passes through fields of milo, a type of cattle feed with the appearance of tasseled corn. And it is also a key site for the reemergence of the logic that punishment is redemptive, that a carceral church produces people with changed hearts, and that faith-based ministries and seminaries are necessary to supervise the reformation of the body and soul.

Our current model of prisons is a fairly modern invention without any analogies in world history. In the colonial era, most crimes were seen as sins, and imprisonment as we know it today was almost nonexistent.[4] Early colonial towns in New England had populations of sometimes fewer than one thousand inhabitants.[5] Institutionalized punishment was too expensive, so when punishment occurred, it was swift and immediate. Transgressors were usually known members of the community, and almost everyone belonged to the church. Given this proximity to others, the punishment most befitting the crime was humiliation through time in stockades or banishment from the community. Being tarred and feathered was also a colonial punishment, and the women and men accused in the Salem witch trials of 1692 were hanged. Colonial models of law and justice were steeped in Calvinist doctrine. John Calvin, the sixteenth-century theologian, argued in *Institutes of the Christian Religion* that all humans were inherently wicked and sinful. Since humans were condemned from birth, the only function of punishment was deterrence. The pious might rejoice only in the more pronounced suffering of the wicked, as all were destined to suffer, and punishment by Calvin's vengeful and fierce God was inevitable.[6] Colonial laws also followed English criminal codes, which listed as many as 160 crimes as capital offenses.[7] Only after the Revolutionary War did laws begin to shift away from the British model, as the states asserted independence. By the late 1700s, new criminal codes in the early republic abolished capital punishment, except for treason and premeditated murder.[8]

In the American South, hangings, whippings, and burnings, often at the hands of lynch mobs, were commonplace brutalities for slaves and even those who might oppose slavery. Bodily torture and humiliation served in the absence of a formal code of law and justice. The newly constructed prisons of the early 1800s, with solitary cells and hard labor, were designed to replace brutal physical punishments, and they wed Calvinist ideas with concepts of individual liberty and optimism spurred by the Second Great Awakening, a Protestant religious revival movement.[9] Quaker faith in the inherent divinity and, thus, goodness in each person was a drastic contrast to Calvinism's pessimistic view of human nature. Prominent Quakers like Thomas Eddy and members of the Philadelphia Society for Alleviating the Miseries of Public Prisons conveyed their belief in the inner divine light carried by all human beings to the prisoner. Early religious reformers affirmed prisoners' reformative potential and argued for a connection between democracy and humane punishment.[10] Prisons might become prayer houses. Criminals were not born, Eddy and others argued; they are molded by social circumstances and could be reformed. The dimmed light might be reignited in the gloom of the modern penitentiary.

Quaker reformers believed that silence, prayer, discipline, and orderliness were methods for fostering a redeemed life in prison.[11] Their theology of redemptive suffering emphasized an unbending faith that God approved of prison and worked through it to reach prisoners, an assumption that continues to resonate with faith-based ministries today. The logic of control emerged in the idea that prisoners' progress in mercy and grace could be measured in their submission to the prison order. In obeying rules of silence and bodily order, prisoners showed their respect for civil authority and, further, their respect for God. Writing of the creation of prisons in France during the same period, philosopher Michel Foucault describes how prisons produced new forms of subjection and power because they governed the body and the soul: docility and obedience were the result of the highly regulated prison system. "Discipline produces subjected and practiced bodies, 'docile' bodies," he writes. "Discipline increases the forces of the body (in economic terms of utility) and diminishes these same forces (in political terms of obedience)."[12] To prison reformers in the early republic, criminals no longer stood for humanity's collected depravity, as Calvin had preached, but represented a Christian's opportunity to convert all sinful people and bolster the discipline of the prison.

In the early 1800s, solitary confinement emerged as a key strategy of control and redemption in Eastern State Penitentiary in Philadelphia and Auburn State Prison in upstate New York. The principles of this new system were isolation and work. The rationale for isolation was to prevent collaboration and recidivism, to promote reformatory practice, and "to create a situation in which the words and power of the imprisoning and reforming power will take on even greater authority due to the relative silence of all others."[13] Eastern State was based on the Quaker model of silence. Designed by architect John Haviland, with walls extending outward, prisoners could not see each other in their cells. They worked and exercised alone in the yards that extended from their cells. Quaker groups, religious men and women, and chaplains who visited would stand and talk to each man individually. They rationalized solitary confinement as a more humane and reformative approach to punishment. Its proponents believed that, in isolation, "the truth lodged deep in the soul could present itself, aided by the encouragement of the bible and the words of the minister."[14]

One journalist opined of the Quaker system, "It showed a touching faith in human nature, although precious little knowledge of it."[15] Isolation in Eastern State Penitentiary drove many to suicide and despair, rather than penitence and reform. Alexis de Tocqueville and Gustave de Beaumont, who had been sent by the government of France in 1831 to survey American penitentiaries, and whose observations still prove eerily prescient today, wrote, "We have often trod during the night those monotonous and dumb galleries, where a lamp is always burning: we felt as if we traversed catacombs; there were a thousand living beings, and yet it was a desert solitude." And, "This absolute solitude, if nothing interrupt it, is beyond the strength of man; it destroys the criminal without intermission and without pity; it does not reform, it kills."[16]

From the time of the first prisons, the aim of redemption always dueled with the rationale of efficiency, control, and profitability. Tocqueville and Beaumont wrote, "The prisoner in the United States breathes in the penitentiary a religious atmosphere that surrounds him on all sides."[17] However, punishment could induce profits and efficiency from prisoner workers, while the missionary might simultaneously evangelize a captive population. If solitary was one method for remaking the prisoner, labor was another, and the contract system in which outside businesses paid a fixed rate for prisoner labor was introduced as early as 1817 in Auburn.[18] Silence was a way to keep prisoners from contaminating each other with

their sins, but it also enabled the keepers of the prison to squeeze productivity from an unruly and unmotivated workforce through increasingly
extreme corporeal punishments.[19] The prisoner's labor and wages became
an incentive for reform of the Quaker model and increased the power
of the prison over the prisoner. At Auburn State Prison, politicians and
prison administrators, eager to make the prison profitable, supplemented
silence at night with communal labor by day.

Punishment and control existed in multiple forms: the lash, labor, or
isolation for the sake of religious transformation. In the same prisons where
ministers stood extolling the virtues of repentance in the dark prison
corridor, with a lantern hanging from the cell bars, prisoners would be
whipped and forced to work all day. Prison authority and God's grace in
Auburn and Eastern were inseparable; submitting to God meant submitting to prison authorities. Neither system—of silent, congregate labor or
separate, solitary cells—allowed any form of communication between the
imprisoned, because it was thought community would lead to corruption
and depravity, and hinder moral reform.[20] For prisoners who resisted religious instruction, the reformers believed that the hours of isolation might
eventually drive them to biblical devotion and reflection, particularly because the Bible was the only book available to them.[21]

Although Eddy, the Quaker, still saw prisoners as human beings, Calvin's notion of an inherently flawed and sinful human nature reigned at
Auburn State Prison. Elam Lynd, the warden of Auburn, himself religious, proved to be despotic and vicious.[22] Lynd rejected the idea of religious reformation. "We must understand each other," he told Tocqueville
and Beaumont. "I do not believe in a complete reform, except with young
delinquents. Nothing, in my opinion, is rarer than to see a convict of
mature age become a religious and virtuous man. I do not put great faith
in the sanctity of those who leave the prison. I do not believe that the
counsels of the chaplain or the meditations of the prisoner, make a good
Christian of him."[23]

Since the prison was meant to be financially viable, any method of
brutality was justified. Lynd introduced the lash as punishment for broken rules. At the sound of a keeper's whistle, men in his prison moved
in lockstep, with their arms held tightly to their chests or with one hand

down and the other resting on the arm or shoulder of the prisoner ahead of him.[24] Prisoners could reclaim their humanity by surrendering their will to God and, more importantly, to the authority of Lynd. In 1825, in his zeal for productivity, Lynd had prisoners floated on barges from Auburn down the Hudson River to Ossining, New York. There, in silence and backbreaking labor, they built Sing Sing Prison. Many of them would go on to live there.

Tocqueville and Beaumont characterized the American system this way: "The Philadelphia system produces more honest men, and that of New York more obedient citizens."[25]

Externally, Auburn's system worked on the body, at the level of movements, gestures, and attitudes: an infinitesimal power over the active body. The constant coercion and supervision of the body's activity was the object, rather than internal or spiritual reform. "The whole duty of a convict in this prison is to obey orders, labor diligently in silence, and whenever it is necessary for him to speak to a keeper, to do it with a humble sense of his degraded situation," Lynd wrote.[26] Life was routinized. Bells rang to determine mealtimes. Keepers kept vigilant watch over the prisoners. The prisoners woke and worked in silence. In her book on the history of religion in prison, Jennifer Graber writes that Auburn's prisoners had become the walking dead—bodies in disciplined motion, without the will to resist.[27] It was no longer the cannon directed at the unruly inmates but a system of discipline, labor, and religious coercion.

After the Civil War, the Quaker model of solitude and individual labor proved more costly and less efficient than Auburn's communal model. As the United States became more religiously, racially, and ethnically diverse, prisons gradually became more punitive.[28] Prisoners who emerged from the hellholes of Auburn and Sing Sing told stories of physical terror that exposed the lie that suffering might be redemptive. Their stories emphasized the concept that prison hardened rather than reformed; it turned men into beasts.[29] And yet a public outcry about the barbarity of the lash at Auburn only engendered more intricate and pernicious forms of brutality: the shower in which a man was tied to a chair and continually doused with cold water; the gag, a metal plate inserted in the mouth and attached to cuffs by a chain; screws and pulleys by which to hang a man by his thumbs. The success and profitability of Auburn and Sing Sing encouraged Maryland, Massachusetts, New Hampshire, New Jersey, Ohio, Vermont, and Virginia to develop similar models.[30]

Around the same time Auburn became a paragon of prison management to extract maximum labor, the model of the prisoner as disposable laborer found its apotheosis in the transition from slavery to convict lease farms in the South. Their models of prisoner control were fueled by Southern ideas of racial subjugation and white supremacy. Southern prisons and work farms were often former plantations, where brutality and horror far eclipsed any idea of redemption. Robert Perkinson, in his book on the history of prisons in Texas, compares the Northern and Southern prisons: "One reformatory; one retributive; one integrationist, one exclusionary; one conceived in northern churches and the other on southern work farms."[31] With the highest rates of incarceration and reputations as the most violent places to do time in the United States, these same Southern prisons are today the sites of religious evangelization and faith-based ministries.

The Reconstruction era after the Civil War marked a moment of hope and possibility for freed African Americans. During this brief period, African American men and women owned land and businesses, and ran for political office; it seemed that democracy might take root in the rubble of the defeated states of the Confederacy.[32] However, Southern white elites struck back, and soon legislatures began criminalizing actions like loitering and vagrancy, behaviors that had never been subject to criminal sanction in the past. Politicians, desperate to maintain white supremacy, and terrified of the newly enfranchised African Americans, sought ways to enslave on work farms those who had once been enslaved on plantations. The black codes or "pig laws" became justification for sending children from the age of eight and adults to the newly built convict lease farms. The pig laws resulted in the record imprisonment of black men during Reconstruction and the Jim Crow era and, along with the convict lease system, restored white-dominated political and social order.[33] W. E. B. Du Bois, one of the foremost African American intellectuals of this period, wrote of Reconstruction, "The slave went free, stood a brief moment in the sun; then moved back again toward slavery."[34]

In his book *Worse Than Slavery*, David Oshinsky describes the horror of the convict lease farms. Men convicted of the increasingly labyrinthine number of crimes targeting African Americans were leased out to work for the benefit of landowners, where overseers whipped and worked convicts to death. The system was maintained by a trustee system in which prisoners called "Big Stripes," armed with guns, guarded other prisoners. However, since prisoners were no longer property, they could be worked to death, discarded, and replaced by new prisoners. The number of African Americans in the convict lease system grew exponentially, while white imprisonment declined during this period. Mary Church Terrell, the first president of the National Association of Colored Women, argued, "In . . . the convict lease camps of the South to-day are thousands of colored people men, women, and children, who are enduring a bondage, in some respects more cruel and crushing than that from which their parents were emancipated forty years ago."[35] Whites received longer sentences because they were usually punished only for the most heinous crimes, and while whites did work on the convict lease farms, they were often kept in the prisons rather than leased out to corporations and landowners. As accounts by white prisoners of their treatment "as slaves" leaked out, the public unleashed its outrage at the specter of white men and women subjected to slavelike conditions.

The only goal in this model of imprisonment was profit, gained through the brutal control of bodies. The South needed to industrialize, and freed slaves became the engine of labor in coal mines, lumber mills, railroad camps, and sugarcane plantations in Alabama, Arkansas, Texas, Virginia, Florida, Georgia, North Carolina, South Carolina, Louisiana, and Mississippi, the same states with the highest presence of faith-based ministries today. The expansion of the Texas prisoner population coincided with the railroad boom of the 1870s. Convicts laid most of the 3,500 miles of track in North Carolina. Modern corporations like US Steel and Imperial Sugar, the railroads, and even the construction of the capital city of Texas were made possible through this system. The South's economic development depended on the sweat and blood of prisoners: between 1866 and 1915, the death toll of men in the convict lease system exceeded thirty thousand.[36]

The system of convict leasing lasted until after 1915, but its legacy has stretched far beyond.[37] Prisons like Parchman Farm became the Mississippi

State Penitentiary, which now has a Baptist seminary. Angola, a slave plantation and convict lease farm, is now the Louisiana State Penitentiary. Still referred to as "the farm," it is the site of the original prisoner missionary program. Darrington Unit in Texas, also originally a plantation and then a convict lease farm, is the latest permutation of the faith-based prison experiment. The application for the Darrington seminary program describes its seminarians as farmhands going out into the fields to harvest, a metaphor supposed to invoke the idea of a missionary field but one that is especially haunting, given the prison's history.

Over time, the penitentiary model declined in favor of labor and profit rather than individual reformation. The term "penitentiary" was rarely used after the Civil War.[38] It was replaced by the word "reformatory." Eastern State Penitentiary, the last of the prisons based on Quaker models of solitary confinement, turned to congregate labor in 1913. The formation of the Prison Association of New York in 1844 and the first national prison conference in Cincinnati in 1870 signaled the institutionalization and professionalization of punishment during the Progressive Era.[39]

The word "reformatory" reflected the shift in thinking to prisons that emphasized education, labor, and training. Increasingly, the public expected bureaucrats and officials to administer the prison, rather than religious reformers. This era ushered in a rehabilitative ethos based on theories of medical, behavioral, and biological science that viewed people in prison as sick and in need of cure rather than religious redemption. Psychotherapeutic treatments became prevalent in prisons, and by 1926, sixty-seven prisons employed psychiatrists and psychologists.[40] Religion was rarely a feature of these new programs, and many prisons were renamed "correctional institutions" in the 1950s as part of the wider hospital metaphor of treatment.[41] In the Northern states, gradually, the idea of "corrections" that we now associate with prisons took precedence.

The idea that prisons would provide job training, basic education and access to recreation infused the carceral system around the middle of the twentieth century.[42] Several trends followed this period of rehabilitation. First, rehabilitative programs began to disappear in the 1970s and 1980s. At the same time, the combination of tougher sentencing laws and the War on Drugs flooded the prison system with predominantly poor and African

American and Latino men and women. As the racially disproportionate behemoth of mass incarceration in the United States that we have today emerged in the 1980s, the state withdrew support for programs in favor of warehousing vast numbers of people. Highly organized and influential prison ministries began to reenter the prison in a more organized manner during this punitive period of massive prison growth and unprecedented numbers of men and women in prisons.

Prison Fellowship (PF) became one of the most prominent, evangelical prison ministry organizations in the United States. Its founder, Chuck Colson, died in 2012, but, as I discuss in chapter 7, his belief in evangelicals as a social force to transform mass incarceration shaped the current conservative coalition around criminal justice reform. Colson was a former Nixon aide, known for his ruthless political tactics, and he served seven months in federal prison for obstruction of justice as part of his Watergate crimes.[43] Upon his release in the late 1970s, he wrote the book *Born Again* and refashioned himself as an advocate for the redemptive power of evangelical Christianity on criminals.[44] He attributed his zeal for prison ministry to the men he met in prison, who, he felt, were often victims of injustice, and to the prison itself, as marked by despair. Colson left prison convinced that secular rehabilitative programs would never succeed. Formally incorporated in August 1976 as Prison Fellowship, Colson's ministry offered prison authorities an alternative to secular rehabilitative programs that were widely judged to have failed, especially in the aftermath of the Attica Prison uprising. His model was based on fellowship groups of prisoners supported by community volunteers, and it coincided with renewed interest by evangelicals in the prison as a mission field.

Colson's faith-based experiment in the United States drew inspiration from a Christian prison in Brazil called Humaita, near Sao Paulo, which was built by the Association for the Protection and Assistance for the Convicted (APAC) in the 1970s.[45] Mario Ottoboni, the founder, attended, with fifteen other couples, a Cursillo, a short course on Christianity consisting of fifteen talks and five meditations spread over three days. At the end of a Cursillo, a person embarks on the "fourth day," considered to be the rest of his life. As part of his fourth day, Ottoboni went to work with prisoners in Brazil. Like the early prison reformers of the 1790s, he had toured a jail in Brazil and was appalled by the conditions there. There were more than 150 men in a space meant for 40, without water, sunlight, or cleaning materials.[46] "It is imperative to restore in the prisoner the sense of human dignity and divine affiliation, so that he can turn himself to goodness," Ottoboni wrote. "It should never be forgotten that the whole of the APAC approach finds its inspiration in the sacrifice on the cross, and in the merciful look of Christ when he turned to the repentant thief and announced his salvation."[47] A judge granted Ottoboni and others un-limited access to the Brazilian prison, with authority over how it would be run, allowing Ottoboni to act as a subsidiary of the justice system.[48] He and others authored a book called *Christ Wept in Jail*, which prompted the Brazilian government in 1976 to reform its penal code and treat prisoners in a more humane manner. After various setbacks, Ottoboni took over Humaita as a private entity in 1984.

Humaita is a "community in perfection," said to be indistinguishable from any other kind of faith-based community. It wants to transform not only the prisoners but the prison environment.[49] Humaita teaches responsi-bility to a community rather than individual tasks or programs. According to the professor of biblical law Jonathan Burnside, "The State can build prisons, nominate agents, assign resources—but cannot give love. It is only we, physical persons . . . that can face the challenge of seeding love in the prisons."[50] Participants at the Humaita program receive judicial, medical and psychological assistance, good food, and a prison free from the cor-rupting influence of the police. They have their own canteen, a barbershop, and a place for families to visit. They also receive sentence reductions for participation; for each day in the program, one day is subtracted from their sentence. Men participate in daily prayers, literacy and professional-skills courses, and the Cursillo course to win unbelievers called Journey with Christ. They also have godmothers and godfathers, community members who agree to sponsor them and visit them throughout their time in prison. In addition to moving through five phases of progressive freedom, the prison has a prisoners' council of one hundred men, including a Council on Sincerity and Security, which enforces the rules and behavior of the community. Those who violate a rule go before the fifteen members of the Council on Sincerity and Security to explain their behavior.[51]

Colson visited Humaita and used it as a model for Prison Fellowship. The first Prison Fellowship faith-based dorm in prisons opened in the United States in 1997, and APAC officially became a part of Prison Fellowship International in 1989. The central part of the fellowship is the InnerChange Freedom Initiative, a twenty-four-hour-a-day Christian immersion program that it later started in prisons around the United States. The fellowship has contracted with state corrections departments to minister to entire wings of men's medium security prisons in Texas, Missouri, Minnesota, Iowa, and Kansas.

The program begins eighteen to twenty-four months before a prisoner is released. To be eligible to join, prisoners must be within two years of parole and must proclaim their status as born-again Christians. Men and women work at a job during the day and attend classes to develop their life skills and spiritual maturity. The classes focus on time management, anger control, family relations, and job preparedness. There are also classes dedicated to biblical doctrine and scripture memorization. Evenings are filled with more Christian teaching and discipleship seminars that run until 10 p.m. During the second phase of the program, prisoners must perform community service, and they are encouraged to apologize and make restitution to their victims in the form of letters or meetings. Six months into the program, each person is matched with a Christian church volunteer who mentors him or her during the remaining time in prison. After release, that person continues to mentor him or her for six to twelve months, during which the former prisoner must hold a job and be an active church member.[52]

During the 1970s, another prison-ministry movement, called Kairos, also inspired by Humaita, spread throughout the United States. The goal of Kairos was not only to help Christ in saving souls, but to transform prison environments; it was based on the idea that religious volunteers and people inside prison could bond despite the disparities in their situations. Kairos began during a weekend at Union Correctional Institution in Raiford, Florida, in 1976. Its stated goal was "to bring Christ's love and forgiveness to all incarcerated individuals, their families, and those who work with them, and to assist in the transition of becoming a productive citizen."[53]

Kairos doesn't create faith-based dorms or prisons, as some ministries do, but it is one of the oldest and most active ministries. Kairos ministries currently operate in over thirty-three states and close to three hundred prisons in the United States and in prisons in Australia, Canada, England, Costa Rica, Peru, Nicaragua, Honduras, and South Africa. Kairos holds approximately 650 weekend gatherings each year and has one of the highest numbers of prison volunteers in the United States, and it organizes 7,000 short courses in Christianity, based on the Cursillo method, during Kairos weekends involving 170,000 people in US prisons.[54]

In order to run a Kairos weekend in a prison, volunteers must commit to forty hours of preparatory community building over a two-week period.[55] Kairos believes the best volunteers have suffered from abuse, addiction to drugs and alcohol, isolation, and abandonment, just like the men and women inside the prison. Often, volunteers are required to make themselves vulnerable by sharing their own struggles in order to build trust and sustain connections. While the volunteers might imagine a compassionate connection with the prisoners, if they have not properly overcome their own problems, they risk reinforcing what has happened to prisoners, rather than being models of transformation. The founder of Kairos argues, "The volunteers are not worth anything to the prisoners unless they are vulnerable and of course that same vulnerability makes them a security risk."[56]

For volunteers, being in the prison must be a willing sacrifice rather than a professional obligation. They are to be authentic and vulnerable, to share the agape love of God, no matter what it costs the volunteer emotionally. The founder of Kairos writes that "when we begin doing it for any other reason, whether it is being paid or moving into that ministry because it feels good to us . . . then we begin to lose track of what we are up to and the authenticity disappears."[57] Kairos welcomes prisoners of any religion, despite its explicit Christianity, and bills itself as broadly ecumenical. The ministry eschews altar calls, overt proselytizing, and speaking in tongues for the sake of this identification. During a Kairos weekend, women and men in prison are led through a structured "encounter" program in which they are introduced to Kairos's philosophy and the volunteers on Thursday night. The next day, they "encounter the self" and scrutinize their own decisions and their relationship with God. On Saturday, they encounter Christ and are required to analyze how Christ resonates as a model for forgiveness in their relationships. Finally, on Sunday, they expand beyond the focus on the self and encounter others, which should launch them into the process of aligning themselves with a fellowship of Kairos graduates as part of a broader religious community within the prison. After the completion of the weekend course, they will participate in another reunion, join a weekly prayer and fellowship group, and finish with a final two-day retreat. The "prayer and share" group produces continuity for prisoners who have completed Kairos trainings.

Kairos chooses prisoners for its three-day weekend courses who are leaders; they do not need to be Christian but must have significant influence over the prison population. Kairos strives to recruit people like gang leaders who might not come to the chapel but who can aid it in transforming the prison.[58] By converting the most powerful and influential prison leaders, Kairos persuades others to become Christians; the prison authorities benefit as well when prisoner leaders are under the sway of a ministry group. Kairos volunteers are forthcoming about their own sins during the weekend courses as a way to encourage prisoners to show vulnerability. The volunteers work on listening skills, disclosing formative life experiences to all who attend. In a meditation called "the Wall," prisoners are supposed to testify about how their behavior has led them to isolate themselves from others. After the weekend, Kairos urges the men and women in the groups to continue meeting together once a week and organizes weekly reunions with outside volunteers. Kairos weekends become the basis for ongoing Bible study.

Thomas Eddy, the Quaker reformer, preached, "Work on the prisoner's soul must be carried out as often as possible. The prison, though an administrative apparatus, will at the same time be a machine for altering minds."[59] Over a hundred years after the first penitentiaries, APAC, Prison Fellowship, and Kairos reintroduced to the prison individual conversion and heart change as the central facet of transformation. The growth of faith-based ministries nationally and the evangelical impulse to remake people into Christians has taken root in prisons where historically reform was never a consideration—prisons like Darrington.

Texas has over one hundred state and private prisons; it is one of the largest prison networks in the United States, and many men and women are serving life terms or the equivalent. During the class I described at the beginning of this chapter, prisoners discussed how to ascertain someone's motives and deal with recalcitrant potential converts. A constant din distinguishes Darrington from other prisons, and the unceasing clamor only abates when the door to the seminary wing closes. Other prisons I've visited did not seem as unremittingly loud. Darrington has one long main corridor, with staircases and rows of barred cells down the central artery. The day rooms, mostly lined with white painted benches and a few tables, are the domain of the prison gangs, according to men in the seminary. The students treat their status as potential missionaries with gravity, and their white jumpsuits and the stark white walls of the windowless classroom gave the classroom an almost monastic appearance. The men I speak with tell me that, once the seminary program was underway, the gang leadership agreed to reserve a special table just for seminary students. The story of Christians being protected and sanctioned by the gangs has become the stuff of legend here, although I am never able to verify if it is true.

Echoing Eddy's sentiments from the early 1800s, Ben Phillips, the seminary director, tells the men at Darrington, "You know when you got into this program that it is largely not to minister to the free world; your assignment—and you're already doing it, I understand, in your cell blocks—you're going to change the culture of this system. It's already happening in Darrington." At Darrington and elsewhere, the purpose of redemption is to manage and contain the sprawling carceral system that exists throughout the United States. Unlike prisoners in the Quaker penitentiary, the students in the prison seminary are to govern themselves and each other. As I discuss in the next chapter, the seminary students forge community and belonging, but they watch each other carefully for lapses in behavior or even belief. Rather than outsiders, seminary students become the religious leaders in the prison, a rare chance for them to have responsibility or to participate in their own governance. Just as the reformers at Eastern State Penitentiary and Auburn State Prison did, Phillips believes he is bringing God's word to the prison, and that it will spread through the influence of the students. The debate about good motives the men engaged in is key, because they must figure out how to shape and influence others within the prison. Keith, who is thirty-five years old and has a life sentence, told me that when they are sent to other Texas prisons as missionaries, their strategy should be to win over the other religious guys first, before they can even start to think about new converts.

The seminary grants the power to minister to others, to monitor each other, and to patrol prisoners' own inner worlds for signs of sin or false motives. They spend their days in a quiet section of the prison, sealed off from the chaos of prison life. A particular officer is assigned to the seminary wing. Often, the students' idea of who has authority over them can conflict with the administration and those paid to guard them. Patricia, from the women's seminary in Louisiana, believes punishment is just, as long as it comes from God, who is an alternate authority to the prison. Many of the men in Darrington echoed that idea. God would enter their hearts and change them, and only God can determine their punishment and redemption, not the guards or the prison or the courts. Patricia and many of the men in the seminar were disdainful of the officers and even the mode of punishment the prison mandated. "Your job is not to punish me," Patricia said. "I was punished when I went to court. I'm punished every day when I can't go home. I'm punished when I talk to my daughter on the phone or my kids, when they have babies and I can't be there. But it's not your job to punish me." For them, punishment is coupled with redemption of the individual by God. The two are inextricable.

Phillips greets everyone with the bantering Southern politeness that later compels him to invite me to dinner. Although he is an avid sports fan and wears a Baltimore Orioles jacket, having grown up in Maryland, he was descended from a long line of Baptist missionaries. "I like to say I was a Baptist before birth," he tells me. Before he started working at Darrington, the only time he'd been to a prison was with the University of Maryland band. They played "Tis the Gift to Be Simple," with the words "Tis the gift to be free," at the opening of a jail in Prince George's County. Phillips's grandparents were Baptist music missionaries who specialized in the trumpet and trombone and traveled all over the world. Despite his specialization in ancient religion, his passion is military history, and he reads Greek. His dream to attend the Naval Academy was scuttled by asthma and poor eyesight, so he immersed himself in the seminary. Prison work was never on his radar until one Saturday, while he was practicing for a piano concert at church, he received a call from the president of the seminary. The president asked Phillips to direct the program and expected an answer right away. As Phillips put it, "Sometimes you know God's will, and sometimes others tell you it."

Inside the prison, Phillips clearly enjoys his authority and showing me around, but he doesn't hover. Darrington is one of the few men's prisons where I could talk to prisoners in a room without anyone else around. However, there are no female faculty members because of the seminary's belief in gender role differentiation. Women, they think, should not have teaching authority over the students. The female correctional officers at Darrington wear a heavy apron-like garment over their uniforms that looks like the X-ray cover at a dentist's office. Sean, the program administrator, says, "I would not recommend that women work in this environment on a regular basis. The things that they have to deal with to me are just really hard. Even if theologically we were cool with women being spiritual authorities, advisors, and whatnot, I still would not practically recommend that it be the case." He emphasizes that the main reason women can't teach is because the men would be uncomfortable.

The program has computers and a library, but the men are limited to the courses the seminary offers and the books available. They are being inducted into a specific worldview, that of the Southwestern Baptist Theological Seminary. Later that day at Darrington Unit, Phillips teaches a class for freshman on virtues. Although he occasionally glances at his tablet, he speaks with the fluency and dynamism of someone accustomed to the pulpit. The men have been reading Aristotle and Aquinas, on reciprocal and individual justice, but today the lesson is on redistributive justice. As I sit at a table with seven men, Phillips hands each a strip of paper with five boxes on it. The boxes represent their happiness index. Then he hands each man a bag of candy. Some have Orange Slices, others Skittles, M&Ms, or Junior Mints. One of the wardens enters the room and watches carefully.

First, Phillips asks them to record their level of happiness, on a scale of one to five, in the first box of the strip. Five is the highest and one is the lowest. Next, the men exchange their bags of candy with someone at their table and then record their happiness level in the second box. After a boisterous five minutes of laughter and talking, Phillips tells them to trade with a person who has the same letter on their strip of paper. Again, they record their happiness index. Finally, Phillips tells them they can trade with anyone in the room. At the end, they subtract the first number from the last to see if their happiness stayed the same, went up, or went down. After all the trading, almost everyone's number increased. Phillips uses this exercise to discuss redistribution and his own particular political views as part of a religious worldview: "The more people you have to trade with, the better chance you have at happiness, to get what you want. When trade is forced, someone outside decides, it decreases happiness." To illustrate, he asks Warden Tucker what he likes, and the men are forced to hand over their Orange Slices. "This is what communism does," Phillips explains to them. The free-market lecture continues as he discusses greed and covetousness, blending the biblical with the economic. The lesson makes his particular views seem biblically supported and mandated, and without access to other classes or information, why would the students think differently? One man asks, "What if we don't start out the same? Some have more and others less." Phillips tells the class it doesn't matter, because we all start out in the image of God. God will provide.

In 1833, George W. Smith, an early commentator on prison life, expressed that the will might be tamed through religious instruction: "Each individual will necessarily be made the instrument of his own punishment—his conscience will be the avenger of society."[60] The men in the class were not being preached to under the threat of a cannon or toiling in the fields of the plantation, but they were still under coercion: the alternative was endless warehousing in the Texas prison system.

In the library where Phillips's virtues class met, men were hanging a large wooden plaque that seminary students at Angola prison had elaborately carved for them. The verse on the plaque was from Matthew 7:7–8: "Ask and it will be given to you; seek and you will find; knock and the door will be opened to you. For everyone who asks receives; the one who seeks finds; and to the one who knocks, the door will be opened." The worldviews presented to them were partial and biased, as was the information they could access. The verse implied that a person might discover something about himself, the divine light of the optimistic Quakers, but his choices were already circumscribed: become a missionary or remain a number in the vast prison system. Today's faith-based ministries are a carceral church, much like the penitentiary. They accept punishment and imprisonment as necessary precursors in order for a person in prison to be redeemed. The Quakers may have initially hoped that through their experiments in redemption and confinement, the prison system might fade away. Instead, they laid the groundwork for mass incarceration. The question then becomes whether a system is justified as long as the people captive within it will find God. The seminary strives to make prisoners into emissaries of Baptist belief, fed back in the vast Texas prison archipelago without questioning why so many people are in prison in the first place.

# CHAPTER 3

# THE MISSIONARIES

*Governing the Prison*

IN A DUSTY PRISON RODEO ARENA, Mother Mary cradles Jesus's head in her lap. Around them, a group of men and women wail; Jesus is about to be crucified on the cross. Susan, the gray-haired woman playing Mary, sobs audibly. When she acts in this scene, she imagines her son serving multiple tours in Iraq and Afghanistan; she doesn't know if he is alive or dead. He no longer speaks to her because she has been sentenced to fifteen years in prison for identity theft. The role of Mary allows her to feel like a mother. Sammy, a slight, middle-aged man with a bushy afro, who wears a T-shirt that says "Malachi Dads," a reference to a Christian parenting program, is playing Jesus. Later, he tells Susan that he feels her love for him as a son every time they rehearse. He also misses his children. He's serving a sixty-six-year sentence for armed robbery.

For almost two years, a group of some seventy men and women practiced the play *Cast the First Stone*, the story of the life of Jesus, at Angola, the Louisiana State Penitentiary. The play is three-and-a-half hours long, with musical interludes and elaborate sets that include enormous crosses, a mule, a camel, and two horses. The women, like Susan and Patricia, the ex-biker who is playing a supporting role, come by bus from LCIW, the women's prison about two hours away. For the first time in decades, some of these prisoners have been allowed to touch or interact with the opposite sex.[1] Sandra, who plays Mary Magdalene, talks with the other women about how unnerving it is to interact with men.

When a man comes into the women's prison, they are supposed to keep their heads down. Sandra is so unused to hearing a man's voice that she tells them, "I almost couldn't understand what he was saying," in reference to the director. Sandra tells me she identifies with Mary Magdalene because she has also been abused and used by men. She killed her boyfriend. Her children were four and seven at the time and now they are in their twenties. "I'd rather take the beatings and be home," she says. One day, when the group practices and has a picnic by the lake at Angola, Patricia comments that she hasn't seen a lake in ten years.

In a prison where everything is circumscribed, the play is a sanctioned environment in which to express and enact the pain and anguish of their lives. They identify their story with something divine and biblical. The play becomes a space of restricted freedom to be something different from what they were and what they may be in the prison. These men and women serving life sentences or the equivalent negotiate what it means to live in a prison for most of their lives without seeing their children or families or a lake.

The director and head of the Angola drama club, Gary Tyler, is acting expert, taskmaster, cheerleader, and confidant to the group. He's chosen and trained all the actors. They include Terrell, a Muslim who is playing Judas, a role that no one wanted because Judas is the original snitch, and Jonathan, who plays the disciple Peter. "Prison makes you better or worse," Jonathan explains. "I'm not who I used to be. Peter was a fisherman and now a disciple. I am something different." When the men playing Jesus, Peter, Joseph, and Judas assemble in one of the prison's rooms to practice, Tyler, who describes himself as spiritual but not religious, has them begin with a chant and exhortation. It is a call and response that the men repeat together after him:

*We are the willing.*
*Doing the impossible*
*For the ungrateful*
*We have done so much*

*with so little, for so long,*
*that we are now qualified*
*to do anything, with nothing.*

The chant showcases the seeming impossibility of men and women condemned to spend their lives behind bars undertaking a play in a prison. Although they repeat it with gusto, the chant is both inspired and beleaguered.

Tyler was the youngest prisoner on death row in Louisiana, sentenced when he was seventeen years old, in 1975. In 1974, Tyler had been one of many black high school students bused to an all-white school. Twenty years after *Brown v. Board of Education*, Louisiana had finally been forced to comply with the law. On the way home from school, a mob of one hundred or so white people, mainly students, attacked the bus. A thirteen-year-old white boy named Timothy, who was standing with his mother, was shot and killed. Although the driver testified that the shot came from outside the bus, and no gun was found on it, police ruthlessly questioned the black kids. Tyler was walking home when he was arrested by a police official. Officers beat him to exact a confession, and an all-white jury tried him as an adult and sentenced him to death. The police produced a gun in the courtroom they claimed killed Timothy, but it later disappeared from the evidence room.[2] Tyler was removed from death row and sentenced to life after the court ruled the death penalty unconstitutional. Tyler rarely talks about himself, except to remark that Jesus was executed because of an allegation, too.

Although the actors only play disciples, men throughout Angola are living this role. For over twenty years, Angola prison has pioneered the faith-based model of redemption and rehabilitation now spreading throughout the Southern prison system. It is the brainchild of Burl Cain, the controversial, now retired warden of Angola prison. The sign above the entrance gate to Angola reads "You Are Entering the Land of New Beginnings." When Warden Cain, a stout authoritative figure in his seventies with flowing white hair and a penchant for aphorisms, became warden in 1995, one of his first actions was to institute "Experiencing God," a yearlong Southern Baptist Convention program for Christians undergoing adversity. Before

long, sixteen hundred men had completed the program, and now it's a re-
quirement for anyone who wants to attend the college program.

The Angola seminary is a result of the withdrawal of state services for
programs inside prison, particularly the dismantlement of higher education. Congress eliminated Pell grants for prisoners in 1994, even though
they made up only 1 percent of the students receiving Pell money to go
to college. The "tough on crime" atmosphere of the period, enflamed
by anti-welfare sentiment, doomed hundreds of prison college-education
programs throughout the United States, including Angola's. Almost immediately, Cain solicited private religious organizations to teach in the
prison to fill the gap left by the state. The New Orleans Baptist Theological
Seminary program (NOBTS) designated Angola as one of its twenty-one
extension sites on September 11, 1995. The program is funded by private
donation, the seminary, Louisiana Baptist Convention, the Baton Rouge
Baptist Association, and individual donors. The program offers the only
way to get a college education in Angola and is the sole educational vehicle
in the prison that avoids opposition from politicians and public resentment
because it is faith-based. Religious groups drawn by Angola's notorious
past and the prominence of the Baptist program send Cain dozens of requests to visit the prison. The films *Out of Sight* and *Monster's Ball* were
filmed there, and *Animal Planet* has a series on Angola about inmates who
farm. Many outsiders are lured by Angola's exceptionalism, and ministers
want the prestige of having ministered to the worst of the worst. As Wilbert Rideau, a writer and former editor of *Angolite Magazine* who spent
forty-four years in Angola, told me, the seminary was an ingenious way
for Cain to create college in the prison through religion. "Most citizens
are not going to criticize an effort that brings prisoners into the folds of
the church," he told me. The program at Angola has inspired similar ones
in Texas, Mississippi, Georgia, West Virginia, and Illinois.

For years, Angola's moniker had been the "bloodiest prison in America."[3] Men slept with catalogues and phone books taped to their chests
as shields against stabbing. Rideau chronicled rampant rape and sexual
exploitation in his memoir and a well-known essay, "Prison: The Sexual
Jungle." The triumphant story Cain tells about his reign is that he turned
prisoners into missionaries, which made the prison safer for all and, by

extension, easier to manage. Almost three hundred men have graduated from the New Orleans Baptist Theological Seminary program, and Cain was heralded by his supporters as a miracle worker who brought order and peace to a previously chaotic and brutal place. Cain believed that, unlike secular college programs, the Baptist seminary college enables men to undergo a spiritual and moral inner transformation. "Without moral rehabilitation, you're just making smarter criminals," Cain says. For Cain, reforming prisons is a matter of reforming prisoners' hearts. When he spoke to the cast of the play, Cain said, "Morality is what works; force doesn't work. This is a test. Your challenge after this is over is how you conduct your life."

One prisoner tells me that the prison no longer has an overseer with a whip as slave plantations did, but the same kind of psychological and theological control is still present. The faith-based volunteers, teachers, and others who oversee the seminary program are now the watchers. The seminary leaders wield extraordinary power and might well be viewed as extensions of the state's disciplinary mechanisms. Whether a sentence is lessened or parole and work release are granted can hinge on the verbal or written support of a volunteer who teaches the class. A religious volunteer or chaplain has the power to decide whether a prisoner is sufficiently re-deemed. In this way, faith-based programs actually increase the number of people who fall under the discipline of the prison, making the seminary a pedagogical tool of the state that determines who and to what extent a person is transformed.

Programs like the seminary create new forms of surveillance, con-temporary forms of the panopticon, from the men who watch each other to the technology used in the prisons. The panopticon encompassed an idea and a physical building, created by Jeremy Bentham, in which cells for prisoners encircled the central tower of the prison. The guards could monitor everyone, and the men in the cells could not tell when they were being watched. The idea was that men would begin to comport them-selves and organize their conduct based on the principle that, at any time, someone might be monitoring them.

At eighteen thousand acres, Angola is nearly the size of Manhattan. It's the largest prison in the world, and its administration has to govern it. At Darrington Unit and the LCIW, the administration installed security cameras at the onset of the seminary program. When I asked if Angola seemed safer after the seminary program became established, one seminary student responded that drug dealing and contraband were less evident, but he hesitated. "Cameras," he said. "This place has got cameras everywhere. There is a change that's taken place here, but I don't know if I see the change from my perspective or the staff's perspective, if you could say it's us or the cameras. I want to give credit to God. I hate bringing the cameras up because that sounds like you're cutting it short." He pointed up at the ceiling in the room where we spoke. "Look up and you'll see their domes."

The ministries become a panopticon-like structure for prisons, particularly in the seminary programs where men live under a Baptist code of conduct and impart those norms to others. Tocqueville and Beaumont wrote, "New rules and regulations are both minute and uniform. It does not break men's will, but softens, bends and guides it; seldom enjoins, but often inhibits, action; it does not destroy anything, but prevents much from being born; it is not at all tyrannical, but it hinders, restrains, stifles and stultifies the potential for disorder."[4] Foucault described how the will of the individual succumbs to the regulations of a prison apparatus; there are parallels to the way the seminary program functions. Foucault chose January 22, 1840, the date of the official opening of Mettray Penal Colony, a prison in France for boys and men between the ages of six and twenty-one, as the date the carceral system reached its apex of control. He described how every part of the day was marked out by bells, and how prisoners had to walk together in lockstep and lived with a military kind of discipline. He called those who built the prison "engineers of conduct."[5] On the walls of the cells were written the words "God sees you." To Foucault, the proof of the total power of this system was that the people of Mettray never rebelled or rioted. The seminarian sent out as a missionary to other prisoners and prisons is supposed to obtain the same result: order and obedience.

A part of controlling the prison is allowing spaces of freedom within unfreedom, such as the seminary for a prisoner who knows he may never leave prison. Despair is a prisoner's most potent enemy; that is one of the few things the prison administration and the men inside seem to agree on. Of the nearly six thousand men in Angola, four thousand are serving life sentences without the possibility of parole. "We have more funerals than we have men going home," Cain told me. To combat disorder and the despair of life without parole, the prison administration believes in giving everyone a job or vocation. As a result, no one is picking grass at Angola, and everyone is supposed to be occupied. Unlike the men at Darrington, who rarely experience fresh air, the men here have at least a limited sense of movement.

The prison trustees are those prisoners who hold the most coveted jobs, earned after decades at Angola. These men have inched their way to the upper echelons of the prison hierarchy as automotive mechanics, newspaper editors, radio DJs, cattle wranglers, horse trainers, preachers, heavy-machinery repairmen, coffin makers, and cowboys who compete in Angola's yearly prison rodeo. They retain some modicum of control over their own lives, a precarious space of sovereignty within the vast prison. In this way, they make time their own and stave off despair. It is the difference between doing time and making a life within captivity.

The trustee system is meant to dole out incentives in the face of hopelessness. Prisoners have responsibilities, jobs, and a modicum of opportunity within the vast Angola prison empire. "They want to have their lives make sense," Cain explains. "There is something for everybody." In most other prisons, it is hard to imagine all these men bustling from place to place. Cain says, "You can move your way up all the way in the system until you almost feel like you're free." The prison is a disorienting world unto itself. When I visited, I was allowed to stay on prison grounds in a cottage designated for visitors. I'd leave the homey cottage with its front porch and rocking chairs, pass a golf course, and five minutes later witness men laboring with hoes in the vast agricultural fields in a tableau from a slave plantation.

In this hierarchical system, the prisoner trustees and administration share an unequal intimacy that enables the trustee system and the contingent sense of freedom within the prison. Big George, who is significantly over six feet tall and close to three hundred pounds, has been in Angola for thirty-five years; he is the cook for the warden, his upper-level staff, and any visitors in the ranch house. No one lives in the ranch house, but friends of Cain, his trusted administrators, and visitors like me have meals there, if invited. George, who at one point worked in the governor's mansion, oversees the kitchen with a proprietary air, and he has the leeway to handpick the other prisoners who work with him. When he's not lumbering around filling plates for dinner guests, he is lounging in a leather recliner watching a giant-screen TV. During one lunch, George carried a bundle of pressed button-down shirts in various colors on hangers past the table where Cain's friends were eating. "Where you going?" asked Cain facetiously, as if Big George were headed to the laundromat or store instead of having been confined almost forty years. As if it were a hilarious joke, the other men at the table laughed and repeated, "Yes, where are you going?"

Joseph, the prison caretaker, has also carved out a space of autonomy inside the prison. He knows each peacock, guinea hen, chicken, flower, and plant because he's been at Angola for thirty-four years. When I met him outside the ranch house, he had been tending the peacocks since dawn. There are dozens of them roaming the expansive grounds, perched on trucks, reclining in tree branches, and pecking around the front porch of the ranch house. Joseph has discovered a nest midway up the hill, and he'll have to cajole the mother and her chicks down to the safety of the hutches and sheds he's built for them over the years, away from the foxes, snakes, and whatever else might nab an unsuspecting peacock at night. Now sixty-four, a slight white man with a stoop and a squinty smile, Joseph spends up to fifteen hours a day in the company of the animals, mowing the lawn and tending the flowers. Cain, an ardent animal lover, brought in the animals, but this is Joseph's tiny domain. After a brief tour and discussion about native Louisiana plants, he reenters his shack to retrieve a battered manila folder. Inside are photos of him with Emily Maw, director of the Innocence Project New Orleans, and her family. The Innocence Project has championed his case, which is marred by evidence suppression and blatant police misconduct.

A life sentence is not just for prisoners, and the lopsided bonds between guards and prisoners persist through generations A few miles from the main prison is B-Line, a town built for prison staff, where grandfathers, fathers, and sons have all worked in the prison. There is a chapel, a pool, a recreation center, and the Prison View golf course. Although the prison began hiring African American correctional staff in 1975, B-Line is still a stronghold for white families who have worked here for generations. Their livelihoods depend on the men who spend their lives in Angola. Joseph and Big George talk about small kids they observed growing up who are now prison lieutenants. More than half of the B-Line population is children under eighteen. To them, Angola represents home and security. The prison has its own post office and a picnic table area where trustees used to be able to meet their families, girlfriends, and wives, until too many were caught having sex in the woods. Now the area is a miniature golf course. One of the communications staff in the prison, Jennifer, is married to a fourth-generation Angola guard whose family lives in B-Line. As a result, she is accepted, but in many ways, she will never be fully embraced because she wasn't born there. Jennifer's mother-in-law, a cook, regularly consults with Big George about menus and catering.

Part of Cain's bravura was that Angola didn't need fences when it had hundreds of men trained as ministers to promote peace, order, and security. Cain and everyone who worked with him all say the same thing. People were punished by the courts, and it wasn't their job to punish them further. They have to have something for everyone or people will be creative in dark ways. Cain understands redemption within the bounds of the prison through finding a life as a cook or groundskeeper or cowboy within Angola. The men in the Baptist seminary have an exalted position, because to Cain, a person can build a life in Angola, but redemption is possible primarily through faith in God. He had to manage a giant prison where few would get out, and the seminary was—and remains—a way to do something with them. The system's effectiveness is measured by the fact that there are no fences in Angola, except those encircling the prison housing camps, spread throughout its eighteen thousand acres.

No one has more contingent freedom than the seminary students and graduates, except possibly the Angola cowboys who herd cattle all day, far from the center of prison life. As with the women at LCIW, Angola's students spend all day in the classrooms, libraries, and computer labs. Dr. John Robson has been the director of NOBTS since the Baptist seminary began at Angola in 1995, and he still teaches regularly. In his seventies,

Robson is a disconcerting mix of piety and frankness. He startled me with a 6 a.m. phone call to make sure I could meet him in time for class. Everywhere he walks in the prison, men greet and petition him: "Hi, Doc," "I sent you a message, Doc," and "See you in class, Doc." Not one to mince words, when one man droned on for ten minutes in class, Robson told him he'd been "shooting the bull" for too long. A veteran preacher and seminary teacher, Robson relishes upending stereotypes of conservative Southern Baptists. "You can't peg me," he said after pointing out his white Prius among the ubiquitous giant trucks and SUVs of the prison staff. Originally from northern Louisiana, Robson had planned to retire in 1995 but took the Angola job instead, and says he has never regretted it. As a student, he had visited the local jail and preached after school, so his return has taken him full circle.

Before his class on the Old Testament, Robson shares with me a book by Russell Nestor, *Ministry from the Inside*. Nestor is a prisoner in a federal penitentiary, but his manual is widely read and circulated. It is an eclectic mix of biblical scripture, facts about prison life, and guidelines for daily conduct. His reference is the *Expositor's Study Bible*, created by Jimmy Swaggart Ministries, which combines Swaggart's words with those of the Bible. Nestor's book is considered the definitive ministry manual for Angola's seminarians; its theology is that faith and faith alone is necessary to be a Christian. As Nestor writes, "The only way to be reconciled with God is through faith in Jesus Christ and His completed work which took place on the Cross at Calvary."[6] He exhorts men to minister to those around them, no matter who they are or what they've done. A Christian cannot look down on fellow prisoners for any reason, according to Nestor, because everyone is a sinner: "If not for the grace of God, you would be involved in and guilty of the worst sin imaginable, including nailing the Lord to the Cross! This means that the moment you look down upon the homosexual, the child molester, the assaulter of the elderly, you have forgotten who you really are: a wretched sinner whom Christ has saved." He writes that they are all undeserving, but that God loves prisoners despite their sin. According to Nestor, the good news that men are expected to share as missionaries is that victory over sin happens by grace through faith in Jesus.

Nestor's book resonates with men in the seminary who adamantly distinguish between their faith and religion, which they define as a control mechanism. They claim that faith liberates through a relationship with God, while religion merely imposes a set of rules without true feeling or engagement. Nestor writes,

A belief based on works or keeping laws is called "religion." Biblical Christianity is not a religion. You must realize that religion of any sort is the greatest enemy of God and mankind that exists today. Why? Because religion is a placebo—a fake pill that claims to cure our ills. Religion posits as being of God but, in fact, is a scheme of Satan to fool the people. And it works! Religion makes people feel good all the way to hell. From the men, the only form of legitimate Christianity involves having a relationship with God through Jesus Christ.[7]

He continues: "It is not about feeding people or trying to change their behavior, or even keeping them out of Hell. It is about the Gospel—the 'Good News.'" Although he emphasizes faith over good works, he is not above offering enticements as part of proselytization. Nestor advises seminary students to maintain a Christian locker filled with the best hygiene items, like toothpaste, soap, shower slides, and deodorant to offer new people coming into prison. (This contradicts the general belief of many men in prison that you should never accept anything from anyone or you will be in debt to them.)

Nestor and the theology of the NOBTS emphasizes faith and private conviction, but much of what men do involves ministering and serving each other when no one else will, and they provide tangible services outside the scope of the seminary, like hospice or funerals. There is a disjuncture between Nestor's teachings and the reality that faith-based work in Angola happens in the daily practice of faith in community. Gary Tyler, the director of *Cast the First Stone*, frequently visits men in the hospice program. One man who had endured cancer three times told Tyler, "I wish I had found God out there or I wouldn't be in here." The men initiated the hospice program years ago. The workers, most of them lifers, are devoted to caring for their brothers who are sick and dying, knowing they will one day take their place. They practice a selflessness rare in the free or unfree world. Tyler would say that they are the willing, doing the impossible. In the morning, they arrive to the stench of men no longer able to control their bodily functions. Human touch is officially prohibited and often furtive and secretive, but in hospice, the men attend to each other's most intimate corporeal needs. They bathe each other's withered bodies. They spoon-feed one another. They change diapers. The patients will never leave hospice, and the kindnesses and intimacies of these men are perhaps the last they will receive. In a no-nonsense manner, Joseph Hawk, a prisoner who works in the hospice, bustles around amid the smells with trays of food. To care for the dying is, of course, a profound act of service. Joseph says he is doing God's work.

The men at Angola have created rituals to mark the time, another way of facing life inside the world of the prison. Angola has a solemn graveyard, Point Lookout, surrounded by white fencing; the headstones date back to 1927. Once, when men died in Angola, they were buried in unmarked graves or with an anonymous cross. It was as if the prison had swallowed them whole and they were forgotten. Because Point Lookout is full, the prison has created a second cemetery, Point Lookout II, with the capacity for seven hundred graves. The prison doesn't arrange funerals, but now death is commemorated with protocols and ceremonies because of the efforts of some of the men in Angola.

Kerry Myers is the official funeral director at Angola, as well as the editor of the *Angolite*, the oldest prison magazine, which has won national awards for reporting. The *Angolite* office has the look of a regular newspaper office, with an old desktop computer, a TV, rows of magazines, pictures of family, and two ivy plants growing up the wall. The wry sign above the clutter reads "Everything Here Is Wonderful." Myers has been in Angola over twenty years and in 2013 received a unanimous commutation recommendation from the Louisiana Board of Pardons. He is awaiting a pardon from the governor. Myers and other men who participate in the Point Lookout project have presided over so many funerals that now they just put the machine in gear when someone dies, he explains. The day I met him, he had arranged a Jewish funeral service. Instead of being anonymous, funerals are now attended and marked. Skilled artisans construct a coffin, and a horse-drawn carriage with a procession of men solemnly bears the coffin to the cemetery. Myers or others say a few words. There are personalized headstones for each man, not the unmarked white crosses of the past. They honor the lives of those almost everyone else has forgotten. The ministry focuses on the dignity and sanctity of life as it can be lived in a prison, from where few will ever embark on a new beginning outside.

Myers, Tyler, and others find fulfillment in the funerals and hospice programs, but since the message of the seminary is that pride causes a person's downfall, even the message of Tyler and the men in the play, that they are "qualified to do anything, with nothing," would seem to violate their code of humility. The play, hospice, and funerals are ways to express the collective emotion and self-introspection of which the seminary disapproves. The seminary teachers also preach against pride, because of its potential for rebellion. Obedience to the teachings of the seminary and to the rules of the prison are foremost.

In Robson's class on the Old Testament, various men take turns at the pulpit expounding on a verse as if conducting a small, impromptu revival. The majority of students wear heavy, black-framed Malcolm X–type glasses, made at the prison. A man gesticulates wildly as he preaches about pride, explaining that it is the ugliest and ultimate sin. It is so dreadful that it created Satan, he tells them. (At Darrington prison, too, the men have posted printed signs all over the seminary wing with dire warnings of the dangers of pride.) Pride is the source of their problems and must be combated. As Nestor writes, "Humility is the grease that allows the wheels of Christian growth to turn."[8]

A lack of pride also means forgoing personal gain or even safety for the sake of others. It can mean putting oneself on the line for another person who is part of a Christian brotherhood. Robson claims that the seminary constructs, however tenuously, a community of accountability in a place where no one trusts anyone. The men are expected to protect and shelter each other. The seminary is meant to function like an ascetic community, a group of men led by absolute certainty in their belief. The men in the seminary have their own set of rules and laws for how to comport themselves, similar to the rules and discipline in the French prison Mettray, as long as they do not contradict those of the prison. Protection and community are by-products of that commitment. The seminary provides the structure so they can keep their vows and avoid the temptations of prison life. Although in the fishbowl of the prison, where men sleep in open dormitories on bunk beds, with just a locker for their belongings, there is particular pressure to embody the monastic life. Robson stresses the concept of community and responsibility to each other: "There is only one liberty, the liberty of Jesus at work in our conscience, enabling us to do what is right."

Protection of the weaker from the stronger is a perennial issue in prison, which Robson also emphasizes in the half sermon, half lecture I listen to during his class in a windowless classroom filled with almost forty men. "It is better to be thrown with a millstone around my neck into the sea than hurt a weaker person," he explains. He uses the example of a little sister: "Would you defraud or hurt your sister? No, the big brother never hurts his little sister." During the lecture, I wonder if the reference to a woman is related to the fact that I'm the lone woman in the class that day.

The communal and ascetic aspect of the seminary modifies how men behave. As part of the seminary, they must refrain from violence; others are watching to ensure that occurs. Robson preaches, "The greatest force of behavior modification is gratitude to Jesus. Do you want to go to sleep with a Sears Roebuck catalogue across your chest?" As Rideau explained to me later, "If you're a born-again inmate, you can't go around raping or assaulting guards." The seminary attempts to forge homogeneity of action within a massive prison population, but there are limitations to the notion of being your brother's keeper. In *Ministry from the Inside*, Nestor warns that each man must weigh being wise versus standing up for what is right.[9] As much as the seminary talks about fellowship, Nestor says that even a Christian can be a confidential informant: "Even if prison is lonely and you want a confidant, that confidant should be Jesus. People take advantage of each other constantly and prey on each other. Don't get in the middle of battles. It's not your place. Tell someone to go to SHU [a solitary security housing unit] or hole for safety."[10] Conversations with other prisoners revealed that seminary men were not always ready to intervene when someone was being attacked or coerced. One man confided that they have a saying in Angola: "You see, but you don't see."

Just as there are limits to the community the seminaries try to construct, there are limits to the independence they are granted. The rules and regulations of prison life are still highly repressive. Outsiders and staff often refer to Angola as a prison farm, and agricultural labor remains the mainstay of the prison economy. The most dreaded work assignment is still in the fields, which stretch for miles, broken only by the immense Lake Killarney, where some prisoners fish. Every day, all year round, hundreds of men march in a line, hoes balanced on their shoulders, to pick beans, okra, squash, cotton, sugarcane, wheat, or corn. If the men don't walk to the fields, they are brought on large flatbed vehicles that everyone calls "hootenanny trucks." None of the twelve hundred guards at Angola carry guns. The exception are the field overseers, who are mounted on horses, with rifles beside them at all times. Men assigned to the fields are often overwhelmed with despair and rage. Derek Mason, a thirty-one-year-old black man from California who is a student in the seminary program, recalled his incredulity at being sent to pick crops when he first arrived at Angola: "I didn't know people were still doing slave-type work. I didn't think they were doing that in America. Period. Until I come down here."

Small acts of rebellion occur regularly, if not in the seminary program. During lunch when I visited, the associate warden's walkie-talkie crackled with the chatter of an altercation in the yard of the main prison. The cause was an attempt to smuggle in synthetic marijuana during a flag football game. Later that day, two emaciated hunger strikers staggered into the infirmary to protest prison conditions. Cain explained that he doesn't talk to hunger strikers and he doesn't listen to ultimatums. If they start eating, he says, he'll hear what they have to say.

The total lack of freedom is most starkly manifest in Camp J. Prisoners refer to it as "the dungeon," "where they take you to crush you." Here, the specter of punishment supersedes everything else. Another former prisoner described Camp J as "where they hate human beings, and they throw feces on you. That is hell on earth, the closest thing to it." On April 2, 2016, two men committed suicide in Camp J by hanging themselves in their cells.[11] At Camp J, men spend twenty-three of twenty-four

hours in a cell with only the company of a metal bed and a toilet. Entering
the cellblock with the associate superintendent, we passed men in orange
jumpsuits, outside for their allotted forty-five minutes of daily exercise
in eight-by-ten-foot cages. Herman Wallace is a former Black Panther
accused of murdering a prison guard. His case, along with that of two
others who became known as the Angola Three, helped ignite a movement against solitary confinement after he spent more than forty years in
solitary in Angola, most of it in Camp J. He was released a day before he
died of pancreatic cancer. The hunger strikers and the men in Camp J are
reminders that if you rebel against the rules of the prison, the punishment
is severe.

Punishment is the motor that drives the business of mass incarceration
in Louisiana. The state is unforgiving, unlike the God of the seminary.
As the prison capital of the United States and the world, Louisiana holds
close to forty thousand people behind bars. African Americans make up
32 percent of the state's population but represent 66 percent of incarcerated
people in the state. Conversely, whites in Louisiana make up 60 percent
of the population but represent only 30 percent of the incarcerated population.[12] The state prisons, however, hold only half the men and women
sentenced to prison terms; Louisiana's numerous parish jails hold the other
half. All prisoners dread time in the parish jails because of overcrowding,
unchecked violence, and a dearth of programs. Since the 1990s, the parish
jail system has become a lucrative enterprise for rural sheriff departments
who secure $24.39 a day in state money for each prisoner. Sheriffs trade
and vie for prisoners from New Orleans and Baton Rouge because body
counts fund police cars, salaries, and equipment. They "treat us like cattle," Monica, the woman from LCIW, told me when I visited the women's
prison. The sheriffs' priority is to fill their facilities, many of which were
built in the past two decades.

The prosecutors, sheriffs, and private prison contractors compose a vociferous lobby against sentencing reform. In Louisiana, first- and second-
degree murder charges result in automatic life without parole, but the
majority of prisoners are in for nonviolent offenses, and Louisiana's mandatory minimum sentencing laws mean that a person can be sentenced for
twenty years to life without parole for drug possession or shoplifting.

The very idea of a life sentence is a relatively new concept. It was a rare penalty before the 1970s. At that time, even with a life sentence, a prisoner had the hope of release because of executive clemency. Today, approximately 160,000 people are serving life sentences in the United States. Even the conservative Texas Public Policy Foundation recently issued a report recommending that Louisiana drastically alter its sentencing guidelines, arguing that the state is out of step with other conservative states, like Georgia and Texas. Clemency, too, is almost nonexistent in Louisiana's current political climate. Between 2008 and 2016, former governor Bobby Jindal pardoned approximately eighty people. His predecessors, former governor Kathleen Blanco, a Democrat, approved clemency for 285 prisoners during her one term in office, and former governor Mike Foster, a Republican, granted clemency to 455 over the course of his two terms.[13] Many of these applicants are doing life or close to it, compared to the few cases in other states. As Monica observed, "You're in Louisiana, girl. You wouldn't be surprised to see a noose hanging from a tree, either."

Cain showcases the success of the seminary by pointing to its exemplary graduates, who are paragons of a redeemed life and guides to other men. Cain and Robson sent some of them on missions, and, currently, almost thirty men from Angola are serving as missionaries in other Louisiana prisons. Whether the missionary experiment will work in other states and prisons depends on prison officials granting authority and privilege to the prisoner missionaries who come from Angola or the women's prisons. Cain's vision of prisoners as missionaries extended beyond Angola, not only to the women's prison but to nine other states: Darrington Unit in Texas, Mississippi's Parchman Farm, and Phillips State Prison in Buford, Georgia, have all graduated men with degrees in Christian ministry.[14]

Thomas Whelan, who supervises close to forty men in the Angola automotive plant, is one of these men. He started in the first seminary class in 1995. His chaotic office is separated from the immense garage by a window. He works on an old desktop computer, the surface barely visible beneath lists, Post-its, calendars, and family pictures. It might be a local mechanic's shop except for how he answers the ever-ringing phone, "Automotive. Inmate Whelan," and the fact that he makes seventy-five cents per hour as the director, considered an excellent prison salary. "I want to be like an outside person. Don't act like you are in prison, act like you are in society," he says. Whelan is a white man in his late fifties with thinning hair, thick glasses, and an avuncular, eager manner. He's lived in Angola for twenty-two years and is quasi-staff in some ways. "This is my church," Whelan tells me. "Ministry is saving people, not the pulpit." Since Angola received an influx of almost twelve hundred men with short-term sentences when Phelps Correctional Center closed, Cain developed a mentor program in which seminary graduates were key. These new prisoners worked in automotive and other industries during the day and took night classes on God, parenting, anger, and life skills taught by seminarians like Whelan. Whelan's mentees spent three months in each section of the garage learning about air-conditioning and heating, brakes, electrics, body, steering, transmissions, and God. Eighty-five percent will pass the state automotive repair test. Whelan is proud of them: "We are blowing the state away," he boasts, referring to the quality of his mechanics.

When Whelan graduated from the prison seminary in 2000, he was sent to Rayburn Correctional Center, one hundred thirty miles from Angola, to work as a missionary. The rationale for the missionary program is derived from Mark 6:7, "Calling the Twelve to him, he began to send them out two by two and gave them authority over impure spirits." Cain believes the men would join chaplains in prisons around the state to build a culture of peace, safety, morality, and spirituality. After the effort of establishing himself in the Angola prison hierarchy, Whelan resisted the transfer: "I was afraid I would lose everything I had here." Initially, Whelan found Rayburn's atmosphere anarchic and stressful. Like cranky elders, Angola trustees complain about the "young 'uns." Rayburn and many of Louisiana's other prisons house younger men with shorter sentences who have a predilection for fighting and gangs. Undaunted, Whelan preached and converted others, until he eventually created a faith-based wing and brought in seven other Angola seminary graduates. "I was like Joseph," he tells me, shepherding other men to Christ and promoting peace. Two years later, he came back to Angola. Whelan still occasionally preaches at Angola's Church of God in Christ congregation. Half of his friends from his seminary graduating class have died.

At Angola, with hundreds of aging lifers, there is a measure of calm and peace for those trustees who have lived there twenty or thirty years. For better or worse, it has become their home. But for other prisoners, men like Whelan evoke the trustees of the convict lease farms without the guns. These men view the seminary graduates as lackeys of the system and call them "Cain's snitches." Cain wanted prisoners to monitor each other in an ecosystem of prisoner governance, quelling violence and disorder. Some, like Whelan, say they believe wholeheartedly in the mission of the seminary. His role as a minister is a mark of being set apart and imbued with trust. For the administration, which has an underpaid and overworked staff, the prisoner missionaries make their jobs easier by becoming behavioral exemplars to those around them. Dennis, a seminary student, tells me, "If you prove yourself, stay the course, they will give you trust. They still have to watch you. They have given us the leeway to pretty much govern ourselves. I give you this liberty. If you screw it up, it's your fault." Cain and his deputies reinforced this accounting of trust by relating how a female officer could be locked into a dormitory with one hundred men each night and nothing would happen because prisoners monitor each other.

His supporters and some prisoners viewed Cain as an iconoclast for championing a program that places faith in individuals whom others treat as less than human. If God functioned like a warden in the earliest penitentiaries, a justification for meting out punishment, at Angola Cain was like a god. Some prisoners referred to Cain as a dictator or "the king," while others called him "Uncle Burl," with equal parts affection and derision. He was both tyrant and patriarch, benevolent father and strict disciplinarian, genial charmer and animal lover, and cunning businessman and political wheeler-dealer. Wilbert Rideau described Angola as Cain's empire, calling it the Government of Corrections in Louisiana. Rideau claimed Cain was one of the most politically powerful individuals in Louisiana, but even his authority wasn't absolute. In late December 2015, Cain abruptly retired after investigations into improper use of prisoner labor, ethics violations, and payroll fraud.[15]

The metaphor of God and warden coalesced in Cain, and the men in the prison unanimously agree that you did not cross him. Calvin Duncan spent almost three decades in Angola, where he became a sought-after lawyer for death-row prisoners. When he arrived at Angola with a ninth-grade education, he had to file a motion to get law books in the prison. Now a Soros Justice fellow who provides legal documents to men inside Angola, Duncan vividly described to me how men flocked to the chapel on the day they knew Warden Cain would be there. As Cain swaggered down the aisle, men surreptitiously handed him carefully folded notes, like supplicants, asking for new teeth or a job transfer. By nightfall, most of their requests were granted. Duncan explained that reciprocity was the only way to work with Cain. If you didn't ever ask him for anything, you were invisible. If you wanted something, you told Cain anything he wanted to know when he wanted to know it. Nestor writes of the value of unconditional surrender and authority: "It is the Lord who puts people into positions of authority. When you rebel against the law and those who uphold them, you are in fact rebelling against the Lord."[16] Before Cain became warden, Duncan filed civil suits. There were allegations that cans of expired food were coming into Angola, and prisoners were placing new labels on them so the prison could resell them. All civil suits stopped after Cain came. Cain told Duncan that he could work on getting people released, but cautioned him not to criticize or interfere with how he ran his prison.

Cain's success was predicated on his assertion that Angola was safer because the seminary had morally rehabilitated men, and they in turn rehabilitated each other. Murders, suicides, escapes, and assaults on staff and prisoners crept downward, according to a chart Robson gave me during my visit. In the 1980s and '90s, Angola was known for violence and corruption: many men in the prison had cell phones, and gangs were moving drugs in and out of the prison. Assaults between prisoners decreased from 743 in 1988 to 195 in 2009. The seminary and Cain were heralded as the heroes of this transformation, and they preached their ideas widely. Cain is now a consultant for similar programs in New Mexico, California, Michigan, and Tennessee, in addition to the programs he's inspired in Texas, Georgia, and Louisiana.

Governing and managing a giant prison colony is a gargantuan operation. Angola has gained fifteen hundred prisoners in recent years. Cain was the longest-serving warden in the United States, approaching twenty years in the job in 2015. Now, half the staff are women, and numerous people, including the associate warden, Cathy Fontenot, tell me that women are more effective guards. At night, a woman guard is locked in a dormitory with ninety-six men; she is safe because they see her as their sister or mother and will protect her against the few "knuckleheads" who try anything. The same is not said about women prisoners. Fontenot claims that women in prison are devious, dangerous, and unpredictable, and she is astounded that I interviewed women alone at LCIW. She says she would never sit in a room alone with a woman prisoner.

Both staff and prisoners agree that Angola is a less brutal place than it was in the seventies and eighties, but the reason is more complicated than the triumphant seminary narrative. As far back as 1932, thirty-one Angola prisoners known as the "Heel String Gang" cut their Achilles tendons to draw attention to the abysmal conditions at the prison. In 1976, Ross Maggio, known as "Boss Ross," became warden and hired guards with college degrees, fired corrupt officers who condoned rape and stabbings, and brought in more weapons. Even before Boss Ross's arrival, the federal government ordered Louisiana to reform Angola after prisoners reported grievances about racial discrimination in job assignments, abuse by guards, and violations of their civil rights. In the mid-seventies, the state hired licensed doctors (a veterinarian had sutured the men for years), constructed new living quarters, and finally hired African American officers onto a previously all-white staff.

Rideau supports the view that administrative changes altered the dynamics of the prison, and he is skeptical of claims about the seminary. It does the seminary a disservice, he explained, when it is presented as "some sort of magical wand that ends violence, transforms everybody, everything is cheaper, and the world is better. The sun will rise in the morning because of this faith-based programming." He argues that its value is that it provides an education when there are no other educational alternatives. Angola's aging population has also meant less violence, according to Rideau, who tracked the age of Angola's prison population while he was editor of the *Angolite*. Prison has always been a young man's game, Rideau says, and the average age of the Angola prison population is forty. As individuals grow older and mature, they become less troublesome.

Norris Henderson says of the seminary and Cain, "If they want to take credit for making the prison safe, so be it. They showed up and the prison was safe." Henderson is now the director of Voice of the Ex-Offender (VOTE) and a highly respected national advocate for criminal justice reform and policy. While in Angola, he founded the hospice program and led the Muslim community. He was freed after going to court fifty-two times between 1990 and 2003. Henderson is an imposing man with a permanent look of skepticism that disguises his indefatigable kindness and compassion for prisoners and those who have been released. He credits the Islamic brothers, educated men like himself, who improved conditions in the prison long before the seminary arrived. "You survived on the strength of someone else who opened a door for you," he said.

Cain was simultaneously expanding the physical structures within Angola and planning how to release some of the thousands of men serving life without parole. In the past fifteen years, there has been frenetic construction at Angola. Henderson, who goes back to Angola frequently for Muslim services, said sardonically, "Everywhere you walk is a chapel and chaplains feeling good about themselves." The main prison is dominated by a large Protestant chapel with an organ donated by George Beverly Shea, longtime organist for Billy Graham. Across the way, prisoners and staff have dubbed the new Catholic chapel "the Alamo" for its pinkish stucco appearance and mammoth size. Men in the prison's Latin American club touched up the paint on the elaborate murals behind the altar. A hologram painting of Jesus worth $30,000 hung nearby. Dedicated in December 2013, prisoners built the entire Alamo in thirty-eight days with funds raised by Warden Cain. Their skill and labor are visible in the painstaking craftsmanship of the wood-hewn pews, stained-glass windows, and the gleaming red-and-white tiled floors.

Henderson questions the religious organizations funding new chapels and pews, asking, "Why don't they build opportunities for guys to get out?" Rideau expressed a similar criticism about giving people in prison the help they need versus the help the faith-based groups think they need: "Sometimes churches come in and want to save the souls. Really what they want to do is make them believe like they do, to be their kind of Christians. I remember one time asking some Christians, hey, would you help me? They were willing to, but only if I'm a born-again Christian. If I'm not a born-again Christian, then the hell with me. Rather than trying to make them some kind of Christian, why not make them be better human beings? They're concerned about the soul. But they're not concerned about the person."

Despite his unbending faith in the seminary as the vehicle of moral transformation at Angola, Cain also had to attend to issues like prison overcrowding and old men dying. Cain wanted to know whether a faith-based group would aid in reentry to civilian life. The question of actual freedom is more pressing as the prison becomes overcrowded. There are only so many new chapels and churches to build. Cain and his staff focused on reentry to deal with a prison of lifers. The reentry program is managed by those men who will probably never leave the prison. Two judges in New Orleans, Arthur Hunter and Laurie White, created a court-ordered program in 2011. Men with ten-year sentences come to Angola, and if they complete the programs with a seminary-trained mentor for two years, they can go home. They are placed in Camp C in two dorms with lifers and trustees to guide them. They work in the automotive shop or other vocational jobs like the horticulture program, or fixing and building bikes, wheelchairs, and the ubiquitous thick, black-framed glasses. These mentees learn about social manners, anger management, substance abuse, and parenting from the seminary graduates. Nevertheless, the turnover is high. Some long-termers resent that the new men are taking programming space.

The bulk of the prison population still comprises men who will spend most of their lives in Angola and die there. *Cast the First Stone* asks whether forgiveness by God is enough when freedom is an impossibility. At the end of the play, Sammy, playing Jesus, is hanging by his wrists and feet on a ten-foot-tall cross that is constructed during the play. The sight is vivid and slightly macabre, and audience members cry. In the play, Jesus returns and tells his disciples to forgive and that they will be forgiven for their sins. The statement is optimistic, given Louisiana's zest for punishment. The play ends with a film montage of a lethal injection table and the scene on the cross. Jonathan, who plays Peter, faces the camera and says, "You can have all the faith in the world, but how can you not think about getting out?" Certainly, prisoners can fashion their lives as missionaries, but to Sammy, Gary Tyler, Patricia, and all the others who still talk of freedom—of their cases winding laboriously through the courts, of a miracle pardon, of the stories of lifers who have gone home—being a missionary in prison or playing Jesus in a play is always a qualified life.

Robson may tell the seminary students, "Spiritually speaking we're all in prison until we get that card from Jesus Christ, 'get out of jail,'" but Thomas Whelan may literally be locked up for his entire life. Russell Nestor's ministry explains that men need to relinquish hope that God will intervene with them personally: "I have seen men who have put themselves on the path of disappointment because they believed that they could somehow get God to do things in their timing. DELIVERING YOU OR ANYONE ELSE FROM PRISON IS NOT GOD'S PRIMARY FOCUS! Delivering you and everyone else from sin is His all consuming objective."[17]

When next year's seminary class members graduate, they'll be trained to counsel and preach the word like missionaries everywhere, but they'll also want to go home. There is the time and the crime, and the remorse for both. The actors in the play are portraying the excruciating tension between their own moral reform as Christians and people with the possibility of ever having a life outside prison. The desire for education and religious devotion is also bound up with prisoners' hope that a clemency board or the governor will bear witness to what they have made of their life. Cain says that the sign at the entrance to Angola means "We don't care about your past; we care about what you become." Yet, redemption as a missionary doesn't lead to actual freedom. It is freedom within unfreedom. "Their chance of a pardon is very slim," Henderson explains. "Nobody has really benefited from the seminary because their chance of a pardon depends on their crime." After forty-one years in Angola, Tyler, the director of the play, was released on May 1, 2016.

On my last evening at Angola, after having observed the seminary program for three days, I stood with Cain outside the ranch house. This was a year before his retirement. It was twilight, and Cain had arrived late to dinner after driving to town to pick up prescription medication for his wife. His beloved peacocks and guinea hens roosted around us on cars, fences, and trees. Cain urged me, "Tell the truth, that moral rehabilitation really does work. Help us out." The sun is setting over Lake Killarney, a deceptively pastoral scene if you ignore the prison camps with their barbed wire. That night, in the dark, with the lights of the prisons blinking like distant towns, all I hear are screams of peacocks and distant yelps of dogs. Joseph approaches us. "I know you're going to get out because you're innocent," Cain tells him, then he turns to me and says, "He really is." Joseph, stone-faced, doesn't respond. Instead, he solemnly tells Cain about the peacock eggs. They had been covered by a tarp, but it blew away in the wind. Now the eggs are broken and the chicks are dead. The warden is more distraught over the peacocks than Joseph's predicament. Joseph at this point has spent most of his life in Angola, where he's built a space for himself, no matter how constrained. "That's bad luck," Cain says. It isn't clear if he's talking about the peacock eggs or Joseph.

# CHAPTER 4

# THE CHAPEL

## *The Predominance of Christianity in Faith-Based Prisons*

AS YOU DRIVE THE HOUR south from Jacksonville, Florida, to Lawtey Correctional Institution, a medium security prison, the only signs of habitation are small billboards advertising fireworks, fresh peaches, the chance to glimpse a fourteen-foot alligator, and churches. There is the Church of Pisgah, the First Baptist Church, the Baptist Church of Lawtey, Florida Baptist Church, and Word of God Church. Lawtey Correctional Institution is located in the "Iron Triangle," an area with a half-dozen prisons, including Florida State Prison, which still has an electric chair on its death row. The prisons in this area add more than seven thousand people to the local population, and the prison system is one of the main employers for the rural communities in the area. Lawtey is one of sixteen state prisons in Florida designated as faith- and character-based institutions (FCBIs) since 2003.[1]

The FCBIs provide a range of secular and religious programming for eligible men and women who have indicated an interest in personal growth and character development. But most faith-based programs remain overwhelmingly Christian, with other religious affiliations an afterthought. Florida's Department of Corrections designed the FBCIs to include all religions, and a prisoner's religious faith, or lack thereof, is not considered in determining eligibility for the programs. The Florida programs, for example, are supposed to be a neutral space for character development, where no one religion is promoted. In actuality, however, the Southern Baptist chaplain and warden have made their form of Protestantism the norm, with all other faiths and theological differences a deviation.

The success of Lawtey as an FCBI depends on religious volunteers, supervised by a chaplain, who function as instructors, group facilitators, seminar presenters, mentors, worship leaders, or musicians. Like most of the volunteers, the warden, chaplain, and staff identify as Southern Baptists. According to the Florida Department of Corrections, close to 70 percent of men at Lawtey characterize their religious orientation as Christian non-Roman Catholic with only 3 percent identified as Muslim and 1 percent as Jewish. Yet, 17 percent of men in the state system report no or unknown religious orientations. Approximately eight hundred men at Lawtey have volunteered and applied to be transferred from other prisons to Lawtey. More than one hundred volunteers visit Lawtey monthly, and the chaplain cannot observe most of the volunteer programs and classes. Therefore, oversight of the programs is sporadic, making it difficult to ascertain whether proselytization for Christian faith does occur, in violation of the Department of Corrections requirements.[2]

The inescapability of Christianity in a faith-based prison and the pretense of a secular character program entirely divorced from religion did not escape local commentary. The *Palm Beach Post* included a parodic schedule of a day at Lawtey when the prison opened under former Governor Jeb Bush in 2003. The daily schedule of events began at 6 a.m. with "Good morning, sinners!"

| | |
|---|---|
| 6:30 a.m. | Sunrise service; weight room. |
| 8:30 a.m. | Cellblock psalms. |
| 10 a.m. | Lecture: Speaking in tongues for confidential informants; law library. |
| 11:30 a.m. | Bringing in the shivs. Last chance to turn in weapons; no questions asked. |
| Noon | Radio club: Learning from Rush "Talent on Loan from God" Limbaugh; detox unit. |

1 p.m.          Seminar: Snake Handling for Dummies. One slot has
                suddenly opened up for this seminar. Admission: one cig-
                arette or two candy bars. Not for beginners; Classroom 2.
1:30 p.m.       Careers seminar: How to run a faith-based school in
                Florida and get state funding, with Gov. Bush on satellite
                linkup; Classroom 3.
2 p.m.          Afternoon shift reports for work; Ten Commandments
                monument construction center (counts for gain time on
                any outstanding Alabama sentence).
3:30 p.m.       Baptisms. (Note: Due to the recent escape, we will no
                longer be going to the lake for this event.)
4 p.m.          Book discussion group: Chicken Soup for the Criminal
                Soul; rec. room.[3]

In most state prisons, depending on proximity to an urban center, you
might encounter some Catholic services, Jehovah's Witnesses, an occa-
sional group from the Church of Jesus Christ of Latter-day Saints (LDS),
Muslim groups, and Wicca and Native American sweat lodges. In prisons
adjacent to urban areas like San Quentin or Graterford, there are Muslim
and Jewish chaplains. However, in the more isolated Bible belt of Louisiana, Texas, Georgia, and Florida, the volunteers reflect only the dominant
religion of the area.

When Quaker silence, Presbyterian prayer, and Methodist discipline
lost their hold on prison cultures, the conditions for the dominance of an
increasingly nonspecific Protestantism within the prison were set. Though
prisons in the United States are saturated by broadly Protestant theological
ideas, mainline Protestants, Unitarians, or Quakers rarely hold services or
studies in prison. Theorists of secularism and religion have argued that the
unstated religious assumptions of secularism in the United States are Protestant, and Christian morality shapes legislation, policy, and jurisprudence
in what scholars have called "stealth Protestantism."[4] In the same way,
religious ideas shape secular laws about punishment.

The decline of mainline Protestant churches since the 1970s and the up-
surge in nondenominational mega-churches are exemplified in the trends
of prison ministry.[5] Mega-churches with memberships in the thousands

have thrived using the model of small groups of engagement. Prison ministry is a natural extension of this model, with a theological emphasis on conversion and Jesus as the original prisoner. Some Christians believe that prisoners have a special place in the Christian imagination because Jesus was a prisoner who died in custody.

Jack Miles, a professor of religious studies and author of *God: A Biography*, writes, "Christianity is a religion founded by men in deep trouble with the law, men familiar with the inside of prisons, whose message was 'the last shall be first, and the first last.'"[6] For many Christians, their religious ethics dictate that what is owed to their neighbor is simultaneously owed to God himself. Miles continues, "When doing good deeds for our fellow human beings, we as Christians seek to imagine that we are simultaneously doing them for Christ in person. Jesus taught his followers to imagine themselves hearing his voice saying, 'I was hungry and you gave me food, I was thirsty and you gave me drink, I was a stranger and you welcomed me, I was naked and you clothed me, I was sick and you came to me,' and finally: 'I was in prison and you visited me' (Matthew 25:35–36)."[7] As a result of this theology and the organizational structure of large churches with individual ministries within them, evangelicals are dominant in prison ministry.

A sampling of the religious program schedule at prisons in Florida, Washington State or Texas, for example, reveals that the majority are made up of Protestant Christian groups. From 9 a.m. to 9 p.m., a prisoner can attend Way of Holiness, Harbor Covenant, Word of Life, New Jerusalem Church, Crossways Discipleship, Alpha Bible Study, Prisoners for Christ, New Life Baptist, Prison Fellowship ministry, Kairos, Spanish Bible group, Greater Life Church, Faith Bible Study, CWays Bible Study with a sprinkling of Jehovah's Witnesses, LDS, and Catholic Mass. There is one Muslim group and a Wiccan meeting. Florida's FCBIs are similar. The guidelines of the Florida Department of Corrections explicitly state, "Staff may not attempt to convert inmates toward a particular secular, faith or religious viewpoint or affiliation. Except as provided by law, state funds may not be expended on programs that further religious indoctrination, or on inherently religious activities such as religious worship, religious instruction or proselytization."[8] This injunction contradicts the basic principle of evangelical and nondenominational Christian ministries, which is to proselytize and convert others. The 2005 Florida statutes also state that "the department shall ensure that state funds are not expended for the purpose of furthering religious indoctrination, but rather, that state funds are expended for purposes of furthering the secular goals of criminal rehabilitation, the successful reintegration of offenders into the community, and the reduction of recidivism." The state continues to open FBCIs based on the Lawtey model.[9]

The presence of state faith-based prisons raises constitutional questions, especially because many programs operate within state prisons, using state property and resources, even though they may not be state funded. Some faith-based groups comprise mainly volunteers, but in Florida or the Baptist seminary programs, the Christian program is an integral part of the prison itself, whether it is providing education, mental health counseling, or building a new chapel. In addressing similar issues, Prison Fellowship claims that it deploys government funds only to buy equipment like computers, while private money funds the religious aspects of the program. Yet, it is almost impossible to make this distinction in a program that believes rehabilitation occurs through faith in Jesus Christ. The principle of non-establishment means that tax dollars are not used to build facilities for religious groups. But Barry Lynn of Americans United for Separation of Church and State makes the case that these programs represent the government paying for a spiritual transformation and conversion: "Prison Fellowship is free to run evangelism programs on its own dime but has no business handing the bill to the taxpayers."[10]

Lawtey is part of a national trend to remake state prisons into religious communities. The Florida Department of Corrections investigated the Prison Fellowship model and decided that a dormitory arrangement with long-term involvement would be the most effective model for its state.[11] Kairos Horizon Prison Initiative became a nonprofit in 2001 and received a grant from Florida's Responsible Fatherhood Initiative to hire a program coordinator to oversee the faith-based dormitories at Tomoka Correctional Institution in 1999.[12] Other faith-based and multifaith units followed in Ohio, Oklahoma, and Texas, and at Wakulla Correctional Institution in Florida.

The Florida version of the faith-based prison began with dorms that were arranged in cubes with eight men making up a family group. Almost all the groups were Christian, although one was primarily Muslim men. The cubes had four double bunks, large lockers to house books and materials, bookshelves, and televisions. The families were based on the model of Kairos weekends, which had taken place for seventeen years in Tomoka before Kairos initiated the faith-based dormitories. All the prisoners attended the three-day weekend before becoming part of the dorms and were familiar with the aim of building trust and community.[13] Initially, the DOC wanted those prisoners with short sentences to take part in the program, but Kairos found that they weren't as serious about the program as those with long-term sentences.

Based on the success of Tomoka, in 2001, the legislature under Jeb Bush mandated establishing the faith-based model in six other Florida prisons, but the plan was suspended after September 11, 2001. That year, the warden of Lawtey requested that Pastor Steve McCoy, head of a nondenominational conservative Christian mega-church of a thousand members—Beaches Chapel Church in Neptune Beach—oversee seven faith-based dormitories operating at Lawtey. A minister for twenty-nine years, McCoy recounts being raised in the 1960s in what he remembers as the streets of a rough neighborhood, and he had a checkered background in drugs until he "found Christ." A large, garrulous man, he relished the chance to transform the prison, viewing his ministry at Lawtey as a natural extension of his personal history. Eventually, as the success of the close-knit dorm programs grew, the program expanded to the entire prison. McCoy's Beaches Chapel congregation has continued as the largest and most influential group at Lawtey. The Lawtey program began Christmas Eve 2003, and as it has become institutionalized, the once-volunteer religious program managers have become employees of the Department of Corrections.[14] The faith-based prisons are now overseen by the individual prison chaplain and, thus, subject to his particular theological view.

When I visited Lawtey, McCoy was preaching to a group of several hundred men scattered among the gleaming wood pews of the modern and airy prison chapel that Beaches had built. In a sermon that had a distinctly pep-talk feel and seemed a clear attempt to generate interest for the Beaches classes and programs, McCoy declaimed, "God does not see you in an endless cycle of incarceration." Beaches Chapel, with an income of $1.7 million, has contributed more than $30,000 to Lawtey, paying for computers, ceiling fans, musical instruments, and the renovation of the chapel, which is the most modern and comfortable building in the prison.[15] Lawtey's chapel boasts an elevated stage with a massive screen for viewing films and a sophisticated sound system. It's also the only air-conditioned building in the central Florida prison.

The chaplain, warden, and McCoy are acutely aware that the prison treads close to promoting state-sanctioned religion and are careful to emphasize that attendance is voluntary, all religious groups are respected, and secular programming for building character is written into the rationale of the prison program. However, in other conversations, they reiterated their belief that rehabilitation is only possible as part of a theology of individual salvation.

When I visited Lawtey, the Muslim study group was meeting in a glorified broom closet without a religious volunteer. The warden was considering eliminating recreation time for the men so they would be forced to go to the Beaches nondenominational Christian services. (Immersion in religious texts, programs, and classes is supposed to reform and better the self.) Lawtey's chapel claims to have weekly Qur'an and Torah study groups, as well as Catholic Mass, Native American pipe ceremony, gatherings for Jehovah's Witnesses, and Hebrew Israel, a religious group based on the belief that African Americans are direct descendants of the ancient Israelites. But the explicitly Christian character of the prison became obvious when the chaplain informed me that many of these groups had not met for some time due to shortages in volunteers. The groups that held regular meetings included Monday-night Bible study, led by Beaches Chapel volunteers in the education building, as well as a class on practical Christian living, Praise and Worship Bible study, the Ken Cooper prison ministry on overcoming addictions, St. Dismas Prison Ministry, and Toastmasters International, an overwhelmingly popular public-speaking group. Many programs in health and wellness, mental health, anger management, and addiction are also administered by Christian faith-based programs. Some examples include a Jesus-centered twelve-step program for overcoming addictions and anger-management classes that are reframed as a religious endeavor with the motto "Only by God's grace can we manage it."

Information about other religions is limited. The chapel library at Lawtey has a more extensive collection than the regular prison library, which contains primarily law books and paperback fiction. Since most materials are donated, they represent the eclectic nature of the donor religious organizations rather than a systematized collection. (In any prison, chapel libraries exhibit the near impossibility of establishing a well-formed collection.) Texts range from a Hasidic Jewish calendar to one shelf containing the Qur'an, Zohar, and books on Scientology. There are multiple copies of the *Left Behind* series and films, and a section of Catholic materials and biographies of saints. The topic of Christianity is organized by subject matter: evangelical witnessing, Holy Spirit, social problems, marriage, conversion biographies, family, parenting, Billy Graham, Chuck Swindoll, Norman Vincent Peale, Christian life, the last days, and spiritual lives.

A controversy over what religious texts a prison should contain gained national attention in 2007. The US Department of Homeland Security ordered prisons to remove certain religious literature it deemed a threat to national security, in direct contradiction to the federal faith-based initiatives goal of providing more opportunities for faith-based learning in prison. The order to confiscate books was implemented and later rescinded due to pressure from various religious groups.[16]

The conundrum for faith-based prisons in Florida and the majority of US prisons located outside urban areas is the inability to find outside volunteers to facilitate a Muslim, Native American, or non-Christian group. Partly, this is due to the structure of religious programming in prisons in which chaplains, primarily Christians, determine the content. More than seven in ten chaplains (73 percent) in a Pew Research Center study on religion in prison consider access to high-quality religion-related programs in prison to be "absolutely critical" for successful rehabilitation and reentry, and about a third of chaplains (32 percent) who are mainly Christian report that some faith groups have more volunteers than are needed to meet inmates' spiritual needs.[17] Over 71 percent of chaplains in the Pew study are Protestant, with 13 percent identifying as Catholics and 7 percent as Muslim.

The role of a chaplain is a hybrid position for a person who is to serve as spiritual and religious advisor in ostensibly secular spaces like hospitals, the military, and prisons. One possible meaning of the term is keeper of the cloak, a Christian designation that may have emerged in the 1400s when a religious order was founded to provide consolation to those condemned to death. Now chaplains oversee religious life in prison chapels. In her book on the role of chaplaincy, religious studies professor Winnifred Sullivan calls a chaplain an explicit broker between the sacred and the secular.[18] The chaplain is paid by secular institutions and beholden to secular authorities, despite the religious character of the work. Chaplains do not report to a church authority.

Many chaplains are trained in their own religious tradition but are required to minister to a wide range of religions. In prisons, chaplains' myriad duties range from leading worship services in their own religion to facilitating volunteers for religious groups and holidays. The list of the chaplain's duties in Florida was a page long and included religious education classes, crisis and bereavement counseling, notification of deaths, self-esteem seminars, anger management, cell-to-cell visitation, Ramadan and Passover services, Kairos weekends, and the chapel choir.

In the mid-twentieth century, patients, inmates, and soldiers thought that chaplains had specific ministerial resources particular to each denomination, such that Catholic priests, for example, could offer services that no other denomination's chaplains could.[19] Contemporary chaplains are trained to deemphasize their individual religious identities so that they can provide a nonimposing, noncoercive presence, letting parishioners instead take the lead in terms of any religious specificity. Chaplains have come to serve a role of ministering to what is increasingly understood as a universal spiritual need, which Sullivan labels "a ministry of presence."[20]

Tom O'Connor, the former head prison chaplain for the state of Oregon, argues that chaplains have to create a pluralistic space for all faiths that is secular and spiritual. He believes that, like doctors helping patients, all chaplains should administer a spiritual questionnaire or history and ask four simple questions: What is your faith or belief? Is it important to your life? Are you part of a spiritual or religious community? How would you like to address these issues in your program/plan?[21] O'Connor says, "Only professional chaplains and other religious services staff are in a position to have the appropriate vision, knowledge, skills and aptitude to engage, train and supervise a wide diversity of religious volunteers in an effective manner for correctional purposes, and in a way that maintains the non-establishment of any given religion and the separation of church and state."[22] This attention to the "spiritual" components of human life—rather than the "religious"—provides chaplaincy programs with legal space in which to maneuver. Spirituality stands for something that is universal and available to all, and thus sidesteps First Amendment restrictions about religion, which can be divisive and partisan.[23]

In their book comparing chaplaincy in the United States to that in the United Kingdom, James Beckford and Sophie Gilliat argue that the UK chaplaincy functions like a patron because of the established Church of England.[24] Everyone is a member of the Church of England by default. It sets up a number of religious options, and prisoners have to accommodate themselves to the categories offered.[25] Chaplaincy in the United States might better be characterized as a middle manager or vice president dealing with religious consumers. Chaplains have to recognize a multitude of religious affiliations, but they can simply deprive them of resources. The role of the US chaplain is thus administrative in some regards. In the United Kingdom, the prison has separate spaces for different religions, controlled by the Church of England, whereas in the United States, the chapel is meant to be a neutral space that accommodates everyone, despite the fact that it has the accoutrements of the Christian chapel. For instance, Jummah—Muslim Friday prayers—often occurs in a traditionally Protestant space.

With an estimated two-thirds of all current chaplains affiliated with evangelical and Pentecostal denominations, which often prioritize conversion and evangelizing, and a marked decline in chaplains from Catholic and mainstream Protestant churches, the ideal of neutrality is fraying. The chaplaincy is a professional organization that bestows necessary credentials and grants membership in the American Correctional Chaplains Association; most chaplains have earned a master's degree and worked for an average of ten years in the prisons.[26] But even if the credentialing process is, in theory, open to any person, from any background, not everyone can actually become a chaplain. Atheists and secular humanists may be consumers of chaplaincy services, but the government does not yet permit them to serve as chaplains in hospitals, prisons, or the military. Even the training of chaplains is uneven. Muslim chaplains must receive special training in Judeo-Christian theology, whereas Christians do not have to study Muslim theology; the rationale is that most prisoners express a preference for Christianity. Christian chaplains are also not required to study the history, theology, and practices of other religions, although some do on their own.[27] Instead, chaplains with a nondenominational Protestant background are at once constrained by law to provide religious opportunities to all and impelled by their faith to believe fervently in a Christian God.

The result of the peculiar role of the chaplain in state prisons is that non-Christian prisoners are often subject to the whims of state law and of the chaplain; they must petition for space and religious texts. In Texas, the state is being sued for not providing adequate services for Muslim inmates, and in May 2014, US District Judge Kenneth Hoyt ruled that the Texas Department of Criminal Justice (TDCJ) had illegally violated the rights of Muslim prisoners by making it almost impossible for them to practice their religion while behind bars.[28] As far back as 1969, Muslim prisoners filed lawsuits to make the prisons comply with their religious requirements, such as meals without pork, and permitting them to receive literature about Islam. The state settled in 1977, but in 2012, Texas attorney general Greg Abbott argued that the state should no longer have to abide by that settlement. From 2012 on, the TDCJ regulations stated that groups of four or more prisoners could not meet without either staff or civilian supervision, and could not engage in religious gatherings for more than one hour a week, except with those same stipulations. In his opinion in 2014, Judge Hoyt wrote that "the TDCJ knowingly adopted a policy it knew would impose requirements on Muslim inmates' religious services that could not be satisfied by volunteers or overcome by Muslim inmates." By contrast, he said, the TDCJ illegally favored Christian inmates because there were ample civilians and chaplains of that faith in the state to conduct services in prisons.[29] (There are only five imams employed by the Texas prison system's 111 prison units.) The TDCJ seemed to target Muslim prisoners in particular: Jewish and Native American prisoners were intentionally grouped at the same facilities to enable them to practice their religions, unlike Muslim prisoners, who were separated.

To be a Muslim prisoner in a Texas prison is to exist at the lowest end of the religious hierarchy. Rodney is a student in the seminary at Darrington Unit, one of six Muslims, but he is the only one in his junior class. Serious, articulate, and thoughtful with deep wrinkles across his forehead, he always yearned to pursue a college degree, but the prison system is quite restricted. Rodney was incarcerated in Texas at age nineteen and is now thirty-four. When we first met, he seemed stunned to have the opportunity to speak with me. He says, "I cannot believe they asked me to talk with you. It is just . . . It is just shocking to me, you know what I mean?" "Why?" I ask. "Because I feel so out of place in a sense," he answers. "You know, I mean, you, you . . . it is like a fish out of water, so to speak, and speaking to the curriculum is . . . like the majority of the curriculum is, I want to say, bashing towards certain pillars of my belief." In order to obtain a college degree, Rodney had requested transfer from another Texas prison where he had been part of a strong, tight-knit Muslim community, but his alienation is intense. "I left a beautiful Muslim community that I was raised as a Muslim in, and I miss my brothers very much, you know. I want to go—I do not want to stay here per se." He says he is toughing it out to get an education, and for the long haul,

> I want to take the things that I am learning here to implement in my family's life and in my personal life, because one day I plan on going home. I have been here my whole life, basically, so I need something to fall back on, you know. . . . What else is there for me to do while I am incarcerated? I cannot work; we do not get paid for working. I cannot go to college, because I do not have the money to pay for it. So, this is the best thing going.

Darrington, he explains, is decrepit, and people are disrespectful. After years of a measure of privacy, he has found it difficult to face the indignities of group showers and smaller cells. "Being incarcerated in Texas is a heck of an experience you know," Rodney says. "So you got to make the best of it."

With the specificity of the convert, Rodney can relate the exact date he became a Muslim: December 29, 2006, immediately after his twenty-sixth birthday. He was impressed by two Muslims he met in a vocational course, one black and the other white. He'd been the top student, but when they arrived, he felt mediocre. "And I was like, 'Mmm, I been here for a while and this one come in running the show, right.'" One of the brothers read him a passage from the Qur'an that he recites to me, "In the name of God most gracious, most merciful, say he is God, the one and only, the absolute, the eternal. And, there is none like unto Him." Rodney read it over and over and felt revolutionized in his thinking. He'd been raised a Baptist and believed vaguely in God, but this spoke to him because he no longer felt he needed a mediator in order to have access to God. He impressed the chaplain when he took a class with her called "The Search for Significance" and decided to apply for the seminary. He explains, "She was a good Christian lady, I guess, and when the applications came around for the rest of the year, I got shot down. The second year I was approved."

In the middle of our conversation, Rodney's lips curl upward and he pauses. "I'm trying not to smile, but I cannot help it," he says. "I am enjoying this. This is, this is so unusual for me, you know." He tells me that he is a stern person and shows me his ID picture; a stone-faced man stares back at me. "This is the most you will ever see me smile," he says. We agree; it's more of a grimace. The reluctant grin still in place, he explains, "Well, we do not have an avenue to speak here, really, you know, as a Muslim. This is a Christian program, funded by Christians. I honestly respect it, because even though I do not agree with everything, I am being allowed, I am afforded an opportunity to make history, so to speak. I do not campaign. I just try to do, try to be sincere, and I want people to respect me for who I am, not kissing their rumps and things of this nature." Clearly, for Rodney, studying in an explicitly Christian program with proselytizing goals creates a constant tension.

Rodney takes a breath. "Okay, I am just going to be one hundred with you; this means me 100 percent real," he says. He describes a hypothetical situation in which a Christian and Muslim debate, and the Muslim is "very sharp in understanding what he believes in and how to apply that," whereas the Christian is "not as crisp as he is." Speaking in the third person, Rodney explains that the Muslim is able to apply history and tangible proof for his beliefs, while the Christian simply relies on his faith. He intimates that it creates a problem with the professors and the students. His anecdote is full of ellipses, pauses, and significant looks because he feels censored, though no one else is in the room. "So this is a stepping stone for me. I am not using it as a platform, but I am using it because it is the best option for me right now. And I think any thinking person will, in my position, do the same. Eat the meat and throw the bones away," he says. "Have you heard that before?" he asks, and when I tell him I haven't, he is inordinately pleased. "Oh good, I want to say something original."

Rodney says he longs for more intellectual discussion and less preaching. In our conversations, Rodney presses me over and over to tell him my religious preference, even when I tell him I am agnostic. "There is nothing that you like more than the other, nothing stands out more than the other to you?" he persists. I tell him that if I had to pick, I would choose Quakers or Buddhists. "I heard about Buddhism," he says, "but I do not know much about them. Anytime we think about Buddhism, we think of some kind of chubby guy, Buddha." I tell him a bit about nonviolence and non-attachment, and how even Buddha's teachings would not constitute a dogma because the idea is to question all things. After considering for a long time, he says, "Yeah, that is good, about letting go of things of the world. We need stuff though." He is obviously interested, yet the seminary has little material that would give him the sense of the teachings of other religions, their history, or how they are practiced today.

Accommodating non-Christians is an underlying anxiety for the seminaries and faith-based programs. At Angola in Louisiana, Cain seemed at pains to assure me that the Baptist seminary was not a partisan program, iterating the idea of moral rehabilitation. He repeated several times that the head of Louisiana's ACLU had trained him well, and that he regularly called her on her cell phone. "Forget religion; it's about morality. As long as it's fair, I don't care," Cain said. However, evangelization to a captive population of prisoners inevitably raises ethical and legal matters; it's a coercive use of power. To underscore the diversity of the seminary program beyond Baptists, Cain produced a list of all religions represented, like Methodists, Presbyterians, and Eastern Orthodox, but the highest percentage was nondenominational Christian.

The lack of books about and educators from other religions means students understand Christianity as the norm and everything else as an exception or aberration. In one seminary class at Angola, Robson asked the students, "How many of you were exposed to spurious belief like Wicca?" A muscular white man with a goatee and tattoos strode to the lectern and proceeded to sermonize about Wicca as brainwashing. He said that as a child he was exposed to Wicca and to the teachings of Aleister Crowley, a famous British practitioner of a religious movement in the early 1900s that combined beliefs about the occult, sexuality, magic, and paganism. With each of his statements about Wicca, most of them exaggerations, there were audible gasps of disbelief from the students in the room. Contrary to what Cain said to me, Robson told his Angola class, "There is only one liberty, the liberty of Jesus at work in our conscience enabling us to do what is right."

Nestor's book has this to say about other religions: "The religions of the world will tell you there are other ways to get to God. They are lying. Buddha, Mohammed, Mary, the Saints, Ellen G. White, Joseph Smith, C. T. Russell, Norman Vincent Peale, L. Ron Hubbard, nor any other religious leader has ever saved a soul from Hell."[30] Nestor's advice to Christian ministry leaders is to never participate in the faith services of another religion, ever. "Do not speak, do not sing, do not play instruments, do not hand out literature, do not lend them financial aid, do not invite. While the invitation to one of these services may give you the opportunity to share the Gospel with someone and allow you to bring them to your service, do not participate in their rituals, or pray to their God." In Nestor's influential book, other forms of Christianity are potentially even more dangerous enemies because their claim to being Christians makes them enticing. These "perversions of Christianity," according to Nestor, include "Word of faith (Name it and claim it or Blab it and Grab it), The Purpose Driven life, Calvinism, Seven Day Adventists, Hebraic Roots."

The legal question is how explicitly Christian programs like the seminary operate in a state prison with private support, but also with the assent of the administration to use the prison space and staff. In an article in the *Louisiana Law Review*, Roy Bergeron, a graduate of Louisiana State University and a lawyer in Baton Rouge, argues that the Angola seminary program would fail both the Endorsement and Lemon tests used by courts to interpret compliance with the First Amendment's Establishment Clause, which states, "Congress shall make no law respecting an establishment of religion." The Lemon test, derived from the 1971 Supreme Court decision *Lemon v. Kurtzman*, has three criteria: Does the government action in question have a bona fide secular purpose? Does it have the effect of advancing or inhibiting religion? Does it excessively entangle religion and government? The Endorsement test simply asks: Does the government action amount to an endorsement of religion? Bergeron argues that the Angola seminary requires that men attest to the exclusivity of Jesus, and they must take the "Experiencing God" course in order to have the privilege of attending college. The seminary's stated purpose is to "fulfill the great commission," which it takes from Jesus ordering his disciples to spread his teachings throughout the world. This means the mandate of the seminary is to spread Baptist Christianity. In addition, the only men who can transfer to other prisons are members of the Baptist seminary. According to Bergeron, the seminary program therefore privileges one kind of religion.

Sitting in Robson's class at Angola was Darren Hayes, arms crossed, a barely detectable annoyed look on his face. Unlike most of the men there, Hayes received a college degree before he was imprisoned at Angola. Now forty years old, he's been in prison for eight years and has already graduated from the Baptist seminary. There have been only a few Muslim prisoners in the Angola seminary program since its inception. Hayes reads Qur'anic Arabic and some Hebrew and Greek and relishes comparing biblical and Qur'anic commentaries. Of his early years in the bachelor's program, Hayes explains, "I was frustrated, and I was argumentative. I wanted to question everything. I had to understand I was a guest in the school. I had choice. They didn't force me to come." Now, he's resigned. The seminary program hasn't altered his beliefs, but he's learned to temper his opinions. Of the five other Muslims who just started as freshmen, he says, "I explained to them they shouldn't be argumentative. Take in the good. You don't have to believe what he's saying, and you can learn from them."

There are approximately 180 Muslims in the main prison of Angola, with close to 300 in the entirety of Angola, including all the prison out-camps, and the prison has a part-time Muslim imam. Cain said, as though it were a positive sign, "We're the only prison where the Muslim population is going down." Recently, after becoming disillusioned with the imam, Hayes attempted to hold a Qur'an study session in the prison yard, but the administration shut the group down. "Security disapproves of a new group, thinks it is terrorism. If they did more research and study, maybe they could reconsider. If this were a Christian group, it would be fine. They have no knowledge of Islam. They don't want groups fighting against each other. But we can have all kinds of Christian groups, right?" Hayes says. I asked Cain why he hadn't built a mosque alongside the many new chapels. He replied that he simply couldn't raise the money from the local Muslim community.

The person who paved the way for Darren Hayes is still at Angola. I met Andre Burns, in the oldest chapel in the prison, where he is the Muslim clerk. The chapel is in the central part of the prison where the main cell blocks are located. The administration and prisoners consider it an interfaith space because Cain authorized the construction of new Christian chapels in distant parts of the prison near its out-camps and other housing units, miles away. Burns, in many ways, represents the history of Islam in American prisons, with its attendant legal and political battles. He's a weathered-looking sixty-five-year-old who has been in Angola for thirty-five years and was in the first Baptist seminary graduating class almost twenty years ago. As a young man in his twenties in 1970s New Orleans, he was a Black Panther party organizer and helped the neighborhood set up food programs for kids. In prison, he became a member of the Nation of Islam, which openly criticized the prison administration and treatment of prisoners. "I wanted a spiritual center to my life," he explains. The Nation brought order to a violent and chaotic prison. "Our religion called for standing up for a person, if we see somebody trying to rape somebody. We were doing a lot to stop that. It's a different atmosphere," he says.

Norris Henderson, his old friend, who visits the prison for Jummah prayers, tells a similar story with more bite. Henderson can afford to, because he's no longer locked up. He vehemently disagrees with the story that the seminary brought peace and order to the prison. "It happened with the black power movement, the Nation, and the idea that they were their brother's keeper," he related. There were five hundred Muslims out of five thousand prisoners, but they were respected, educated, and organized. Others knew that the Muslims improved conditions in the prison by brokering prisoner rights with the administration and different factions in the prison.

Henderson explains that Muslims have always been in the vanguard: "We were the ones to establish things legally, to get legislation for the right to meet." Everything they have now, the institutional recognition, the Muslims got through struggle. For years, during Ramadan, the Muslims at Angola would have nothing but cornflakes to break their fast each day. Now they have specific meals that are held for them. When Cain arrived, he recognized that the Muslims were serious. Cain knew where they stood and respected them. Unlike Henderson, who completed every program at Angola except the Baptist seminary, Burns entered the seminary only when other educational opportunities dried up. It didn't change his beliefs, but he says, "I see a lot of similarities between religions. I see there is one God." The seminary provided Burns with a way to continue his education. Now he assists the imam, makes rounds to the cell blocks, and places people on the call-outs, the lists generated so officers know who should be permitted in which classes or religious services.

Henderson's advocacy for Muslim prisoners and Burns's journey from the Nation of Islam to more traditional Sunni Islam is part of a broader history of Muslim legal organizing and institutional shifts in the prison and beyond. The circumscribed diversity of the Angola chapel owes a debt to the Muslim prisoners, who waged an arduous campaign for freedom of religious expression in the 1950s and '60s and pioneered the recognition of non-Christian practices in prison.[31]

The Nation of Islam grew simultaneously in the urban black neighborhoods of the North and the prisons that began to fill with black men between the 1950s and 1970s, but it emerged in Depression-era Detroit. It was a religion of resistance to white supremacy and prejudice as well as a new identity for African Americans who were beleaguered and oppressed by the institutional racism of white society.[32] From the start, the Nation's members positioned themselves as religious outsiders. When Elijah Muhammad, a fervent convert, took over from the enigmatic founder W. D. Fard, he solidified the teachings and assumed leadership. Muhammad taught followers a peculiarly American form of Islam, forged in the Southern Baptist church and the racism of his youth.[33] His most controversial teaching was about Yacub, an evil scientist banished to an island where he created a bleached-out race of white people as revenge. This wicked race overran superior blacks and ruled the world through cruel oppression. A redeemer would appear after six thousand years in North America in the form of W. D. Fard to help oppressed people rise up.[34]

In 1942, Muhammad and others resisted the World War II draft and were imprisoned in large numbers. Sentenced to three years in a Maryland federal prison, Muhammad used the time in prison to recruit and to teach others within the degradation of prison. Also in prison in the late 1940s, Malcolm X, serving time for petty theft, encountered the Nation and, upon release, became Muhammad's deputy and spokesman. The Nation of Islam took root in the prisons of the North, particularly, where they were influenced by Jehovah's Witnesses, whose members were imprisoned for their refusal to salute the flag and serve in the military.[35] Each group found allies in the other as religious outsiders fighting to practice and live separate and religiously focused lives, even in prison. The Nation struggled to prove it was a legitimate religion, when others saw it as a political movement.[36]

The Nation was one of the original faith-based organizations in prison. Both democratic and secretive, it provided protection to those within it and forbid violence unless necessary. Its members prohibited homosexuality and embodied the idea of being "their brother's keeper." Their outside temple supported communication with prisoners and provided them with religious training materials and financial assistance, while offering a broader critique of American society. Malcolm X wrote, "The black prisoner symbolized white society's crime of keeping black men oppressed and deprived and ignorant, and unable to get decent jobs, turning them into criminals."[37] Prisoners stuck together, existing within and apart from prison population, and their members numbered between sixty-five thousand and a hundred thousand by 1960.

For their political and legal commitments, prison authorities did not want Nation leaders like Malcolm X in their prisons.[38] The Nation advised and paid for lawsuits and organizing activities in the prison. The Nation's foremost battles were legal, paving the way for freedom of religious practice for other religious groups in the future. According to nineteenth-century Virginia case law, prisoners were "slaves of the state."[39] Until the 1960s, prison administrators invoked the master-subject relationship to make sense of the status imposed by incarceration. By 1961, the Nation had one hundred separate lawsuits from prisoners for constitutional protection as a religious group, and it challenged the idea of the slave relationship through claims to religious freedom as a liberating force, even within the confines of prison. In New York, prisoners filed suit, saying that they had been unable to buy the Qur'an and communicate with their spiritual advisors. Prisoners at Green Haven Correctional Facility in New York filed petitions objecting to their inability to have religious services from a clergyman of their own religion. Authorities continued to argue that the Nation was political rather than religious, and newspapers smeared them as radical and potentially dangerous to prison society.[40]

The prisoners' rights movement was built upon the activism of Muslim prisoners, who also lobbied for better prison conditions, the right to education, and the right to be free from violence. By 1966, the New York commissioners of the prison system had created a proposal to protect the rights of Muslim prisoners to practice, to recognize Islam as a legitimate religion, and to accommodate dietary needs. The ruling included the right to have Muslim teachers visit the prison, to hold weekly services, to wear religious insignia, to recruit new members, and to receive Muslim materials. The Muslim prisoners' political agitation and savvy legal work had paved the way for access and the right to practice to all religious groups.

After Nation of Islam prisoners Martin Sostre and James Pierce were placed in segregation at New York's Green Haven prison because the warden cited them as security risks, they filed suit for persecution and religious discrimination. Judge John Henderson, a federal district judge, ruled that they were members of a legitimate religion but decided against their claim of persecution. After more than a year in segregation, Sostre was transferred to Attica Prison, where he continued his organizing. The Attica uprising of 1971, one of the largest prisoner rebellions for education, resources, and religious accommodation, was organized and peacefully maintained by Muslim prisoners until the state violently quashed it.[41]

The radical politics of Malcolm X and other black Muslims has been largely repressed by the institutionalization of Islam as just another part of the prison chapel.[42] After Elijah Muhammad's death, his heir, Warith Deen, renounced his father's version of Islam, while maintaining his social teachings of empowerment and unity. He established the American Muslim Mission and sent members to Islamic universities to study. Over time, the Nation became aligned with more traditional Sunni Islam. Louis Farrakhan, who viewed the mission as too integrationist, maintained the Nation of Islam as a separatist movement against white oppression, arguing that W. D. Fard was a prophet of God.

Men like Henderson and Burns, who came of age in the Nation, moved toward more traditional versions of Islam, while retaining the belief in the importance of unity and social organizing.[43] Most Muslim men in prison today are members of traditional Sunni groups, although the Moorish Science Temple of America, a movement founded in 1913 that taught that African Americans were originally Moorish but their heritage was lost during slavery, and the Five Percenters, a Muslim group that splintered from the Nation of Islam in 1964, still have adherents. The other notable shift has been that Muslim groups and leaders are under the direction of the Christian chaplains in most prisons, rendering the group controllable and easily observable. They hire the religious leaders they deem appropriate to come to the prison and administer their programs.

Despite the roots of chaplaincy in the Christian tradition, Muslim chaplains are in prisons in California, New York, and elsewhere. As I've noted, even Angola contracts with imams. Through the National Association of Muslim Chaplains, a professional organization started in 2011, Muslim chaplains work in prisons, hospitals, universities, and the military.

While the early focus of the Nation was on outreach, or *da'wah*, to prisoners who might never have heard about Islam, today chaplains and imams stress support and pastoral care. Most chaplains serve a Muslim community in which multiple interpretations of Islam coexist. But, still, Muslim chaplains in correctional facilities are sometimes accused of spreading a radical, dangerous interpretation of Islam to prisoners.

Chuck Colson, the former head of Prison Fellowship who vocally supported religious rights for prisoners, promulgated the idea of Islam as inherently dangerous. He once wrote in a Prison Fellowship newsletter that prisons are "breeding grounds for future terrorists."[44] Colson warned, "No religious sect should be allowed to preach a doctrine that promotes violence, especially in prison." His solution: "The surest antidote to the poison of hatred and revenge spread by some radical Islamists is Christ's message of love, forgiveness, and peace." Colson made it clear that he would not support state funding for an Islamic immersion program in America's prisons. In the 2012 Pew survey of chaplains, it was primarily the Christian chaplains who saw the potential for extremism in Islam.[45]

This perception of extremism exists at the faith-based prisons and seminaries I visited in Texas and Louisiana. At Darrington, Rodney told me he was frustrated that Islam is viewed negatively because of stereotypes regarding fundamentalist groups, while Christians escape the same judgments.

> You never see the Christian people or whatever, religion being scrutinized as much. Catholics, sometimes because of the, the hanky-panky and stuff that is going on with the pedophiles and stuff like that. I am not being disrespectful, just being honest. But anytime someone commits a crime in America, religion never plays a part unless they are Islamic fundamentalists or someone practic[ing] Islam, and that is the very first thing they will say, instead of just saying this guy pulled a burglary or committed a robbery or something. When a Christian goes out and kills everybody in Columbine, they do not say he is a Christian terrorist. You see, and I think that people need to be more aware of how the media paints pictures of individuals first and foremost.

Christian groups have also played a strange role by arguing for religious liberty cases in prison while railing against Islam as a practice. The work of early Nation of Islam activists like Sostre lives on in contemporary cases about religious freedom, legitimacy, and expression in prisons. There is some irony to the fact that Colson's InnerChange Freedom Initiative (IFI), a twenty-four-hour Christian immersion program sponsored by Prison Fellowship, owes its ability to practice and meet to the legal agitation of Muslim prisoners.

The contention over religious freedom within prisons is exemplified in the court case brought by Americans United for Separation of Church and State in 2006 against IFI program. The case claimed IFI owed the state of Iowa money for running a partisan Christian program in an entire wing of its state prison, which required participants to become evangelical Christians with attendant benefits and privileges. In June 2006, US District judge Robert W. Pratt ordered IFI to shut down and reimburse the state of Iowa the $1.5 million it had received to fund the program in the Newton Correctional Facility.[46] The lawsuit argued that the program promoted evangelical Christianity at state expense. Coercion was a factor in the decision, as people in the program frequently received favorable recommendations from the parole board based on their enrollment and completion of the IFI program. Budgetary constraints had eliminated other programming, and men in the IFI program had larger cells, televisions, and better access to release. Judge Pratt wrote in his decision, "Left with only one true option with which to complete required programming, non-Christian, atheist and agnostic inmates were presented with the dilemma of choosing between early release and personal beliefs; it is understandable why an inmate would choose to compromise the latter."[47] The ruling further reads:

> For all practical purposes, the state has literally established an Evangelical Christian congregation within the walls of one its penal institutions, giving the leaders of that congregation, i.e., InnerChange employees, authority to control the spiritual, emotional, and physical lives of hundreds of Iowa inmates. There are no adequate safeguards present, nor could there be, to ensure that state funds are not being directly spent to indoctrinate Iowa inmates.[48]

Colson and PF president Mark Early launched a campaign to discredit the ruling, solicit funding, and appeal the decision. Although IFI had existed for almost ten years, with six years in Iowa, Judge Pratt wrote: "There was no information presented at trial about whether InnerChange participants are more or less prone to recidivism than other inmates." Colson and Early also argued that revoking the federal funds they received for IFI was an instance of discrimination and a violation of their religious freedom.[49] Early wrote:

> Prison Fellowship wants to see a level playing field for people of faith. People of faith should not be excluded from providing services in the public square to those who have volunteered to receive them. We want prisoners to be able to take part in a program—yes, even a Christ-centered one—that will help them change their lives for the better if they desire to do so.[50]

Neither Early nor Colson envisioned a level playing field for all faiths in prison. The idea of an all-Muslim faith-based prison or program would present an interesting challenge to their arguments. The US Court of Appeals for the Eighth Circuit subsequently confirmed the judge's ruling, but reversed the part of his decision that ordered Prison Fellowship to terminate the program and return state monies already paid to it. The program continued, without state funds, until 2008, when state authorities ended it.

To survive such constitutional scrutiny, many evangelical faith-based groups began to offer intense immersion programs on a volunteer basis, free of charge to prisons, emphasizing the character-building aspect of the programs, suitable for either religious or secular participation. State funds are now typically not allocated to pay staff or supply religiously oriented materials. Indeed, prisons often claim that community volunteers and prison chaplains can adequately and appropriately meet the diverse spiritual needs of inmates. Non-Christian groups still face obstacles at the state level when recalcitrant or hostile chaplains and prison administrations do not recognize their work as the norm.

The experience of Buddhists in prison is another example of the lack of equality for different religious and spiritual groups. In Donaldson

Correctional Facility, a maximum-security prison near Birmingham, Alabama, two men from a Massachusetts-based Vipassana Buddhist center ran a three-day silent-meditation retreat. The prison psychologist had seen the film *Doing Time, Doing Vipassana*, about a prisoners' meditation program in India. He had encouraged the practice in the prison, and once a critical mass of men had become interested in Buddhism over time, the psychologist invited the Massachusetts leaders to visit. The prison officials allowed a member of the Vipassana center to film the retreat, and it eventually became the documentary *The Dhamma Brothers*, a name chosen by the men who participated in the retreat and went on to meet regularly to practice meditation together. I participated in a panel discussion with the filmmaker in 2009, and we discussed what had occurred.

During the retreat, the group of men spent three days in silent meditation, living and sleeping together the entire time with the Vipassana practitioners in a part of the prison gym that had been cordoned off for that purpose. It was a rare and unusual occurrence. The film follows the prisoners from their trepidation to the profound inner shifts they report as a result of meditation: "When someone cuts in front of you in the chow line, the first reaction is to push him. The Vipassana technique gives you a mental tool to observe the situation. If you give yourself time to think, you are gonna come up with a better solution." In their interviews, the leaders and the men never uttered the word "Buddhism," even when they wrote Buddhist teachings and ideas on paper on the walls. They spoke of the Vipassana program in secular language, stating that meditation was a therapeutic, pragmatic, and scientific technique, avoiding any reference to Buddhism as a religion.

Nevertheless, the Christian chaplain shut down the program and forbid the Dhamma Brothers from meeting informally together once the retreat was over and the psychologist had left. The men had to practice in secret or alone. Three years later, in 2006, when a new warden and commissioner who were more sympathetic took over, they allowed the meditation group to resume. Now they are considering establishing a Dhamma Brothers cell block.[51] In the meantime, some of the original Dhamma Brothers were intentionally transferred to other prisons away from their brethren. The chaplain had to decide whether the group was legitimate or not. The chaplain who dismantled the group felt that the Vipassana program competed with his ability to minister to prisoners about Christianity, while the next superintendent viewed it as helpful to a safer-functioning prison.

The courts have a difficult task when asked to decide between the legitimate interests of inmates and the correctional facility. In deciding such cases, the courts now rely on a "balancing test" to help them weigh conflicting issues. The test, decided by the US Supreme Court in 1987 in the case *Turner v. Safley*, consists of four questions:

1. Is there a valid connection between the regulation restricting a religious practice and a legitimate correctional interest?
2. Are inmates allowed other ways of exercising their right?
3. How much will allowing the inmates to exercise their right affect others in the correctional facility?
4. Are there available alternatives that accommodate both interests?[52]

The Turner test stood until 1993, when Congress drafted another law that was to restore certain religious freedoms to all Americans, called the Religious Freedom and Restoration Act (RFRA). The act was passed and signed into law in November 1993. Under RFRA, restrictions on religious freedoms in prisons and jails would be upheld only if the government could show that the restrictions served a "compelling government interest." Further, RFRA required that the religious restriction in question must be the "least restrictive means of furthering that interest." However, in 1997, the US Supreme Court ruled that RFRA was unconstitutional because it did not maintain the separation of powers necessary in the federal government. The RFRA would apply to the federal government but not to the states. State correctional authorities returned to the guidelines outlined in the Turner test for regulating religion in prison.

The most recent legal ruling related to religion in correctional facilities was developed in the year 2000. The Religious Land Use and Institutionalized Persons Act (RLUIPA) was adopted by a unanimous vote in both the US Senate and the House of Representatives in July 2000 and later signed into law by President Bill Clinton. Among other issues, the act ensured that those confined in government institutions such as prisons would be protected in the practice of their faith.[53] Evangelical groups such as Prison Fellowship helped draft RLUIPA. In January 2015, the Supreme Court heard another case based on RLUIPA. In *Holt v. Hobbs*, Gregory Holt, a Muslim prisoner, sued the Arkansas Department of Corrections for prohibiting him from wearing a half-inch beard, which was necessary according to his religious beliefs. The prison warden argued that contraband could be hidden in a beard and thus presented a security risk to the prison.

Today, access to prisoners, money, corporate power, and political influence is not uniform for all prison ministries, and the concept of religious freedom can be used to trump the religious and civil rights and liberties of some groups. The Supreme Court ruled in Holt's favor, citing the protection of the act, but even in her concurring agreement, Justice Ruth Bader Ginsburg stated that the protection extended to Holt because it was not harming anyone else. Just months before, in *Burwell v. Hobby Lobby Stores*, the legal team for Hobby Lobby used RLUIPA to argue that Hobby Lobby had the right to refuse health insurance coverage for employees based on its Christian religious principles. Justice Ginsburg, who wrote the primary dissent in the Hobby Lobby ruling, stated that the Hobby Lobby decision could present harm to employees for whom it refused to cover birth-control coverage, and thus the outcome was against the right to religious freedom. The RLUIPA gathers disparate political actors (Prison Fellowship and Americans United both supported the Holt decisions), while having the potential to promote forms of conservative evangelical Christianity. The various cases argued under RLUIPA exemplify the differing legal premises of what exactly constitutes "religion" and the freedom to embrace certain practices within prison.[54]

While the absolute certainty of Baptists and evangelicals often forecloses curiosity about other religions, for those men like Rodney, marginalized for his race, religion, and foreignness to the prison, his outsider status seems to provide him with the ability to think more critically about religion and the prison in general. He discusses how meeting different people did not close him off, but enabled him to constantly grow and change: "It blessed me with the opportunity to step outside of my own lenses to look at it through your lenses, you see. And from this I have a better understanding of who people are." Later he admitted, "I thought you were a law officer or some Christian lady from a magazine when I first met you. . . . So, it is always good to give a person the benefit of the doubt. I am not saying be crazy or be foolish, but, you know, give the same measure that you would like to receive, you know what I mean."

Rodney tells me he is frustrated by the fact that people in prison cling to their own religious certainty and lack curiosity about others. He would prefer a more open educational space where the premise is to question and learn.

> If a person will talk to me open-minded, an open-end conversation, I will try to get a feel for where he is and vice versa. But a lot of times, you do not have that, because people are so close-minded. One thing that helped me to accept this was that, just because I was taught something, does not necessarily mean that it is true. So I can kind of identify with the Buddhist by questioning all things. If it cannot stand some scrutiny, maybe it should not [be] taken to be something that [you] placed your entire foundation upon.

Rodney's implication was that the prison seminary discourages diversity of opinion and viewpoint, thus constricting the men's view of the world. As Rodney and others noted, despite the history and current cases of legislation around religious freedom and practice in the prison, within most American prisons Christianity is dominant. The idea of the chapel, chaplain, and the concept of "faith" reinforces the assumption that Christianity is the norm. The warden at Lawtey once asked me if men should lose their recreation time so they'd be forced to attend services in the chapel.

Yet, even in a religiously diverse prison in which all groups were represented, with adequate space and time to meet, the deeper question returns to the first penitentiaries in the 1800s, and the role of religious groups within a deeply unjust system. Individual faith is meaningless when there is a lack of access to non-contaminated food or the ability to remain safe and free from violence inside. Record numbers of people are dying in Florida prisons for lack of decent health care. Florida contracted health care to private companies, and now the US Department of Justice may indict the state for violating the constitutional rights of prisoners. Allison DeFoor, director of the Project on Accountable Justice, says of Florida, exemplar of faith-based reform, "If the prison system were a person, it would be screaming for help."[55]

# CHAPTER 5

# THE FATHER AND SON AND THE LIMITED POWER OF FORGIVENESS

AT TWENTY-FIVE, SHAWN IS THE youngest member of the seminary in Texas's Darrington Unit. He's been in prison since he was sixteen for killing his mother. To make sense of what his life has become, Shawn dove into writing, penning both a memoir and works of fiction. In his memoir, which he asked me to read after we met, he retells this story of crime.

Growing up on a ranch in Llano County, he is isolated and forced to do chores most of the day. A love triangle between him and two girls develops, and his mother doesn't approve of one of them. His father is distant and doesn't value school; his mother yells at him and at times seems unstable. He breaks up with the girl he loves because his mother forbids him to see her. Then, in a strangely removed way, Shawn describes returning home and shooting his mother. The section is written in the passive voice, as if he didn't pull the trigger. Local police found the family home burning after Shawn returned to school and accused him of setting fire to his mother's body.

In person and on paper, Shawn shows a curious lack of remorse and a sense of distance from the person in the story. He admits to pulling the trigger but not to setting the fire. "I pulled the trigger of a gun that I should not have pulled the trigger of in the first place, and I bear blame for that," he says, but he claims his mother had threatened him with a knife.

He distances himself from culpability. He continues, "I was a relatively good kid up until this crime. I mean, I was never involved with the police. I was never arrested, I was well-liked in the community, had good friends and stuff. And, certain . . . certain events happened with me and my mom and she ended up attacking me with a knife and I panicked, the knife, acted in self-defense, and I, and I deal with that every day, knowing that I killed my mom. But, so, that is, that is . . ." He trails off and his eyes slide away behind wire-rimmed glasses.

Before he found God, Shawn had tattooed the words "Lost Hope" across the knuckles of his hand. Slender and severe, in his white prisoner's uniform, he's so pale he appears almost translucent. Although he speaks constantly and with a practiced eloquence, never once did he look directly at me. The effect is that he sometimes seems to be disappearing or blending in with his surroundings. I see his memoir as a way he can tell his side of the story. Shawn clearly feels wronged by the narrative the state and the prison have created about him:

> Because, they said I murdered my mother, whereas I did not, and I am trying to tell my side of the story, except, even when I went to trial, I could not, I could not take the stand. My lawyer would not let me, and nobody knows my side of the story, not even my dad. Because, he does not, he never really wants to talk about it. And, my lawyer even said in trial, he even told the jury to find me guilty for murder, or for arson and stuff like that.

Shawn has found solace in the seminary program because, through his relationship with God, he feels forgiven and absolved. Evangelical faith-based ministries facilitate a way to think about forgiveness, victimhood, and restoration for the individual, but this limited mode is predicated on the individual. Although Shawn lives in the suffocating density of a maximum-security prison and escapes briefly each day as part of the tight community of seminarians, his grace and transformation, according to the program, come from within or from a relationship with God.

As previously noted, faith-based prison ministries emphasize the idea that the individual is not incorrigible or fundamentally evil, but they also support the role of the criminal justice system in meting out punishment. The theology that undergirds the work of the seminary and other ministries is a contradictory hybrid of New Testament forgiveness and Old Testament vengeance. The traditional script we expect contains a victim; the prosecutor who often fervently goes to any length to convict the person who has allegedly committed harm; the victim's loved ones pushing for justice, which often takes the form of vengeance; and the idea that proper resolution means the perpetrator is punished by time in prison, by what happens to him in prison, and possibly even by death.

The place of forgiveness and resolution in this process is murky. Release from prison is supposed to signal a form of absolution, a pardon for the crime for which someone was convicted. However, former prisoners continue to be punished and stigmatized in myriad ways. They cannot vote or obtain public housing in some states. They may lose custody of their children or become estranged after years of enforced separation. Certain businesses will not hire them; they have to check a box on an application that means their conviction will affect their ability to get a job or go to school. Doing so lessens their chances for meaningful education or employment. Restrictions on travel and parole violations also hinder them. Their crime and experience of imprisonment follow and haunt them outside the gates in the form of these barriers and prison's lasting psychological and personal toll.

The idea that forgiveness or resolution only occurs as a result of punishment, or after a certain amount of punishment, has roots in Christian theology. Timothy Gorringe, an English theologian, writes in *God's Just Vengeance* that the Christian belief in the crucifixion of Christ reinforces the retributive notion that sin or crime have to be punished, and cannot properly be dealt with in any other way.[1] In the United States, when we think about prisons, we almost universally assume that "justice" for wrongdoing requires retribution or punishment, repaying wrongdoing with pain. Gorringe argues that this cultural approval and support for retribution emerges from a Western Christian belief that retribution is God's will. "The logic of retribution" underlies many rationales for the use of violence: God is impersonal and holy, God's law is a standard by which we measure sin, and God's response to sin is punitive. The central narrative stems from the Christian idea of atonement. Jesus's death on the cross is necessary as a sacrifice to provide the only basis for sinful humans to escape deserved punishment. According to Gorringe, the focus on Jesus's death reinforces the need for a scapegoat in human society, and the prisoner becomes the scapegoat. Gorringe writes, "Could it be that the preaching of the cross not only desensitized us to judicial violence but even lent it sanction?"[2] The theological rationale for punishment rests on the view that appropriate punishment reflects God's character, because God does not countenance any kind of sin. Justice, in this theological framework, works to sustain the moral balance of the universe. If we upset the balance, justice requires payment to restore equilibrium.[3] This payment is made through punishment and pain for wrongdoing.

The close connection between Western political philosophy and Christian theology dates back to the early fourth century with the first Christian emperor, Constantine, and the work of Augustine. Their views of God and justice continue to be foundational in present-day practices of punitive criminal justice.[4] Gorringe also claims that the key impact Greek philosophy had on theology may be seen in emerging notions of God's impassivity, the growing abstraction of concepts of justice, and the objectifying or "othering" of offenders (in Augustine's case—and in the following generations—especially the objectification of "heretics" providing the basis for their severe punishment). Justice became a matter of applying rules, establishing guilt, and fixing penalties, without reference to finding healing for the victim or the relationship between victim and offender. Canon law and the parallel theology began to identify crime as wrong against a moral or metaphysical order. Increasingly, focus centered on punishment by established authorities as a way of doing justice.

Our punitive criminal system is predicated on the expectation that someone will suffer through isolation, banishment from loved ones, violence, and deprivation of intimacy, health care, and freedom as expiation for crime. In this vengeance-centered logic is an expectation that the person in turn will be harmed, humiliated, and injured. To pay for their sins, prisoners need to be expelled, transported, locked out of sight behind walls, prevented from having human contact, and hanged, Gorringe writes. The answer to violence is the violence of sacrificial death as taught to Christian society by its faith.[5] This thinking is reflected in a quote by Simone Weil that claims the necessity of punishment for the transformation of the individual:

> The art of punishing is the art of awakening in a criminal, by pain or even death, the desire for pure good. Those who are so estranged from the good must be reintegrated with it by having harm inflicted upon them. This must be done until the completely innocent part of the criminal's soul awakens with the surprised cry, "Why am I being hurt?" This innocent part of the soul must then be nurtured until it becomes able to judge and condemn past crimes and attain forgiveness.[6]

Today, many nondenominational and evangelical Christians seem wedded to the idea that punishment awakens good and the biblical idea of God's law as retribution, whether it is imprisonment or the death penalty. The chaplain at Lawtey Correctional Institution in Florida, a Southern Baptist who believes wholeheartedly in heart change and transformation, still insists on the necessity of the death penalty. When I asked the chaplain about Karla Faye Tucker, who was executed by the state of Texas in 1998 after becoming a devoted Christian, he responded, "You pay the Old Testament price even if transformed. There is still a penalty to pay." The chaplain recalled how he broke down crying when he had to minister to Ricky Sanchez, a Cuban who came to the United States on the Mariel boatlift in the 1980s and was going to be put to death. "God's Law," he explained to me. "It's not about getting even; it's about fulfilling the law."

Both Gorringe and Mark Taylor, a professor of theology at Princeton Theological Seminary and critic of mass incarceration, argue that remembering the executed Jesus is crucial for mobilizing resistance to mass incarceration.[7] Instead of focusing on the crucifixion and the violence of atonement, Christians could highlight Jesus's teachings and words. Jesus was a criminal who resisted the Roman authorities and preached a practice of forgiveness and fellowship that is absent from the theological underpinnings of punishment today.[8] Gorringe, however, argues that, to a human being who has wronged his fellow man, forgiveness is an infinitely more convincing proof of love than punishment can ever be and may, therefore, touch the heart as punishment cannot.[9]

The faith-based ministries reinforce some of the retributive and vengeance-centered ideas about punishment. In their view, a person like Shawn must suffer and find forgiveness solely through God, rather than in relationship with other people, including those he has harmed. However, the origins of the Darrington seminary, where Shawn lives, grew out of an unlikely story of vengeance and forgiveness between two Christians, the father of a murdered daughter and the man who killed her. Grove Norwood funded and conceived of the seminary in Texas after his personal history of tragedy led him to believe faith-based programs in prison were the solution to changing the hearts of prisoners. Norwood is a rangy former fighter pilot and Vietnam vet in his seventies with a lined, weathered face and a shock of stark white hair. He's a self-described country boy from the small Texas town of Simonton, south of Houston (population approximately 720), who worked at an insurance company before becoming an unlikely champion of faith-based ministries in prison. As he recounts, one day while driving, Norwood passed two men and a child staring at a hole in the side of a small ramshackle wall of St. Andrew's Church. In Norwood's small town, African Americans attended St. Andrew's, while white people went to the fancier church across town that could seat 350 people.

One of the men staring at the hole was the church pastor, and the other was a congregant and deacon named Ulice Parker, who had with him his four-year-old son. After Norwood stopped and convinced Parker and the pastor that he wasn't a politician running for election, they explained that the air conditioner had been pilfered from the church. This was no small thing in the one-hundred-degree heat. Norwood had always wanted to help out some of the poor African American families he'd seen in town. He immediately hopped back in his car and purchased an air conditioner, and that afternoon, all three men installed it with an extra bolt and chain to keep it secure. "I was really excited, because I had been praying, 'Lord, let me meet someone. Let me meet someone outside of my circle that could use a helping hand.' I felt that God was answering my prayers," says Norwood.

Someone again stole the air conditioner two weeks later, but Norwood and Parker became hesitant friends across racial divides that seemed insurmountable in Simonton. According to Norwood, over the years, his own small children, Graham and Joy, visited Parker's house, where he lived with his wife, Carrie, and their children. Parker, who had labored picking cotton in South Texas most of his life, had a slight speech impediment and had never been outside the four square miles of his town, but he kept a prodigious community garden, mowed the St. Andrew's lawn, and took up the plate collection every Sunday. Norwood couldn't help noticing that the home Parker shared with his wife and their children never had hot water, and the rain drizzled onto a mattress through a section of the roof. The refrigerator had stopped functioning long ago. It was only chilly enough to keep milk slightly cold.

Norwood helped out Parker's family from time to time, bringing them a Kenmore stove or helping repair his roof. Their kids played with each other, and Norwood occasionally attended Sunday services at St. Andrew's, the only white person in town to do so. Parker had become a Christian as a boy and Norwood as an adult, but they were both fervent believers.

On April 10, 2000, Norwood's wife, Jill, was driving four-year-old Joy and her brother home from a baseball game around twilight. She pulled their passenger van over to the side of the road because four-year-old Joy had to go to the bathroom. In the confusion of noisy and jostling kids, Joy hopped out of the van on the wrong side. Within seconds, a car hit her, tossing her little body eighty feet in the air. The car sped by into the night. On the country road, without white lines and street lights, Jill could barely see what had happened. She just held Joy in her arms and wailed. Norwood was in Houston, and when he returned to Simonton, helicopters were lifting off the prairie like a painful flashback to Vietnam. Joy died that night.

The town sheriff and police began to hunt for the hit-and-run driver. The pastor of Norwood's church, police officers, and others called for vengeance for the death of a child. A few days later, Norwood's phone rang, and a police officer told him, "We know who hit Joy." They had matched headlight fragments scattered on the road. "The driver remembers hitting something, but seemed shocked it was a little girl," the officer

told Norwood. On unlit Texas country roads, it wasn't uncommon to ac-
cidentally hit an armadillo, stray dog, or varmint. Norwood hung up. The
phone rang again, and it was Carrie Parker, Ulice's wife. "Mr. Grove," she
sobbed, "they tell me my Ulice killed baby Joy."

With an outraged town and a black man responsible for killing a white
little girl, the situation was extremely combustible. That night Norwood
and his brother, Steve, drove to Ulice's house. "I know Ulice is going to
be scared to death," he told him. When they arrived, Parker was slouched
in a chair staring at the floor, unable to articulate his overwhelming remorse and shame. He'd never had a driver's license, and his lights were low
that night. He shouldn't have been driving because he was almost legally
blind. Norwood hugged Parker, consoling him that it would be all right,
that they were friends and would get through this. Norwood says, "I felt
sorry for both of us. I looked at him, and it was like looking at myself. He
was broken, and I was broken. I hugged him as we both cried."

At Joy's funeral, Ulice Parker and his family sat next to Grove Norwood and his wife in the front pew of the church. Norwood had his arms
around both his wife and Parker. When Carrie Parker didn't have a dress
to wear to the funeral, Norwood's relatives drove her to a department
store and bought her one. Norwood wanted everyone to know that he
forgave Parker. Pastor Clay Spears of Parker's church was less certain of
Norwood's motives. "I couldn't figure out any reason why a white man
would invite this black man who killed his child to the funeral, unless it
was for revenge," says Pastor Spears, who is in his late sixties. "I grew up
with that kind of white violence."

Later, Norwood testified to the grand jury that he wanted it to drop all
charges; it eventually did. "I wanted them to know that I held no grudge
against Parker. That I knew it was an accident, and that he was my friend,"
says Norwood. District Attorney Travis J. Koehn says he had never seen
anything like this situation: "It would be more usual for someone to come
to my doorway and say, 'He killed my little girl; I want him in prison.'" In
2001, Norwood convinced his friends at his church to help him construct
a new home for Ulice Parker's family. Eventually, almost one hundred
volunteers joined in the house building. When someone expressed be-
wilderment that Norwood would pay to build a home for the man who

killed his daughter, Norwood answered that it was because the house was dilapidated and Parker was their brother.

That might have been an unusual end to a tragic story except that a man from Promise Keepers, the national men's ministry, heard about it from someone in Norwood's church. Incredulous, he decided to verify its authenticity and then raised funds to make a film about Norwood, Parker, and Joy called *The Heart of Texas*. Norwood was initially reluctant to participate. In a letter to Norwood, the man from Promise Keepers argued that men in America needed to see this story. The film eventually aired on TBN and other Christian networks. In the film is a vivid scene in which Norwood recalls escaping to the lake and weeping on the night of Joy's funeral, his nearby house filled with family and friends. As he railed against God, he recalls asking, "You cannot possibly do anything that is such a greater good here that would make this all worthwhile. How could any good ever come out of this?" Years went by and one day a man tapped Norwood on the shoulder at church. "He asked me if I was Norwood. I said yes, and he thanked me for his new life in Christ, that he had found as a result of the film," says Norwood. The man had driven across the state to thank him. When Norwood politely inquired what church he was from, the man replied that he'd seen the movie in the Huntsville prison when he had been incarcerated there. The same thing happened again to Norwood four months later. "When you come to know the God of the Bible and the way He works, you suddenly start seeing that this is not a coincidence," he says.

Norwood and the filmmakers never intended the film to become a prison sensation. Invitations to speak in prison kept pouring in, and Norwood says he reluctantly began to discern the larger purpose behind Joy's death that he had prayed for. Norwood believes God knew and understood his heart, because he and God had both experienced the trauma of losing a child. He says it made him love God even more. Chaplains and prison ministries now show the film in hundreds of prisons in Texas and across the South. Norwood frequently says, "Joy got into prison," as way of expressing how her senseless death took on meaning. When we talked at Darrington, he said, "I am thankful that it happened the way it did, and I can now see the greater good that came out of the worst night of my life.

I am not trying to dictate what God is going to do here, because I respond to the movement that I see He is making, rather than try to make it myself. And, that is how this whole thing started, with a tap on my shoulder, and invitation to have a dialogue with somebody, an invitation to go into a prison. I have never made a phone call to say, 'Can I come to your prison, or can I come to your church?'"

From the standpoint of an incarcerated woman or man, the film represents central issues of crime, punishment, and forgiveness, with all the characters present: the victim, the victimizer, the law, the clergy, the neighborhood. Norwood says most who watch are stunned that a black man is sitting next to him at the funeral and find his forgiveness of Parker astonishing and even unfathomable. In the American criminal legal system, the usual conclusion to the story of Grove Norwood and Ulice Parker is the incarceration of Parker. The norm would be that imprisonment of Ulice is a form of vengeance and just punishment for Norwood's immense loss. According to Norwood, men and women in prison see it and think, "I wish somebody had gone to bat for me like that. Maybe I would not be in here. I just needed one friend. Nobody embraced me. I am sorry for what I did, and nobody cares."

Eventually, a chaplain at Angola prison in Louisiana asked Norwood to visit and discuss the film, and Norwood marveled at the transformation he witnessed there. Given his curiosity, he wanted to know how things had changed at Angola, which he sees as a model for altering the hearts and morality of men and women in prison.

> And, I realized the lifers who started fifteen years ago, they are still there, and they have been passing this new morality through the bars twenty-four hours a day, seven days a week for fifteen years, while the warden goes home. And, all the volunteers like me, we go home for the night. All the staff shifts and they come in with their own things, but there is the continuity with these men who did not just talk about Jesus, they talked about what does the Bible say about fatherhood and manhood and integrity and truthfulness and being a friend to others. This whole new morality that is also in the Bible.

Norwood now considers former Angola warden Burl Cain one of his best friends and equates Angola's transformation under Cain to the parable of David and Goliath, with Cain as David and the prison as Goliath, even though Cain was hardly small or lacking in power. Once Norwood was convinced that seminary was the way to reform men in prison, he started the Heart of Texas Foundation to raise money for a seminary program in Texas, and began escorting groups of religious leaders and politicians from Texas to visit Angola for three days every month. Two of Norwood's initial guests were Texas state senators Dan Patrick, a Republican, and John Whitmire, a Democrat. Whitmire, the longest-serving member of the Texas legislature, had authored the penal code that sent the prison population soaring in the 1990s, but he became a convert to the seminary idea. Within ten months of the visit to Angola, Darrington prison had a seminary program. Through church and individual donations, Norwood is now raising the funds for the $2 million chapel addition to Darrington prison. Combining the language of faith and economics, Norwood and Cain would like the seminary to become a franchise, a model for prisons everywhere.

Norwood believes in the concept of forgiveness, while acknowledging that he was able to forgive because Parker was a friend. Men and women in prison ask many of the same questions about forgiveness, such as, How do you forgive someone you hate? Norwood has collected these questions: "That began the movement of God in my heart to go back and talk to them, to find out real answers, not sermons." People ask him how he would have reacted if the culprit had been a gang member or a "drug-crazed person." He says he doesn't know: "I have no idea. I hope that I would be able to get over it in due time. I probably would be angry. I would be just like anybody else. I cannot tell you the answer to that. I would not presume to do so." However, Norwood continues, "But even then I would have been called on to forgive. The bottom line is that every Christian is called to offer forgiveness. The Bible tells us to forgive as God has forgiven us. And the prayer I have to say every day is this: 'O God, I do want your forgiveness. I understand that as I do this, I am a new person in your eyes. As Jesus said in John 5:24: I have crossed over from eternal death to eternal life. Thank you!'"

Ulice Parker died of a heart attack, planting okra in his garden five hundred yards up the road from where Joy had died three years earlier. His wife, Carrie, died of cancer in their home. Parker is only the subject of the film, not a speaking participant in Norwood's story. Norwood acknowledges that reform happens soul by soul; the situation was personal rather than something to apply more broadly. He says, "As I told you earlier, it was an accident and he was my friend." His story shows us that forgiveness is not univocal or simple. When a victim chooses to release the perpetrator of a crime, as Norwood released Parker from guilt, and gives up his own feelings of ill will or desire to hurt or damage the perpetrator, it clears the way for reconciliation and the restoration of relationships, theologian Christopher Marshall argues.[10] Forgiveness has to be initiated by the person who was harmed and given freely; in so doing, Norwood relinquished the power his daughter's death had over his life as a negative force. His history with Parker was a source of his own healing.

But forgiveness is not natural or instinctive, because our first impulse is always to inflict equal suffering on those who have harmed us. Marshall writes,

> Retaliation promises satisfaction, a discharging of the burden of pain and resentment. But it fails to deliver real freedom, for even when the victim has hurt the offender, he or she is still cursed with the memory of the offense, which still brings feelings of anger and disgust. So evil multiplies.[11]

When Norwood rejected the idea of equivalence, or an eye for an eye, he committed a creative act of forgiveness.

Despite Norwood's forgiveness of Parker, the work of the Heart of Texas Foundation is not to keep people from prison. Norwood doesn't think that the men in prison should be forgiven enough to leave prison, but he does believe they can be morally reformed. This distinguishes evangelical teachings from those of other progressive Christians, like Gorringe and Taylor, who view forgiveness, not retribution, as an integral part of justice and urge a reconceptualization of how justice is applied. Evangelicalism places primary emphasis on the individual's reformation, and a relationship with God. In Catholicism and other traditions, there is more emphasis on the obligations to the community, family, or others who are implicated in and affected by the prisoner's situation.

Dennis Pierce, a former Catholic chaplain in Joliet Correctional Center, a maximum-security prison in Illinois, argues in his book *Prison Ministry: Hope Behind the Wall* that volunteers who work in prisons should apply the principles of unconditional compassion as manifested in liberation theology.[12] He stresses mutuality in working with prisoners, the idea that you can try to peer into a prisoner's inner world and see how it connects to your own. Unlike the belief of other prison ministries, Pierce does not see the work of ministry as furthering punishment: "The church needs to assure the incarcerated that oppression and human breakdown are not an integral part of the punishment for their crimes."[13] The sacrifice of dignity, self-worth, and the sense of being human should not be part of prison. He disputes the need for vengeance, iterating God's work as that of helping the oppressed. Pierce says, "Sooner or later being human leads the oppressed to struggle to have meaning, the oppressed must not, in seeking to regain their humanity become in turn the oppressors of the oppressors, but rather restorers of humanity for both. Only power that springs from the weakness of the oppressed will be sufficiently strong to free both."[14]

Pierce criticizes those churches that accept the rationale of the prison system: "One of the decisive areas that has allowed our society to embrace the concept of substantial evil as our operating system has been the churches' willingness to participate in this dysfunctional system. This participation has allowed us to forget that Christ's life, teachings and his execution as a criminal were to guide us to live our lives filled with justice, forgiveness and humility."[15] Faith-based ministries upend the dichotomous concept of good people and evil people, but they do not take the next step as Pierce and others do, viewing both the system and each person as flawed and redeemable. Pierce also blames the church for being enmeshed in a capitalist desire for wealth and individual success: "The suburban churches have moved from the scriptural call to engage society as a whole, not as individuals."[16] For many faith-based ministries, the emphasis on the individual rather than the community justifies mass incarceration. This results in charity instead of justice. Charity is episodic; justice is ongoing. The one changes individuals, the other societies.[17]

Volunteering in prison as part of faith-based ministry enacts the charitable impulse, but it can enable people to move beyond simplistic understandings of victims and criminals, punishment and forgiveness. Norwood's work has emboldened hundreds of men and women in prisons around Texas and the South to volunteer to work with prisoners and their families, and in the process, a form of identification and compassion occurs that leads them to think more critically about incarceration.

At Freedom Center Church in Texas, about forty minutes from Darrington, approximately fifty women are being treated to a spa day. Their children's fathers are in prison, and they are their children's sole caregivers. Ranging from age thirty to sixty, they have spent the morning getting manicures or massages in one of the church rooms. They each have a "glamour shot" taken by a professional photographer, which will be framed and ready for them to take home when they leave. The backroom of the church has become "the Boutique of Blessing," where women can shop, but not pay, for twelve items each. Members of the church have donated jewelry, purses, scarves, clothing, and makeup, which are meticulously displayed in boxes on tables in a simulacrum of a department store.

Tricia Howard, the wife of Freedom Center's pastor, which has over one thousand members, organized women from fourteen neighboring churches, like Sugar Creek Baptist Church, Sienna Ranch Church, First Baptist Houston, and Colony Baptist, to offer a day of rest and rejuvenation for the caregivers. Today's theme is "Returning Hearts." "He will turn the hearts of the parents to their children and the hearts of children to their parents," Malachi 4:6, is projected on the wall. The team of church volunteers has spent six months contacting women who are caregivers to children with fathers in prison. In order to ensure that the caregivers, often from other parts of the state, would come to "Returning Hearts," they sent cards and letters, made phone calls, and arranged transportation and lodging for many. Howard says, "It was very strategic, so that we knew that these walls would eventually come down, and they would understand we were their friend, we were not just another agency trying to do this event to make us feel good about ourselves. And, so [we] built this rapport with the women."

The event is based on the idea that interactions between prisoners and volunteers can produce compassion and identification, but it bespeaks the difference between charity and justice. These churchwomen volunteer their time and energies to the caregivers, but what impels them to do so? Laura McTighe, a scholar of religion and prison activist, asks of people ministering in prisons, "Do we just feel sorry for people in prison? Or do we feel personally impacted by their struggles?"[18] The first response engenders sympathy and the second engenders compassion. She argues that most of us would affirm that our intentions are compassionate. "But living true compassion requires far more than not buying into the belief that prisoners are bad people," she says. "True compassion is as much about challenging our own attitudes and assumptions as it is about the support we offer to people in prison." Often the racial imbalances between the white evangelicals and the overwhelmingly black and Latino prison population exacerbate the dynamic of difference.

Tricia Howard, who has long brown hair and immaculately applied makeup, could, at age forty-eight, pass for someone a decade younger. "I want them to bless me," says Tricia, speaking of the caregivers. "And I would want to go shopping. I like to go have my nails done, because these are luxuries; they are luxuries for me, they are luxuries for these women as well." She tells them, "Take care of yourself, because if you do not, you are not going to be able to take care of the child. So, you must; it is important for you to take care of your soul, and so we are giving them some tools for that." In this case, the soul-tending comes with a manicure.

Before the women sit down to lunch of chicken salad on croissants, fruit salad, pasta salad, and banana pudding served by volunteers, Tricia comes to the microphone and asks, "Ya'll look so beautiful. Did you enjoy your spa treatments?" Several volunteers sit with the women. Bowls of candy are everywhere: on the tables, along the sides of the room, and in the spa. Tricia believes that lavishing the women with small gifts is a way to minister to their spirit, soul, and body. With that, they can inject the spiritual side of things: "Being here for prayer, or being here to talk things out for the what-ifs or whatever is going on in their lives. Or if they cannot deal with something, we can assist them in that." Terry, a woman with long brown hair in ringlets and carrying a fuchsia purse, begins weeping during lunch. One of the volunteers pats her back and talks quietly to her. Terry's husband is in the first year of the seminary program.

Norwood had long felt that the labor of the caregivers was as important as anything done for the fathers: "Because all the children go back to those people and this is not something they signed up for, the grandmothers and aunts that are having to reach into their pockets and do it over again. You know that." Tricia Howard and her husband heard Norwood speak at a Heart of Texas event and were moved by his story and ministry work. Norwood convinced Tricia to provide the hands-on planning for the caregiver event, especially because it is consistent with his conservative Baptist sense of the proper, gendered division of labor. He appeared at the spa event later on, when they screened *The Heart of Texas*.

Earlier that day, Norwood had been in Darrington Unit for the annual "Day with Dad" event, when men in the seminary with good behavior can spend one day with their children. Local churches organized games and events, and women volunteers filled plates with mammoth pieces of fried chicken, mashed potatoes, green beans, a roll, and apple or peach cobbler for dessert. The volunteers all wore identical white polo shirts with the tag "Mike Wingman" or "Jeff Wingman" on them. For Norwood, who flew fighter planes in Vietnam, the wingman, the person who is indispensable in supporting you through a tough job, is a crucial social role. Here, it was also a less intrusive term for someone interfering with an intimate day between men and their children. The men who volunteered for Day with Dad were members of local churches, but they didn't necessarily have training in family counseling. They stayed near the fathers in prison as they played and talked with their kids, often facilitating their interactions.

Just as the volunteers are supposed to view the dads in prison as fathers like themselves, women like Tricia more easily find common ground with women caring for children, even if they are doing it alone. Tricia feels she can identify with the women who have come to her church while their children meet their fathers in prison. During the morning of the spa event, small groups discussed overcoming obstacles in finances, raising rebellious kids, and being a single parent or a grandparent raising young children. Tricia says, "And, you know, all of these things that they have to face. I mean, parenting is hard enough, but they just bring up a differ-ent level when they have this responsibility of being caregiver. For me, I have always had an understanding just, if it were not for the grace of God, and, you know, the environment and upbringing that I was in, I was born blessed to have that, but, by the grace of God, I could have been in prison. I understand that they are people just like me, and they are facing the con-sequences for some of their mistakes."

Rather than viewing the caregivers related to men in prison as other than herself, Tricia claims that they are all alike. "God has allowed me to have eyes to see them and identify. I really identify with them truly. I want to be more in tune with their needs and give them stuff, which is what we are doing right now." Eight years earlier, she had returned to school for a teaching degree in order to help her family through some financial difficulties. She was in her forties, and the experience was unfamiliar and humiliating. She recalls it as a time of deep distress and feels that "the Lord just really hugged me through my time of suffering."

She doesn't acknowledge differences of race and class, quite evident at this event. Viewing herself as similar to the wife or mother of a man in prison is also not the same as connecting with the prisoner himself, who is sometimes less sympathetic or accessible. Tricia also doesn't talk about women in prison. The caregivers might be "crippled on the inside," she says, but everyone has wounds or struggles. "And I just get that. And I just try to be real. I do not want anyone here to think that we have got it all together, because that would be so wrong. That is such a huge fallacy. We are all in need of Christ to give us strength, help, support, give us hope, to even give us faith."

Even if Tricia sees her own struggles mirrored by the women at the care-giver event, the other women do not always share her view. At the spa day, a woman named Melissa, standing at the side of the room, seemed to be avoiding everyone. For twelve years, she'd been taking her son to visit his father in prison. She was seven months pregnant at the time of his im-prisonment, and without any resources, she was forced to return to work within six weeks of his birth. Leaving him in child care was so wrenching and stressful that she sobbed on her way to work. Melissa's story is mostly about balancing her son's early years with being a single working mother. The happiest time in her life was when she could bring him to a day-care facility at her job and see him during the day. Even if it took them hours to get home, they were together. Melissa resists the idea that she has a particular fellowship or kinship with the church volunteers or the potential of building a network of other caregivers. She's too exhausted by daily life and resigned to frequent trips to the prison.

The volunteer women are doing the labor of spa attendants, spiritual mentors, and mental health counselors in the space of a weekend. Tricia advises the caregivers to write in journals, think about taking walks, and talk with God about their problems. She gives the women several devotional books with encouraging words and urges them to build a support group of their own. "That is one of the really important things as far as good soul care. Have a good, healthy support group, and have a support group that is faith-based, that will encourage you and will speak truth into you," says Tricia. "The world will do enough speaking negative to us, and so we really need to watch who we let into our circle of trust." When the caregivers are depressed, she urges them to turn on religious music to change the atmosphere of their house. It will even help the kids, she tells them: "I mean, we are trying to give them some tools to say we love you, take care of yourself."

Tricia and her volunteers presume that what works for them—spa days and shopping, journaling and praise music—is what works for these women, and that may be the case. Having a day when other people lavish care upon you is certainly a gift, but the children these women care for will grow up, and their fathers will still be in the prison. The church volunteers may have identified with the women and thus become more compassionate toward those in prison, but it is an individualistic mode of helping. They view the women as victims, but they don't analyze the ideas and social structures that have made the women's lives so difficult. There is a potential for building support networks for child care, jobs, and housing, but the event is a one-time thing. Tricia says they will send the caregivers Thanksgiving and Christmas cards, "just to let them know, 'Hey, we are praying for you, you are doing a good job.'" After that, the women are on their own.

———————

Evangelical faith-based groups contend with the questions of victimhood, forgiveness, and vengeance by focusing on the individual, but other ministries address it as a way of connecting the harmed and the perpetrator. In Darrington Unit, volunteers from Bridges to Life, an ecumenical faith-based organization that remains heavily Protestant and Christian, organize weekly sessions for men in the prison where they listen to the stories of crime victims. One woman describes how she was kept in an attic by a pimp. Another woman shows a video of her vivacious ten-year-old daughter doing gymnastic routines on a balance beam; she was stabbed ninety-seven times by a twelve-year-old neighbor. A couple describes how their four children were killed driving home from a football game by a local man who had been drinking. A woman moves the long hair off her neck to show the men the places where she was shot through the neck and collarbone. For the past sixteen years, over five hundred volunteers from Bridges to Life, two-thirds of whom are women, have come to talk to prisoners about the ways they had been harmed, hoping that it would repair them and the men with whom they speak.[19]

The word "victim" implies suffering, but it has two meanings. The first is the victim of an assault, rape, or some other cruel or malicious treatment. The second is a collateral victim, who endures the loss of another. In impact statements, the meaning of "victim" is important, because it connotes both physical pain and mental or emotional suffering. The creation of the victim rights movement and victim impact statements profoundly altered how we view incarceration and punishment. In 1982, the president's task force on victims of crime proposed that the Sixth Amendment to the Constitution have the following addition: "Likewise the victim in every criminal prosecution shall have the right to be present and to be heard at all critical stages of judicial proceedings."[20] Although no amendment has been passed, forty-nine states and the federal government have passed provisions giving extensive rights to victims. The Victims' Rights Clarification Act of 1997 expanded the way victims could be involved in court and criminal proceedings. Victim impact statements became legal in death penalty cases in 1991. In *Payne v. Tennessee*, Chief Justice William Rehnquist argued that evidence about the impact of a murder on the family of a victim could be used in deciding whether to impose the death penalty. In his dissent to *Payne*, Justice John Paul Stevens asserted that victim impact statements serve no other purpose than to encourage jurors to decide in favor of death rather than life on the basis of their emotions rather than their reason.

Where does forgiveness figure in property crime or possession of illegal drugs or when profound harm has occurred with loss of life, murder, rape, or physical injury? There is little in the process that enables some kind of resolution or forgiveness, and it is rarely granted by those who have been harmed by what has occurred, because the courts, the prosecutor, and the web of laws keep them separate unless they meet in a courtroom. Punishment is meted out in the prison, invisible to the person harmed, the courts, and the prosecutor, except in the sensationalized images we consume on television and in popular culture. The binary terminology of victim and perpetrator simplifies the vector of forces that lead one to commit harm against another, even if it doesn't excuse that harm. It erases the fact that many who harm may have also been victimized. A woman who is abused as a child and takes drugs and enters into an unhealthy relationship with a man who will in turn abuse her and her children is also shaped by those forces, just as she is responsible for harm to others. The American criminal legal system is not equipped to contend with these nuances or to offer a forum in which to think about forgiveness.

During a meal at Angola, Warden Cain ranted about the officers who wouldn't let a prisoner who had been allowed to attend his mother's funeral take a picture with his family. The warden thought this was unnecessarily harsh and asked that the officers involved be brought to him for a reprimand. However, his human resources manager, a woman married to a prison lieutenant, reminded him gently that they had to think about the victim of the crime the man had committed. What would be the victim's perception if she could see the man at the funeral with his family, she asks Cain. The problem, she explained, is that someone could post it to social media. Cain thought for moment and reluctantly replied, "Well, I guess you are right." But it didn't sit well with him. Why couldn't the victim come to the prison, he wondered? She should meet and talk with the man, he thought, so that she might work on letting go, if not forgiving. "Would someone really care if a man took a picture with his family at his own mother's funeral?" he wondered aloud.

In *Inferno: An Anatomy of American Punishment*, law professor Robert Ferguson argues that "articulation in court of the pain and suffering of the collateral victim, the mourning survivor, has a transferring purpose. Everything the victim records about the pain felt is meant to increase the pain to be inflicted on the convicted offender. . . . The role of reason in conviction gives way to an emotional narrative in favor of punishment."[21] In the daily news, it's as if the victims, not the defendant, have had their day in court. The visible anguish of the survivors takes precedence, and no amount of suffering by the prisoner is enough to appease the victim.

Grove Norwood and Ulice Parker's story subverts these expectations. Bridges to Life was also born of another tragedy. In 1993, two nineteen-year-olds stabbed and bludgeoned to death a woman named Marilyn Sage in her apartment during a robbery. Both were placed on death row. Marilyn's brother, John Sage, was devastated. They had grown up in a large Irish Catholic family in Texas and had been inseparable. John raged and fantasized about taking justice into his own hands. Instead, he joined a Bible study group. But he wanted to do more than just accept God's love. A savvy businessman who had worked in finance, John was aghast at the numbers of people who left prison and committed more crimes. He decided he wanted to help people so they could stay out of prison and to help those who had been affected by crime to heal.[22]

Bridges to Life is the result. Groups of prisoners meet with two victim volunteers and a trained facilitator and undergo a fourteen-week curriculum together. They open their meetings with a prayer and touch on topics like crime and its effects, responsibility, accountability, confession, repentance, forgiveness, reconciliation, and restitution. Over four thousand men have completed the program, which operates throughout the Texas prison system; there are plans to replicate the model in other states. At the beginning of the program, only men within a year of release were eligible, but it has expanded to include anyone except for sex offenders and people with mental illness. Although traditionally law enforcement officials have disdained victim encounter groups, calling them "hug a thug," Bridges to

Life has won support from prison wardens and elected officials who attend the program graduations.

The goal of the program is to reduce recidivism, increase public safety, and promote healing. The mission is also spiritual. John felt moved by the Holy Spirit to do this work and to model the teaching of Christ. The Bible is the basis for most of the curriculum. Although belief in God is the foundation of the program, John is clear that Bridges to Life is not there to convert or proselytize: "Our primary emphasis is to save lives, rather than souls, although the two work together like the blades of scissors, and neither works without the other." The program is ecumenical. Anyone, regardless of religious background, can participate, and volunteers don't have to be Christian, although most are. Occasionally, problems arise when volunteers violate the rule against proselytizing, and John is always quick to remind them that this is not the purpose. Love and forgiveness are part of the transforming power of God, John believes, but it doesn't mean that others are excluded from them. He often emphasizes the idea of spirituality in the deepest sense of belonging and inclusiveness, rather than dogma.

The premise of Bridge to Life is that telling stories engenders participants' healing and transformation. Prisoners and volunteers speak candidly in a small, confidential group. They encounter acceptance without judgment, the love of volunteers, and the power of God working in their lives. One volunteer says, "They expect me to be vindictive. My purpose is to help them." John believes that victims are empowered by telling their stories, and prisoners feel the impact of their own crimes. Although the groups never place the people who have committed crimes directly with their victims, the idea is that, by hearing the stories of others, they are forced to confront whatever they have done. Each story is unique, but it can build a bridge between the teller and listener. The storytelling functions like therapy for victims, and many discuss how their families and friends tire of hearing them talk about what happened to them. The program grants those people whose loss or trauma doesn't abate in the proscribed time new audiences of captive listeners. One man listening to a woman talk about the death of her daughter says, "If victims forgive, I can forgive."

The Bridges to Life program is part of a wider movement for restorative justice with both secular and religious roots across the United States.

If legal justice operates on the impersonal level, restorative justice operates at the personal. It is based on the idea that forgiveness is fulfilled by bringing people into relationship no matter how uninvited its origins, rather than just with God. The premise is that justice can best be served by repairing the harm caused by a crime, and it must be accomplished through cooperative processes that include all stakeholders: the accused, the victim, the collateral victims, the prosecutor, and even the judge. Often, the process entails mediation between the victim and person who committed the crime. Sujatha Baliga, director of the Restorative Justice Project at Impact Justice, and Howard Zehr at the Zehr Institute for Restorative Justice have pioneered approaches for having claimants and defendants meet.[23] Many states and prisons now have offices of victim and offender mediation dialogue and restorative circles.[24] They can also include indirect communication through third parties or restitution or reparation payments ordered by courts or referral panels.

Baliga describes restorative justice as a way to think about what is best for all those affected when a crime occurs and to better address victims, their offenders, and the criminal justice process. Instead of the way the current system works, Baliga argues that those most affected by crime should have the opportunity to participate fully in the response to a crime and its resolution. Most of the processes involve encounters between those involved to discuss the crime and the aftermath. Restorative justice raises questions that are distinct from the criminal legal process: What are we restoring and to whom? Why should the prosecutor have the final say in punishment? Is society the victim in the case of robbery or theft? The language of amends is central to the process, and it means people must acknowledge the harm they have caused. It asks us to think more expansively about whether victims and those who commit crimes are fundamentally different from the rest of us.

The current legal process often obscures the reality that most people in prison have also been victims. Over 85 percent of women in prison, for instance, report experiences of domestic violence and sexual or physical abuse. If people were to recognize that they had more in common, they might be able to forge social bonds. Restorative justice upends conventional assumptions that the harmed and the person who did the harm are natural enemies, and that victims are always retributive in their view of justice. Most victims, in fact, report being unsatisfied with punishment as we know it.[25] Restorative justice also assumes that prisons are not necessarily the best way to prevent repeat crime.

A person can more readily imagine repair and restitution for a stolen car than for a rape or murder.[26] However, for people who have survived rape, assault, murder, and other crimes, the process can entail encounters between parties in order to hear a confession.[27] In the case of restorative justice mediation, the harmed person may never be able to get to a point of forgiveness, but often the person or loved one who was harmed wants the answer to basic questions that only the person who committed the crime can tell them. Why? What were my loved one's last words? Sometimes there is a need to force people to hear about the repercussions of their actions, and it's a way for a harmed person to regain control.[28] It similarly forces the person who did harm to witness and experience the impact those actions have on a real person.

In restorative justice, the person who was harmed must initiate the mediation. The process can take months or years, with meetings and preparation on both sides.[29] The person in prison doesn't have to agree to meet, and there is a risk that the process will end in disappointment. What if the person seems remorseless? Or is merely reciting a script? What if the person harmed is incapable of forgiveness? But the mediation can be powerful.

Patty, a woman I know through my work teaching in a prison, has been imprisoned for thirteen years since becoming addicted to drugs at age nineteen. She has a twenty-year sentence. One night, high on meth and other substances, she fled in her car from the police. Speeding through a red light, she hit another car and killed the couple inside. Gloria, the daughter of the couple, was initially filled with bitterness and anger, which ate away at her over the years.[30] Through mediation, a form of restorative justice, she began counseling, and wrote to Patty to ask to meet. Since it was her mother and stepfather who were killed, Gloria asked her father to accompany her. He did not say much at all, but his presence emboldened her. Gloria and Patty met on and off for years and exchanged letters. Their wary friendship enabled Gloria to see Patty as a troubled and abused teenager who made a terrible mistake. When Patty spoke of her remorse some of Gloria's antagonism evaporated. Together they gave a talk about their process in a TEDx event at the women's prison in Washington State. Their relationship was messy, but they had become reconciled to the past and each other. In order to do so, they first had to acknowledge that the situation needed forgiveness and be open to each other's pain and hostility. What both women did in this instance was to commit themselves to a new relationship. Gloria's forgiveness was a process.

One case mediated by Sujatha Baliga involved a young man, Conor, who had murdered his girlfriend, Ann Margaret Grosmaire, in a rage.[31] The families of the two had been friends for a long time. Baliga facilitated their meetings with each other and with Conor so that the families could truly participate and deliberate in the process of punishment. Initially, the prosecutor was reluctant to agree to this process. Prosecutors are often so intent on a conviction that they can prohibit a restorative justice mediation process or the input of the victims' families. The mother of the young woman who had been killed described how the process enabled her to find forgiveness and how it "frees us, frees us from going to prison with Conor. Because we could forgive, people can say her name. ... I can be sad, but I don't have to stay stuck in that moment where this awful thing happened. Because if I do, I may never come out of it. Forgiveness for me was self-preservation."[32] Their forgiveness affected Conor, too, and not only in the obvious way of reducing his sentence from life to twenty years. "With the Grosmaires' forgiveness," he explained, "I could accept the responsibility and not be condemned." Forgiveness doesn't make him any less guilty, and it doesn't absolve him of what he did, but in refusing to become Conor's enemy, the Grosmaires deprived him of a certain kind of refuge—of feeling abandoned and hated, the way that Shawn in Darrington feels—and placed the reckoning for the crime squarely in his hands.

Shawn, discussed at the beginning of this chapter, views himself as a victim. In some ways, he is a victim of a cruel system, his youth, and murderous impulses. The forgiveness of God he finds in the seminary also perpetuates his narcissism and inability to acknowledge his own culpability, because he doesn't face anyone but himself and God. Although he says the men in the seminary program are like brothers and family, he does not look to them for absolution. He discusses his own anger and hate at the time he killed his mother as an adolescent, but he still justifies what happened through his mother's actions. He says, "My mom when she did that, she, you know, she put me in the circumstance, and it seems like it was a lose-lose either way. And, I do not know if she would have gone through with it, but my instincts just took control." Now he says he could have had more control over his panic and handled the situation differently: "I had a lot of anger at first. I had a lot of hate and stuff dealing with that, too. But, it was God that took all that away from me, all the hate and anger. And, that is why it took me so long to accept God as God." When he turned twenty-two, he felt that he needed a savior: "I need somebody to forgive me for my sins and help me." No one else would forgive him or take him seriously, so God was the only resort.

Norwood's tragedy shows that forgiveness is not a sign of weakness, and that it is easier to hate or retaliate than to forgive, which requires immense courage and strength. Norwood recognized Parker's common humanity because he knew him. Forgiveness didn't excuse the wrong, but it found another outlet. In contrast, Shawn has personal faith but not accountability or reconciliation with his family or himself. His mother's family has disowned him. His father's life has deteriorated, and he has lost almost all his land. He visited Shawn for the first ten years of his incarceration, but he doesn't any longer. Shawn thinks his dad wants to forget and move on. Shawn found grace and forgiveness from God but not a sense of amends or restoration. If someone had intervened before sentencing, his family might have discussed together what had occurred. If he had been given a space to find a truer story of himself, separated from his pain and anger as a sixteen-year-old, he might have acknowledged fully the harm he caused, rather than deflecting blame. Even if his father hadn't forgiven him, he could have vented and expressed his conflicted feelings to Shawn with the help of a facilitator. This might have led to more accountability, even if Shawn's family wouldn't forgive him or reconcile. If his mother's relatives had had the opportunity to face him and discuss what happened, they could possibly have progressed through the arduous process of confession, responsibility, and accountability to some kind of reconciliation. Shawn might still have a family outside the prison.

# CHAPTER 6

# MOTHERS AND SERVANTS IN THE SAVIOR PRISON

IN AN OHIO PRISON CHAPEL, twenty-three women are trying to form a circle but are constrained by the rigidity of the pews. Behind the pulpit, the group leader, Diana, stands in front of the large stained-glass window depicting a flower-entwined cross. A few minutes earlier, the room had been filled with boisterous clusters of women enjoying the temporary release from physical restrictions during the fifteen minutes allotted for movement. Then the buzzer blasts through the omnipresent loudspeakers, indicating that everyone must be at her destination or incur an infraction or disciplinary measure. The women bow their heads and pray, while Diana asks that the Lord bless this meeting: "Bless these women. They are struggling, but we place our faith in you."

Diana shows up once a week to lead this group, informally known as the Way Forward. They're at the prison other days as well, to lead small Kairos prayer groups and the longer three-day Kairos weekends. For the past month, the theme of Thursday night meetings has been "Disgrace and Grace," with a specific emphasis on overcoming histories of violence. Many women inside the prison have been the victims of abuse, rape, and domestic violence. According to the Center for American Progress, the vast majority of women in prison—85 percent to 90 percent—have a history of being victims of violence prior to their incarceration, including domestic violence, rape, sexual assault, and child abuse.[1] In her book *Arrested Justice*, about black women in the American prison system, Beth E. Richie reports that at least half of female prisoners experienced sexual abuse before incarceration.[2] According to the most recent Bureau of Justice Statistics report, nearly 6 in 10 women in state prisons had experienced physical or sexual abuse in the past.[3] Deb, a group regular, greets the theme with the skeptical comment that "everyone here has been abused or raped. Show me one person who hasn't," as if such violence were so commonplace at the prison that it hardly merits further discussion. At the same time, many of these women have felt that their experiences are not "real" or legitimate because they have been disavowed in familial, cultural, political, and legal arenas. The abuse, however, is at the root of many of their crimes. Women are the fastest-growing part of the prison population, and many of the reasons for that have to do with underlying issues of abuse and violence before they even went to prison. Women tell stories of having their nose and ribs broken while seven months pregnant, running away from home at age thirteen to avoid rape, surviving on the streets through prostitution, and making it through childhoods stolen by horrific sexual abuse at the hands of relatives or acquaintances.[4]

Because of cuts to mental health staffing, few counselors are available to serve the hundreds of women in prison who suffer from the trauma of sexual abuse. Only the most drastic cases of psychosis or schizophrenia have priority for counseling. The options for everyone else are the volunteer-run Christian groups like the Way Forward, medication, or nothing.

When she first came to the prison, Deb had crouched on her bunk shaking, with sweat pooling on her lower back. She was going to spend the next ten years of her life here, but it was the heroin habit she arrived with, more than the prospect of her sentence, that caused the shudders. Depressed and heartbroken, she worried about who would care for her children. Despite her mental distress, she was unable to see a counselor because of the waiting list. After a few painful months, she'd flushed the drugs from her system, started working in maintenance, and was hoping to join a culinary arts program. Then a cousin wrote that her mother wouldn't take in her children. If her kids went to foster care, she could lose them. The federal Adoption and Safe Families Act of 1997 stipulates that if an incarcerated parent does not have contact with his or her child for six months, he or she can be charged with abandonment and lose parental rights.[5]

Deb became catatonic, refusing to leave her cell and spending most of her time sleeping. When she told a prison officer she was depressed, the harried mental health counselor eventually prescribed Seroquel, a drug used for severe schizophrenia and psychotic disorders. Deb joined the pill-line shuffle every evening. Like so many women who can't otherwise cope in a system that wants a complacent population, she was "one of the zombies." She told me she felt "fuzzy" most of the time, but the dull ache was preferable to the jagged memories of the children she'd left behind.

Janine, an officer at the prison for twenty-six years, saw her role as both maternal and disciplinarian. "I hear about medications that offenders are on," she says. "I think that a lot of them come to prison with a lot of problems, and that is one way to help with the problem. If they have problems sleeping, waking up, being depressed or anxious, the women are given pills." Janine went on to acknowledge that "we only have so many mental health counselors." When someone is having a bad day, when a family member dies, when someone is going through menopause or suffering from post-traumatic stress disorder, she often won't be seen by a mental health counselor. Consequently, the prison relies on faith-based volunteers, particularly pastoral care like the Way Forward.

Diana, leader of the Way Forward, tells the women that overcoming their problems and pasts ensues from relinquishing the will to heal, to transform, and to overcome. Only in submission to God can healing and transformation occur. The group has been reading 2 Samuel 13:2, the biblical account of Tamar, who is assaulted by her half-brother Amnon. The story is supposed to illustrate the necessity of heart change, and Diana guides the women in an interpretation that explicitly critiques therapeutic culture. Grace, she notes, is "one-way love" from God, and only this love will transform them—just as it did Tamar. She explains that survivors of sexual assault are normally expected to heal through support groups and conscious attempts to change their thinking. But grace, Diana admonishes, "does not come from reading Oprah's latest book" (this is a calculated jab, since many of the women revere Oprah Winfrey). A transformed heart will not be found in the latest women's magazine. Instead, Diana says, "grace floods in from the outside when hope to change oneself is lost. . . . One-way love from God does not command 'heal thyself' but declares 'You will be healed.'" God's love and grace purportedly work on the women's hearts, guiding them on what Diana calls, "the true path to healing."

Diana warns the women that trying to heal themselves through their own efforts is at best a temporary solution and, at worst, a delusion. Healing, according to Diana, "only comes by laying down your life and picking up His. It comes by saying, 'God, I am tired of doing things my way. I need you. I want you.' It comes by surrendering your heart to the one who can heal it." Self-help techniques, she says, will succeed only superficially, and a person's failure to overcome the repercussions of violence entirely through her own efforts will ultimately produce more shame, in a never-ending downward spiral. If she submits to God, however, she will encounter her unblemished, pure self, separate from her crimes. As one student articulated, "I found myself in myself."

Whereas the punitive discourse of the prison is focused on the individual as criminal, Diana claims to remove this burden by emphasizing that God can take over responsibility for his or her life. Participants read Jeremiah 17:14, which promises, "Heal me, O Lord, and I shall be healed; save me and I shall be saved, for you are my praise." The women pray together in order to heal the disgrace of sexual assault: "I am not damaged goods. I was sinned against." The alleviation of shame, what most women report as the overwhelming emotion that both incarceration and sexual violence engender, resonates deeply for the group.

Many women come to view the prison as the first place where they can talk about their issues and feel relatively safe from their abuser. Once there, they are told that yielding to God is the only way to heal from sexual abuse. The premise is that they are incomplete without God. However, surrender to God is a vexed concept, because, like so many other conservative Christian ideas, surrender is predicated on a belief in males as leaders: men are God's representatives on earth. They are supposed to assert leadership in loving ways, but women should always follow. Diana seems unable to explain what to do when the person who is God's representative on earth is also punching or raping you. The ministry established to provide counseling and support for abused women is based on the idea of submitting to men.

Everyone bows her head in prayer. "Simply ask him to be the Lord of your life," Diana reminds them. "Invite him to sit on the throne of your heart." The loving and sexualized nature of some of these prayers reflects how Jesus or God becomes a repository for longing and desires that cannot be fulfilled by human love. One woman tells us that she has a heart "head over heels in love with the Lord, completely focused on him and his will for my life." There is a measure of safety in their desires. God's love, unlike many of their real relationships before and during imprisonment, is condoned and without risks.

One woman talks of completely abandoning herself to his love. Another, Jessica, a fervent Christian with a life sentence, reads from her journal: "I promise, it is a *wild* ride—the greatest adventure you will ever have. It is joy unspeakable—impossible to find the words to express it. He will fill you with such love, such joy, such *hope*, such peace. Ask Him to be the Lord of your life today. Open your heart to Him. Let Him in." As part of the prayer, Diana says, "Yes, he will ask you to change. But, he gives you the grace and the power to do it." By abandoning themselves to God, the women unleash their pain and open their hearts to transformation.

The Way Forward disparages twelve-step programs since heart change requires faith in something beyond the self. Yet, it operates on a contradiction that even while assuring prisoners that God will spark the revolution within, Diana reminds them that a changed heart also emerges from the effort of the self. A necessary set of actions and disciplines is required. "Even God is not willing to mend or repair a heart that you have corrupted or messed up with your evil desires," Diana reminds her charges. Thus, the program also relies on strategies to promote personal change, such as taking a self-inventory, maintaining bodily discipline, exploring one's life history, listening to other testimonies, and revising one's identity according to a coherent narrative of transformed hearts and personhood. Women have to apply themselves to Bible study, come to services, and pray as hard as they can.

We live, Diana explains, in an age of makeovers, and we are always looking for ways to transform ourselves. Since women in particular are not satisfied with staying the same and are searching for ways to improve, they often focus on outward appearance. Diana chides the group for this, reminding them that the Bible says to concentrate on inner beauty. She paraphrases Peter: "Your beauty should not come from outward adornment, such as braided hair and the wearing of fine jewelry and fine clothes. Instead, your beauty should be that of your inner self, the unfading beauty of a gentle and quiet spirit" (1 Peter 3:3–4).

In her introductory welcome packet, she urges women to undergo the "makeover of the heart" that is the key to such beauty:

> If you are like me, I didn't even realize I needed to change my heart! I thought, "My heart's OK. I'm a good person. I love God." But, over the years, I have had a total transformation of my heart. My heart has opened to a new Truth, a new joy, a new love, and a new way of life. I have had a complete MAKEOVER of my heart! I want you to experience the ultimate makeover—to become a new creation in Christ starting with your heart.

From here, Diana breaks down the process, in which each week is devoted to a different heart theme: delightful hearts, healed hearts, committed hearts, and prayerful hearts. First, the heart transplant occurs, and women relinquish their fear, selfishness, and stubbornness. Diana compares her heart pre-makeover to a spoiled two-year-old throwing a temper tantrum "who wants what it wants and wants it now," and many women laugh in agreement. They analyze the heart-change verse in Ezekiel 36:26–28, in which God speaks about giving each person a new heart.

But while God will transplant women's hearts, the makeover requires prayer, participation, focus, and effort as well as a relentless and constant self-inventory of the familial dysfunction and moral failings that led inexorably to prison. The women learn practical ways to incorporate prayer into daily routines, including "praying Scripture into your life," which means inserting your own name into generic prayers as part of personal devotion time. For instance, "I pray that God will give me (or your name here) a Spirit of wisdom and revelation."

Another class, with the clunky title "How to Choose Your Own Change," exhorts women to alter their thoughts, actions, and ways of speaking until they are habituated into a specific mode of biblical living. Discipline is required for the task of enacting these principles in everyday life. It means compelling themselves to forgo girlfriend drama, fighting, drugs, and the dayroom, where all of the above are most likely to occur. Diana expounds on the steps, telling the women to search through the Bible for verses related to what they want to achieve and memorize and repeat them to themselves. They should run from anything that tempts them to do otherwise. God hears us, she reminds the group, so pray regularly and without ceasing.

To help retrain the mind and body in these new paths, Diana encourages a practice similar to that of many secular and New Age therapies: journal writing. Embossed with a heart clasped between two hands, the journals she donates are cherished commodities, given the prison's restrictions on notebooks with metal binder rings, which are viewed as potential safety hazards. She gives the group writing prompts intended to shore up and strengthen their new hearts, encouraging them to ponder: What are the desires of your heart? How do you want God to change you? What are your personal expectations?

Sharing their writings solidifies their commitments to change. As one woman reads, "I believe God is taking me on a transformation where Paula diminishes and Jesus increases. I'd love to get to the place where there is nothing left of Paula!" Charlese, a young woman who is serving an eighteen-year sentence, articulates a typical mix of cognitive and spiritual goals when she reads of her desire "to love and be loved with an unconditional love with no strings attached or controlling issues with humans the way that Christ loves me . . . to not let emotions rule my life or ruin it, to break free from past and walk in that freedom not just talk about it!"

Sharla, another participant, reads,

My personal goals are to be transformed and to stay transformed. I want to be rid of my selfish heart. I guess all of my "hang-ups" could be attributed to my childhood. I could put the blame on my broken childhood, the absence of a father, abuse by a stepfather. These things created a longing in me, but instead of turning to God, I turned to the world to satisfy me. I was seeking my identity and my worth in these things. Instead of filling the emptiness I felt and giving me a lasting satisfaction, these only created more of a longing, a deeper hole to be filled.

Writing and sharing such stories not only prepare the spirit but retrain the mind and discipline the body; in Diana's ministry, all three activities are necessary for a makeover of the heart. The self requires therapeutic effort in order to bend one's will to God's will.[6]

Although the Way Forward leaders don't stress victimization, they assume that women will always bear the taint of shame and disgrace unless they work on themselves and prepare for God to take over. In this way, the group overlooks the social factors that led to the women's abuse in the first place and preach self-surrender. The idea that women are essentially good and need only God's grace and forgiveness, rather than secular work on the self, is central to faith-based ministries. For them, work on the self is only appropriate in the context of God.

The idea that women in prison are inherently good but need God's direction to be redeemed has not always been the case. The idea of women as "good girls" or "bad criminals" has dictated the ways the United States has punished them since the earliest reformatories, and these meanings have shaped how the system has punished black and white women differently.[7] The earliest prisons for women were custodial, often attached to a separate section of a men's prison, with poorly paid matrons to supervise the women. Sometimes women, especially black women and poor white women, were sent to penal farms in the convict lease system.

Historian Jill McCorkel dates the shift that refigured women as victims or errant children to the first few decades of the twentieth century, when ideas of rehabilitative paternalism reigned.[8] The premise of punishment for white women was that they were unfortunate victims of bad men or of circumstance, rather than evil. Women were convicted for crimes of morality, like prostitution, sexual misconduct, alcohol consumption, child abuse, or transgressions against the norms of feminine behavior, in far greater numbers than men. Therefore, moral reformers and social feminists focused on the idea that women in prison could be retrained to adhere to middle-class norms.[9]

Horrified at the neglect of women in primarily male prisons, reformers created the reformatory and the cottage system, where they tried to instill a familial atmosphere in which women lived together under the tutelage of a matron who taught them domestic skills like sewing, housekeeping, and proper child care. Women were trained to accept standards of propriety and virtue, and ideas about child raising and marriage. Staff regarded inmates as girls whose moral accountability for their crimes was diminished by their feminine subjectivity and past victimization.[10] They were infantilized as fallen women in need of rescue and uplift, and were urged to seek simultaneously to embody childlike submissiveness and true womanhood. However, black women were excluded from this model and from the system of reformatories, as the idea persisted in prison administration that they were not good girls who had been victimized but rather, in keeping with the sexualized and racist ideas of black women at the time, bad girls who simply could not be reformed.

At the same time that they were incarcerated, women prisoners were subject to tests and medical experimentation. Bedford Hills Correctional Facility for Women, an hour from New York City, now considered one of the most progressive women's prisons in the country, had a laboratory for testing intelligence, feeble-mindedness, and venereal diseases. The goal of the reformatory was to experiment and to produce virtuous women who had assimilated white middle-class values. It hoped these women could become a cheap labor pool, the servants, washerwomen, and housekeepers to the upper class, who might replace the young working-class women who were leaving home to work in factories.[11]

Gradually, all women were transferred to reformatories because they were cheaper. Prisons became more racially and religiously diverse, and they became expensive to run. The cottage system was dismantled, and prisons returned to being primarily custodial institutions for women, the forerunners of prisons today. The narratives about women prisoners also underwent a shift in the 1960s, as prisons filled with more black and Latina women. Instead of the childlike victim, the criminological literature began to portray women in prison as deviants who were angry, antisocial, hypersexual, and violent.[12] Race and racist assumptions about black and white women became central to the distinction between good girls and real criminals.[13]

The Way Forward and other faith-based parenting and trauma groups view marriage and respectability as central to women in prison, just as the cottage system taught their prisoners to become law-abiding middle-class women. Since so many of the Way Forward's members are mothers, parenting comes up constantly, especially because many have children who cannot visit them due to the distance and expense.[14] In one session, Charlese, a bright-eyed and positive young woman, spoke of her worries about what would become of her teenage daughter, as her elderly parents, who had severe health issues, had become increasingly unable to take care of her. She was terrified of losing her child to the foster-care system. Diana's response was for everyone to pray for Charlese and her daughter. God would find a solution. Women murmured their prayers, and then Christy spoke.

Christy had become the focal point for a lot of the women's resentment and anxieties in the group because she had recently entered into a relationship with a woman. She frequently missed group meetings. The group confronted her during the confession time. Why wasn't she there? What was she doing? For years, she had been the epitome of a good Christian, spending time with her husband and daughter during precious trailer visits, when a prisoner's family members can visit overnight in designated trailers in the prison. Unlike so many of the women in the group, she had never had a girlfriend or a sexual relationship with anyone at the prison.

At first, Christy crossed her arms and remained stoic, refusing to respond. As the questions and other confessions escalated about the effect of Christy's actions on the group, she began to crack. Someone mentioned her daughter, and Christy began to cry. It was the response that Diana wanted. Her story emerged stiltedly: she and her husband were divorcing. After years of trying to make her marriage work, she'd learned that he had cheated with her close friend on the outside. Diana did not condone same-sex relationships, even though they were common at the prison.

The Way Forward had a strict antigay policy, mirroring the anxiety of the prison administration about lesbianism. Unlike many men's prisons, women were open and affectionate with each other and would proudly boast about how long they'd been in a relationship with another woman. At the same time, most of the conflicts and fights among the women had to do with jealousy and girlfriend issues. However, once Christy confessed her shame to the group, the negativity faded. As long as she repented and asked for help, Diana welcomed and supported her.

During that session, Diana discussed how women became responsible parents: by learning to access their innate "servant heart" and move from rebellion to surrender. God, Diana argued, would resolve Christy's conflict, not Christy herself, and she should submit to God's will, which was to keep her family intact despite her husband's cheating. The women were enjoined that if they could understand their selves and their own spirituality, they might excavate their "genuine desire for servanthood." The class began with biblical references to servanthood and the elements of what this might mean in the Bible: submission to authority (1 Peter 2:13–17), labor (John 9:4), joy (John 15:11), peacefulness (John 14:27), faithfulness (Matthew 25:21), love (Galatians 5:13), duty (Luke 17: 9–10), grace (1 Peter 4:10), and kindness (2 Timothy 2: 24). The ultimate example, Diana explained, was given to us by Christ when he modeled servanthood by washing his disciples' feet (John 13:1–17).

Diana explained that Christ is not just a savior, "he is a Lord." A person can only be a true servant if Christ is also the Lord of her life, and that is what it means to be an authentic Christian. Diana espoused the idea that a woman who is a servant to her husband is a servant to God as he is also a servant to God, a theory of female submission prevalent in other ministries.[15] She defended the idea that servanthood is about sharing God's love with others, and the biggest stumbling block is prisoners' own sense of "who we are." The implication is that once women relinquish their sense of being in control of their own lives and acknowledge the "power of God's love in their lives," this godly power will instill hope and a sense of internal freedom, even while they remain incarcerated. The group prayed for Christy as if their prayers and Christy's surrender to God would suffice to counter her husband's transgressions. Diana also implied that Christy's relationship with a woman was a harmful distraction from her relationship with God. Any personal agency was suspect without surrendering her actions to divine will. Christy didn't return for the next meeting.

Like Christy, most women in prison are the primary caregivers for their children when they are incarcerated. Seventy-three percent of mothers in federal prisons and over 60 percent of mothers in state prisons report that they lived with their children before their arrest, as opposed to 47.2 percent of incarcerated fathers in federal and 35.6 percent in state prisons.[16] Almost all incarcerated fathers report their children's mother as the primary caregiver, while most incarcerated mothers report other relatives, rather than fathers, as the primary caregiver.[17] The incarceration of a mother may cause more disruptions for children than the incarceration of a father, and that child is more likely to have contact with the criminal legal system and end up in prison.[18]

Despite their growing numbers in prison, many faith-based groups devote their resources to the problem of incarcerated fathers, rather than incarcerated mothers, and the impact of their imprisonment on their children. The initial faith-based dormitories in Florida were funded by a grant from the Florida Commission on Responsible Fatherhood.[19] At Lawtey Correctional Institution, one of the faith-based prisons in Florida, the warden was vehement that the reason men end up at this prison is because they lacked a father figure as children. According to him, men become prisoners because they grow up without a masculine disciplinarian. Without a father, men become criminals, because women lack the ability to function as adequate or compelling role models. Twenty years as a correctional officer and warden has taught him the simple truth he relays: the influx of men into the prison system is a direct result of the breakdown of the heterosexual two-parent family and the failure of men to be responsible fathers.

Pat Nolan of Prison Fellowship writes, "Most importantly, the church can water the seeds of healthy parent-child relationships. Incarceration doesn't change a father's status as a father. They're still a parent. The strongest bond in the world is that parental bond. And we need to strengthen that, reaffirm them as the father."[20] This assessment neglects the fact that most people in prison are unmarried and view marriage as an unrealistic panacea. It also devotes resources and policies to men in prison, while neglecting the plethora of issues women face, particularly that most of the violence they suffered was at the hands of a boyfriend or husband. From the federal level to the local practices of faith-based programs and volunteers, the focus is to promote a standard of married heterosexual families and transformed fathers, rather than discovering ways to make the more common and arduous process of mothering from inside feasible.

Nolan's focus resonates on a national scale. President Barack Obama, delivering a Father's Day speech in June 2008 at the Apostolic Church of God in Chicago, quoted from the Sermon on the Mount: "Whoever hears these words of mine, and does them, shall be likened to a wise man who built his house upon a rock: and the rain descended, and the floods came, and the winds blew, and beat upon that house, and it fell not, for it was founded upon a rock." Heralding his administration's fatherhood initiative, a centerpiece of the Office of Faith-Based and Neighborhood Partnerships (FBNP), President Obama continued,

> Of all the rocks upon which we build our lives, we are reminded today that family is the most important. And we are called to recognize and honor how critical every father is to that foundation. . . . But if we are honest with ourselves, we'll admit that what too many fathers also are is missing—missing from too many lives and too many homes. They have abandoned their responsibilities, acting like boys instead of men. And the foundations of our families are weaker because of it.[21]

Obama's investment in the issue led to the creation of the National Responsible Fatherhood Clearinghouse (NRFC), which works within several federal agencies to promote and support responsible fatherhood by providing grantees and faith-based organizations with financial resources to work within prisons and other locations.[22] Despite the demographic and political distinctions between the prison warden and President Obama's speech, they represent a shared sense that the solution to imprisonment in the United States lies in faith-based modes of transformation that emphasize fatherhood.

These models of faith-based transformation often exist in tandem with fatherhood initiatives that treat imprisonment as a problem due to the lack of male role models.[23] At the same time that faith-based programs claim that they can perform the work of the state more cheaply and engender more profound means of transformation, they promote the idea that fathers and, by extension, heterosexual nuclear families will render the need for prisons obsolete. From the federal level to local practices of faith-based prison programming in ministries such as InsideOut Dad and Kairos, fatherhood initiatives claim to solve recidivism and enact a lasting transformation that reshapes prisoners into fathers and citizens. Many programs understand imprisonment as a problem of masculine irresponsibility, remedied by bolstering fatherhood and driven by the premise that children of incarcerated parents desperately need a two-parent household to avoid incarceration themselves.[24]

The FBNP's particular fixation on fatherhood has earlier antecedents in the 1996 reform of Temporary Assistance for Needy Families (TANF) that included promotion of healthy marriage to address welfare. In 2002, the Administration for Children and Families (ACF) within the Department of Health and Human Services designed a healthy-marriage initiative, including allocation of federal grants to states and communities to test new ways to promote married parent families and encourage responsible fatherhood.[25] Currently, the FBNP sponsors the NRFC, whose purpose is to support responsible fatherhood by enabling organizations to receive grants from the ACF.

The NRFC issues statistics on incarcerated fathers and advice for fathers in prison through a program called Spotlight on Dads (Get Creative, Stay Connected, Steps in the Right Direction, etc.), and includes a report on promising practices in programs serving fathers in prison.[26] For programs in prisons, the NRFC recommends relying on faith-based groups and spiritual personnel like chaplains, since they are an integral part of the prison environment. The NRFC dispenses practical advice to dads in prison on how to stay in touch with their children, continue to become better fathers, and strengthen their marriages. One handout, "Stay Connected," relates how a group of fathers in a Missouri state prison purchased plain white pillowcases from the prison store, decorated them with markers, and mailed them to their children with a handmade card.

The National Fatherhood Initiative (NFI), a corollary and advisor to the federal program, bills itself as a means of improving the well-being of children by "connecting children and fathers, heart to heart." NFI works with ministries and organizations to "educate fathers and strengthen families." The NFI has similar goals to the federal fatherhood initiative; by reconnecting prisoners to their families or the mother of their children, it will reduce recidivism and end the intergenerational cycle of crime and incarceration. The NFI sponsors InsideOut Dad to remake prisoners into model fathers who are unlikely to return to prison. The program has several versions: one emphasizes spirituality, another is an explicitly Christian "biblically based" version developed by Prison Fellowship to "introduce inmates to the transforming power of the Gospel," and another is translated into Spanish under the name Padre Adentro y Afuera.

InsideOut is ubiquitous in prisons throughout the United States, with programs in over four hundred state and federal prisons, prerelease programs, and community organizations in twenty-two states. The curriculum, available on its website, purports to foster the motivation for fathers "to get out and stay out." "Through practical, engaging material, InsideOut Dad increases inmates' self-worth and gives them valuable relationship skills." The program includes twelve core sessions such as "What Is a Man?," "Expressing Anger," "Discipline," "Creating a Fathering Plan from the Inside," and "Remembering My Past." They are designed to touch on topics considered crucial for rebuilding and rediscovering fatherhood, such as masculinity, communication skills, and physical and mental health. The idea is that there are universal characteristics of fatherhood and one ideal familial configuration, regardless of race, class, or nationality. The program is designed to point out the importance of spiritual cultivation in order for fathers to commit to something called religion. To be a dad, to be transformed, one must access the nebulous spirituality rooted within each person and cultivate it until it thrives. Given the coercion, violence, and lack of control endemic to the prison experience, the idea that there is something embedded in the individual, a force untarnished by the carceral system, is deeply appealing for men in the group. It bestows a sense of power in a space of relative powerlessness.

At an InsideOut session at a correctional facility in Florida, fatherhood was explicitly linked to recuperating masculinity and recovering a man's spiritual core. During the class, "Being a Man," the group of eleven men—many veterans of anger management, Bible study, Toastmasters, and other programs—brainstormed characteristics they admired in other men. The workbook identifies seven traits to describe masculinity—self-confident, courageous, leadership, dependable, successful, self-reliant, controlling (situations or other people)—and asks the men to rate themselves on how they identify with the traits on a scale of zero to three (zero is "not at all identifying," and three is "a lot"). A key contention of InsideOut Dad is that a spiritual or religious man is also better equipped to realize his potential as a father. The idea is that the cultivation of a man's soul, heart, and inner world will transform him into a model father and citizen because an ideal father is inherently spiritual and filled with faith. A class prompt such as "To me, spirituality means _____" is a tool for men to learn to patrol their inner worlds in a form of self-governance or self-scrutiny.[27] The men complete the following statements: "Two ways I express my spirituality as a man are _____ and _____." and "Two ways I express my spirituality as a father are _____ and _____."

InsideOut emphasizes that spirituality is the basis for families and the underlying force that enables those families to flourish and men to lead them. By employing the self-discipline to access their spirituality, prisoners transform their selves and their families. A "spiritual family" is one that feels a bond between all its members and where the members feel that they belong. The program teaches that when "family spirituality" is present, cooperation, love, respect, and communication are natural outcomes. Fathers complete a family spirituality checklist in their workbook. The group leader of InsideOut asks the men to rate their "family spirituality" on the statements as they were before this incarceration, as they are now, and how they would like to be in the future. Men are required to share their checklists with each other and discuss how to build their family's spirituality.

The responsibility for fathers is considerable, but in the NFI model, mothers also harbor responsibility of a different sort. The InsideOut Dad program understands the role of mothers as that of a gatekeeper who does not allow a man to achieve his full potential as a father. A gatekeeper is a person who controls access. According to the InsideOut curriculum, "Maternal gatekeeping refers to a mother's protective beliefs about the desirability of a father's involvement in their child's life, and the behaviors acted upon that either facilitate or hinder childrearing between the parents." A mother's responsibility consists of relinquishing her gatekeeping power to unleash the potential for successful fatherhood. In a seminar on "Involving Moms," led by the NFI, "maternal gatekeeping" is cited as the central force inhibiting fathers' involvement with children. The epidemic of absent and inadequate fathers is partially blamed on a mother's unwillingness to grant access to their children or on those women who engage in "excessive" gatekeeping.

Mothers are granted the illusion of lopsided power in this scenario. Many fatherhood programs view the preponderance of female-headed households and single motherhood as a cause of incarceration. The NFI also claims that "maternal perceptions of the paternal role are a better predictor of father involvement than the father's actions." According to this model, mothers can damage the father-child relationship and pose a threat to the overall well-being and adjustment of the child. Women govern the family, and a mother's refusal to relinquish familial responsibility and her need for validation as a mother hinder father-child relationships. The NFI is developing a series of classes that would encourage behaviors to facilitate "the reduction of restrictive maternal gatekeeping" with mothers. The NFI presumes not just that mothers only exist outside of prison but also that abdicating the gatekeeper role rehabilitates fatherhood. There is no federal program or clearinghouse for women, and it is often in faith-based groups in prisons like the Way Forward that gender issues related to women are addressed, if at all.

The narrative of women relinquishing familial control has earlier antecedents in the Promise Keepers, the men's movement that flourished in the 1990s. Promise Keepers made the related argument that men had to take back responsibility for their families, but this narrative can be traced back to the 1910s, when Billy Sunday, a popular revival preacher who commanded crowds of thousands, excoriated men for their "sissification" and succumbing to what he viewed as the undue feminizing influence of women in the home and the church. One hallmark of the politics of the Promise Keepers that lingers in the notion of gatekeeping mothers is the idea that only through women submitting to men's presumed natural leadership abilities can men reclaim their rightful place as fathers and leaders. InsideOut Dad redefines masculinity as wresting control of their families from women in order to become loving and dedicated fathers. Leadership of families belongs to men and is transmitted to sons in the next generation, whereas daughters are to be protected and cherished.

Most women in the Way Forward group fervently sought to encounter ways to support their children during their sentences and once released. Despite Diana's assertion that all Christians are servants, many women refuted the implication that servanthood within marriage and responsible fathers could end the cycle of incarceration. During the discussion, one woman, a mother of three children under age twelve, retorted, "I don't know where my kids' daddy is, and I don't care anyway. He isn't around, right? So I know he isn't responsible. This is about me. I'm the one leaving here." However, the general dearth of any prison programming meant that the time and space the Way Forward group offered for introspection and discussion on parenting, spirituality, and the self was valued as a way for women to talk about mothering. Often the discussion would revert to swapping advice about ways to connect with children, how to arrange visits with the cheapest forms of transportation, stories about children in school, gripes about relatives, and anxiety about reuniting with children upon release. As Megan Sweeney, a professor of English, has written of women's reading practices in prison, these opportunities for communal discussion might not have produced servant mothers, but they enabled women to find spaces for what Sweeney calls "self-invention, self-education and self-repair."[28]

The women found that the Way Forward provided resources for them despite its insistence on surrender and servanthood. According to Deb, reading and hearing about other women's experiences of molestation, drug use, abuse, law breaking, and incarceration help her to situate her experiences in relation to broader social patterns; she learns that "there's other people outside of me that are like me" and develops a greater understanding of her own experiences. Transformation does not occur alone but with others who have already changed themselves or can potentially change along with you. Once the women open their hearts to God's will, they also become selves in relation, animated by conscious mutuality and joined in a broader community. This challenges a punitive model that holds individual prisoners solely responsible for their actions and seeks to isolate them from the larger society that they have wronged. Deb and Charlese could engage directly with women whose experiences overlapped their own. For women who have felt intensely isolated in their intimate family domains, and women who have felt disenfranchised and dehumanized for much of their lives, the group enabled them to learn from others' experiences and feel like citizens of a community that recognizes their stories and their humanity.

The assumptions about women in prison I often heard from administration and staff in women's prisons I visited and worked in were that they were disorganized, catty, violent, and constantly questioned orders and rules. Correctional officers commonly complained that women prisoners were much more difficult than men. Yet, that impression was contradicted by women's efforts to build a college program in prison in the Washington State prison where I taught and to lead a community organization called the "Women's Village." The genesis of the organization began with a group of women prisoners who wanted to address the problems of violence, mental health, lack of education, and other pressing issues that the prison either ignored or underserviced. In 2010, the Washington Corrections Center for Women had the dubious distinction of being the most violent in the state, even more so than the sixteen other men's prisons, because of the sheer numbers of women housed in minimum- to maximum-security areas who interacted with each other in programs. It was also the subject of a major lawsuit in 2007, in which male officers were accused of numerous instances of abuse and inappropriate relationships with women prisoners.[29]

Now, there are more female staff, and men are never allowed to be alone with women in the prison or perform strip searches.

The Women's Village motto provides a counterpoint to the idea of surrender and servanthood, because rather than following God's will, the women themselves must create the conditions they want to live in. One woman in prison explained, "When you improve yourself, you are indeed improving the entire world. Therefore there is no need waiting on the world to change. Simply improve yourself and your world would change." The Women's Village now includes almost two hundred members, with subcouncils on violence reduction, peer support for mental health issues, family support, education, reentry, and spirituality. Anyone can join, no matter who they are or what their crime, and although many of its leaders are Christian, the focus is not on religion but on the work of giving meaning to daily life, a ministry on the ground.

The organization is built on the shared values of respect for themselves and others, honesty, compassion, diversity, and self-empowerment, and the rationale is that "as women are empowered to change, the environment will change, as well."[30] Sanctioned and, to a degree, supported by the prison administration, the Women's Village assists with orientation when a woman enters the prison, counsels prisoners in segregation and those who are taking violence-reduction classes, performs mental health assessments and referrals, works on family reunification, organizes anti-violence campaigns, spearheads sustainability projects, and offers GED tutoring. Inspired by the Women's Village, women have initiated similar collectives in other prisons as a result of transfers from one institution to another. Members write that they desire "freedom to be me, to realize and experience my full potential as a person and understand and embrace that discipline is freedom."

The Women's Village relies then on the individualist language of the reformed self, but its aims are collective; members seek to foster a "sense of empathy and communal purpose." They also do not merely replicate or facilitate the disciplinary dimensions of the penal system; in fact, by counseling and educating, they are also helping each other maintain their sense of humanity and citizenship in a space of violence and coercion. In doing so, they do not simply act as the prison's servants but counter its atomizing and dehumanizing forces. Their networks extend beyond the prison to community and social justice organizations, which then participate in programs—like a recent antiviolence forum—"inside." The Women's Village is a direct challenge to the idea that prayer will suffice and only surrender and servanthood is possible, remaking faith-based groups into something more powerfully communal.

# CHAPTER 7

# THE REFORMERS

*The Religious Politics of Prison Reform*

IN A NEWSLETTER ARTICLE, Jim Liske, the director of Prison Fellowship, recounted the difficulty that researchers faced when they tried to statistically measure the intrinsic motivation for someone in prison to change. "They were having a hard time," according to Liske, "because they were trying to analyze the supernatural—the unique power of God's Holy Spirit to transform hearts [and renew] the spirits of men and women from the inside out."[1] Faith-based ministries serve the age-old Christian purpose of rebirthing the self and they save money for the prison system. They use empirical arguments about heart change to say that faith-based programming reduces recidivism and use supernatural arguments to say that prison ministry enacts a more profound change than anything else.

When I visited Lawtey Correctional Institution in Florida, a group of around two hundred men gathered in the prison chapel to see their fellow prisoners enact this very idea. Everyone watched raptly as the Christian-based drama group His Majesty's Ministries performed *One Thing*. The stage set looked like the prison yard, where three groups of men bantered with one another. As one group began speaking, the other two froze into tableaus. In the first exchange, the character Buster says to Jim that when he gets out, he's never coming back. "Yeah, how do you know that?" Jim asks skeptically. "Because I'm smarter now." "Oh, really?" "Yep, I've learned all kinds of new things in here. Ways to buy and sell dope without getting caught. Can't miss." Jim replies, "Uh-huh, that's what they all say, but they end up right back here anyway." "Not me, I'm too smart now." "Tell me about it," Jim asks, and they huddle together and freeze. The next pair, playing Butch and Mickey, repeats the conversation, except Butch declares that he is smarter because he has learned how to rob banks without getting caught. The final two men, Tony and Jack, again repeat the conversation verbatim, until its end, when Tony explains, "I've learned all kinds of new things in here. Things I never knew before." Jack retorts that they all say the same thing and they all end up back in prison. Tony replies, "Not me. I met this man named Jesus and I don't even want to do the things I used to do." "Tell me about it," says Jack.

Measuring heart change empirically has proved elusive and contested. Byron Johnson, a professor at Baylor University, has conducted studies of the Prison Fellowship InnerChange program and Humaita Prison in Brazil, and is currently conducting a study at Louisiana State Penitentiary and Darrington in Texas over time to determine prisoners' transformation through the seminary programs.[2] In his book, *More God, Less Crime*, Johnson, a strong proponent of Christian ministries, argues that "the conversion experience in and of itself is not enough to protect ex-prisoners from all manner of missteps they might take following release from prison." He goes on to say that in-prison programs are a start but that ex-prisoners need "significantly more support" in order for there to be an impact on recidivism.[3] Johnson contends that even if spiritual or religious conversions do not necessarily relate to reduced reincarceration and arrests, and that more research is needed, "I do believe that 'finding God' or becoming a born-again Christian can play a critically important role as a starting point in the process of long-term change and reform."[4] Whatever the data may reveal, Johnson wants to make the case that the effect of prison ministries is still profound. The issue with evaluation of prison ministry relates to broader questions of how we define what it is to "become a new person" and what metrics determine that transformation.[5] Similarly, if recidivism is the sole measure of a program's impact, someone could be homeless on the outside, lacking a job or struggling with mental health issues, but still be considered a success.

In fact, studies on the effect of faith-based prison programs are inconclusive and often show no correlation between participation in faith-based programs and recidivism. Mark Kleiman, at New York University's Marron Institute of Urban Management, analyzed a study from the University of Pennsylvania's Center for Research on Religion and Urban Civil Society reporting that InnerChange graduates had been rearrested and reimprisoned at dramatically lower rates than a matched control group in 2003.[6] He found that the study showed selection bias: it focused on graduates who kept a job after release, while ignoring those who didn't finish the program.[7] The InnerChange study started with 177 volunteer prisoners; 75 graduated. A graduate was defined as someone who found a job upon release. Getting a job is one of the best predictors of who stays out of prison. Thus, the study focused on the success of the successes, according to Kleiman and ignored those who dropped out, were kicked out, or received early parole and thus didn't finish the program. A 2007 study of Florida's faith-based prisons by the Urban Institute presented similar problems.[8]

Since then, Alexander Volokh, a law professor, has undertaken a comprehensive evaluation of all the studies that claim faith-based groups reduce recidivism and compared them with similar studies on private education.[9] Volokh examined studies of Humaita Prison in Brazil, the Florida faith-based prison programs, Life Horizons in the federal system, Prison Fellowship InnerChange and Discipleship programs, Kairos Horizons in two prisons, a religious program at the Mississippi State Penitentiary, and a religious group at Lieber Correctional Institute in South Carolina. All, he found, lacked validity because of selection bias. The studies simply compared faith-based participants with nonparticipants, and the former skew results because the programs are voluntary and volunteers are more likely to be motivated to change. The only credible studies, Volokh argues, are comparisons of participants with nonparticipants who volunteered for the same programs but were rejected, which would eliminate selection bias. "After discarding the faith-based prison studies tainted by self-selection bias," he says, "we're left with two studies that find no effect of faith-based programs, one study that's too small to be meaningful, and three studies that find some effect, even if the effect is quite weak." Of the three that found some effect, two were after-care release programs rather than programs in prisons. The third didn't show any effect once the prisoners were released from prison. Volokh concludes, "So we have no study that actually finds a significant effect of an in-prison faith-based program on recidivism."[10]

When recidivism isn't the only measure of success, some studies of faith-based groups have claimed that religious groups in prisons are effective. One study by the Manhattan Institute in 2005 argued that religiosity reduces the likelihood of fighting and arguing.[11] Another report claimed that higher levels of religion in prison correlate with higher levels of mental and physical health, and that faith-based groups "dispense services more effectively than their secular and governmental counterparts."[12] Volokh concedes that, while the studies don't demonstrate a reduction in recidivism, we don't have to dismiss them outright: "It may be that a faith-based program is better than nothing. . . . But, at the same time, the program may be no better than a comparably funded secular program."[13] To answer this question, Volokh believes we need comparative studies of secular and religious programs with volunteers who were rejected from a religious group and assigned to a comparable secular program. The problem is that, in prison, the programs are rarely comparable. The reality is that the alternative to a religious group is often nothing at all.

Nevertheless, states view faith-based groups as the ideal solution to prison overcrowding, management, and the increasing lack of state resources for any programs. In May 2011, after hearing arguments in a case about abysmal medical conditions and overcrowding in California state prisons, the US Supreme Court ordered the state to release thirty thousand prisoners from its behemoth penal system. The dissent included remarks by Justice Antonin Scalia, who warned that "most of them will be prisoners with medical conditions or severe mental illness; and many will undoubtedly be fine physical specimens who have developed intimidating muscles pumping iron in the prison gym." The legal case was notable for its mandate to free so many, a rarity given the political risks of being "soft on crime." The decision reflected California's acute budget crisis and the fact that conditions in some of the prisons are what sociologist Loïc Wacquant has described as "a murky factory for social pain and human destruction, silently grinding away."[14] A few days after the historic decision, Pat Nolan of Prison Fellowship issued a press statement in which he applauded the decision and stressed how organizations like Prison Fellowship must now "find ways to help the California Department of Corrections and Rehabilitation comply with the Court's order without putting the public at risk," because California and most states lacked sufficient funds to prepare incarcerated men and women for release. Nolan wrote, "Fortunately, faith-based and community groups have been stepping up to do this work at no cost to the government!"[15]

As states face budget constraints coincident with decarceration, proponents of faith-based imprisonment claim they can transform prisoners into citizens more effectively and at a lower cost. In 2003, Ellsworth Correctional Facility in Kansas cut its GED program in half and eliminated the substance-abuse program, but opened a Prison Fellowship ministry. Jerry Wilger, head of InnerChange, said, "We already offer GED, substance-abuse, and pre-release programs. If we get sex-offender treatment, we'll have the whole ball of wax for the state at a bargain-basement price." "We have a very positive relationship with the board. Sometimes they just give our inmates a green light and say, 'See you at work release,'" said Larry Furnish, former InnerChange program manager at Ellsworth. Kansas has only 298 coveted work-release positions for about nine thousand former prisoners.

Nolan asserts that not only can his organization perform the work of the state more cheaply and efficiently, reducing recidivism, it can also enact a powerful, life-changing transformation within prisoners. In one newsletter, Nolan recalls being at an Out4Life conference sponsored by Prison Fellowship with Matt Cate, California's secretary of corrections and rehabilitation.[16] At the conference, hundreds of leaders from faith-based and community groups met with corrections officials and law enforcement leaders to build local coalitions for providing reentry services both before and after release. Moving into the vacuum left by the rise of the punitive model of incarceration, Prison Fellowship and other groups now organize job training, GED and college classes, and work-release and other programs. The state saves precious money by outsourcing the labor of running programs in prison to religious volunteers. With few other options, prisoners apply to get into the coveted faith-based prisons and programs with larger cells, less crowding and violence, coveted work-release assignments, air-conditioning, and other perks.

Religious groups that take over social services once provided by state and federal agencies fulfill two goals: bringing more people to Christ and shrinking government. As Chuck Colson once elaborated in a radio interview, "What's at stake is not just a prison program, but how we deal with social problems in our country. Do we do it through grassroots organizations or big government? We know what works."[17] This is the rationale for the conservative momentum toward criminal justice and prison reform. The faith-based ministries and Right on Crime, the coalition of conservative leaders, espouse policies based on the idea that social welfare is not about governmental responsibility, and that religious organizations are best suited to create the conditions of institutional care giving and moral community in a prison setting.

The Right on Crime coalition emerged in 2010 when the Federal Bureau of Prisons and individual states came under intense political pressure to tighten budgets in a time of economic recession.[18] In early 2011, Newt Gingrich and Pat Nolan wrote an article entitled "Prison Reform: A Smart Way for States to Save Money and Lives."[19] Breaking ranks with fellow Republicans, the editorial urged conservative legislators to lead the charge in reforming prisons as states faced severe budget shortfalls. They announced the Right on Crime movement to encourage states to reform their criminal justice systems without compromising public safety. Signatories included Republican economic and social luminaries such as Grover Norquist of Americans for Tax Reform, Richard Viguerie, Jeb Bush, and Ed Meese. In 2012, the Pew Research Center issued the results of a survey on sentencing and corrections policy in the United States that implied the public was ready for policies that reduce prison populations and spending.[20]

The coalition reframed prison reform as a fiscal imperative, aligning it with limited government, individual liberty, personal responsibility, and free enterprise. It cited the same statistics as the opponents of prison did: $68 billion were spent on prisons in 2010, 300 percent more than twenty-five years ago, and even as crime rates plummeted, incarceration rates continued to rise.[21] Nolan and Gingrich argued that prisons might be worth the cost if the recidivism rate was not so high. The system is broken, they wrote, and conservatives must fix it through cost-effective approaches that enhance public safety. At the state level, Right on Crime has supported decarceration for drug offenders, minimum wage compensation for prison labor, prison construction moratoriums, eradication of "zero tolerance" policies in public schools, more drug courts, better probation systems, and community treatment centers for the mentally ill and drug addicts.

Many organizations traditionally associated with the Right and the Left now support much of the Right on Crime agenda. The Coalition for Public Safety now includes the NAACP, Americans for Tax Reform, the Faith & Freedom Coalition, the Center for American Progress, Freedom-Works, the Koch brothers, the ACLU, and Families Against Mandatory Minimums.[22] The coalition's mandate is to bring "together the nation's most prominent conservative and progressive organizations to pursue an aggressive criminal justice reform effort."[23] The coalition had an initial funding of $5 million from Koch Industries, Laura and John Arnold, the John D. and Catherine T. MacArthur Foundation, and the Ford Foundation. Coalition director Christine Leonard says, "There are different reasons why people come into this conversation. At the end of the day, it doesn't really matter why they're at the table, because I think when they get there, they find there's more they agree upon than they disagree on."[24] A summit on criminal justice led by political activist Van Jones; Democratic senators Cory Booker, Patrick Leahy, and Sheldon Whitehouse; and Republican counterparts Rand Paul, Mike Lee, Rob Portman, and John Cornyn occurred in March 2015.[25]

In 2011, Pat Robertson, a prominent leader of the Christian Right, announced to his undoubtedly startled audience on his conservative Christian program *The 700 Club* that he supported the legalization of marijuana and an end to long prison sentences for drug offenses. He told them, "I really believe we should treat marijuana the way we treat beverage alcohol. I've never used marijuana and I don't intend to, but it's just one of those things that I think, this war on drugs just hasn't succeeded. I believe in working with the hearts of people, and not locking them up."

He continued, "Prisons are being overcrowded, and the penalties, the maximums, some of them could get ten years for possession of a joint of marijuana. It makes no sense at all. If people can go into a liquor store and buy a bottle of alcohol and drink it at home legally, then why do we say that the use of this other substance is somehow criminal?"[26]

Robertson seems an unlikely champion of the decriminalization of drugs and of prison reform, but his confession bespeaks the notable shift in the rhetoric of some Republicans and elite Christian conservatives who historically shied away from the taboo topic of emptying prisons in favor of tough-on-crime policies. Robertson ended his segment by noting, "If you follow the teaching of Christ, you know that Christ is a compassionate man," he said. "And he would not condone the imprisoning of people for nonviolent offenses."

Underlying the conservative movement for prison reform and Robertson's statement are decades of work by Christian conservatives such as Chuck Colson and Pat Nolan, who long argued that people in prison can experience an inner revolution and remake themselves through faith. Their notion of religious transformation fits neatly with the conservative consensus on prison reform. Both, for instance, espouse individual effort, responsibility, and a resistance to state programs. In an era in which privatization is championed as a solution to bureaucratic excess, Right on Crime advocates argue that the problems created by the astronomical numbers of incarcerated men and women and dwindling state budgets can be remedied through a combination of private religious organizations and state and federal funds to transform convicts into religiously redeemed citizens. Faith-based imprisonment is also part of a broader conservative impulse to reframe welfare, drug abuse, and incarceration as individual problems of self-transformation and self-responsibility. One man, who was not in the Prison Fellowship InnerChange program, noted, "The Christians do lots of stuff the state used to do, like vocational programs, but now they're only for believers."[27]

The conservative consensus on prison reform is a result of alliances between evangelicals in prison ministry like Nolan and free-market policy analysts like Marc Levin. Levin's office at the Texas Public Policy Foundation (TPPF) in downtown Austin is remarkably messy for a man who has organized a national coalition on prison reform and is flying out to advise Paul Ryan, Speaker of the House of Representatives, on the same issues the next day. When I meet him there, Levin looks as if he has been hunkered down in his office for weeks instead of arriving twenty minutes earlier. Piles of paper verging on the brink of collapse are everywhere and food containers monopolize every other bit of conceivable space. Levin's law degree certificate and a certificate from the Order of the Coil peek out from amid the clutter on the wall.

The TPPF is part of a network of state public-policy centers and think tanks, connected by free-market ideology and funded by Colson and Nolan's Justice Fellowship and the Heritage Foundation. Levin miraculously cleared some space for both of us and related the origins of what has become a national movement for prison reform. Texas, where Levin and others engineered what became known as the "Texas Turnaround," is an unlikely leader in prison reform, given its vast prison system and punitive history. Since the Supreme Court reinstated capital punishment in 1976, Texas has executed more people in prison than the next six states combined. More than one in ten prisoners in the United States are incarcerated in Texas, with the prison population there nearly tripling since 1992. The prison population in Texas grew from about 50,000 in 1990 to a peak of 173,000 in 2010, according to the Texas Department of Criminal Justice, a 346 percent increase; during the same period, the overall US prison population doubled, to 1.5 million.[28] The War on Drugs was in full swing and crime rates were high; Texas couldn't build prisons fast enough to accommodate the growing number of prisoners. The state began shipping some people to county prisons. Private, for-profit prisons sprang up to handle the overflow.

During Democratic governor Ann Richards's administration, Texas installed a hundred thousand new beds and, by 2006, even those beds were full. The same year, the Texas Department of Criminal Justice director Brad Livingston approached state legislators with a problem: outside observers were projecting the state's prison population would grow by fifteen thousand inmates in the following six years. He would need $523 million to build a sufficient number of prison beds to house those potential prisoners. Levin worked with Dr. Ana Yáñez-Correa, former executive director of the progressive Texas Criminal Justice Coalition; state senator John Whitmire and state representative Jerry Madden, both law-and-order advocates; and Tony Fabelo, a twenty-year veteran of the Texas Criminal Justice Policy Council to create new criminal justice policies for Texas that would include privately run drug treatment programs for people who violated parole, pretrial diversion for the mentally ill, and more options for people on parole and probation. Their proposals were contentious politically, but in 2011, the state legislature voted to close a prison in Sugar Land, near Houston, the first time Texas had shut a prison in 166 years.[29] They were not, however, able to reduce sentencing laws that keep people in prison for their entire lives.

Around the same time, Levin began meeting with prominent national leaders like Nolan and Eugene Meyer of the Federalist Society. Nolan was an invaluable ally because he already possessed an extensive network of friends in Washington from his days as a politician.[30] Their objective was to build a conservative consensus on prison reform.[31] It was an effort to shift not just policy but ideology and change influential conservative politicians' and policymakers' minds about the purpose of prisons. The language of "tough on crime" was supplanted by "right on crime" and now "smart on crime." (The framing of the issue creates a dichotomy in which, if you aren't tough on crime, you are weak on crime, and now, if you aren't right or smart on crime, you're simply wrong.) Levin and Nolan's coalition has enabled prominent politicians and leaders to sign on to Right on Crime without feeling they are compromising public safety and economic austerity.

Levin advises and speaks throughout the country, conferring with senators, congressional representatives, state governors, and others about how to save money for their states by reducing expenditures on prisons. He is emphatic that the coalition is not a centrist effort. He won't sign on to a policy or initiative if Right on Crime is the only conservative organization participating, because it will undermine the conservative credentials of the movement. Right on Crime and the conservative prison-reform movement in general focus predominantly on drug offenses, interrupting the school-to-prison pipeline, removing juveniles from the system, increasing the parole rate, and restoring justice initiatives. When confronted with the bleakest prison issues, like solitary confinement, Levin favors a finance and safety argument rather than one that addresses the ethics of solitary confinement, which philosopher Lisa Guenther terms a "social death" and "an assault on being."[32] Levin advocates a step-down approach in which a person moves from solitary confinement to limited contact to the general population because a person recently discharged from solitary will have mental health issues and isn't fit to be released into public life. Levin's policy initiatives and those of the broader Coalition for Public Safety lack any critique of the ethics of solitary confinement or the incarceration of juveniles.

Some have argued that diversion programs and new parole systems merely recreate a prison beyond the walls. Proposals like privatized, for-profit halfway houses and treatment centers, and parole monitoring and tracking only expand the supervisory state.[33] They are also ripe for abuse. If the goal is to fill a private addiction program or parole program, then what incentive would those programs have to help people get out? They need to fill spaces to continue to be profitable. Jill McCorkel describes this scenario in a women's prison in Pennsylvania that contracted with a private drug treatment program.[34] A central question is whether community supervision, expanded treatment, and increased use of sanctions other than prison for minor parole and probation violations effectively addresses the system of mass incarceration in the United States or merely compounds and supplements.

Mark Kleiman recently proposed dealing with people who commit violent crimes without reducing public safety by monitoring them in their homes 24/7. This would reduce the prison population by 80 percent, he argues. He posted a provocative proposal on *Vox*, suggesting that people would be released from prison before their sentences were up and placed in apartments rented by the government.[35] Once there, they would be monitored continuously via web cam, while being assigned public-service jobs. They would retain their status as prisoners and be subject to strict rules regarding things like curfew, drug use, and geographic location. Each apartment would be located in a community otherwise populated by fully free citizens and would function, in the words of Kleiman and his coauthors, "as a prison without bars."[36] Kleiman's slightly dystopian proposal isn't so farfetched, considering the technology now employed to maintain our current system of security, such as E-Verify, drones and aerial surveillance, GPS and neighborhood lockdown, handheld fingerprint machines, facial recognition, weaponized ankle bracelets, and cell-phone tracking.

The faith-based strand of prison reform in Texas also has a long history of receiving federal funds. As governor of Texas, George W. Bush supported and promoted the Prison Fellowship pilot programs in a Texas prison. In 1996, the Texas Governor's Advisory Task Force on Faith-Based Community Service Groups, appointed by Bush, issued *Faith in Action: A New Vision for Church-State Cooperation*, a report that identified pressing social problems, attacked "today's welfare system," called for the privatization of welfare, and announced that government had a key role to play as an "enabler" of faith-based groups that could respond more effectively to those problems.[37]

When he became president, Bush signed an executive order creating the White House Office of Faith-Based and Community Initiatives (OFBCI) in January 2001. The rationale behind the faith-based policies was to ensure that religious organizations were equal competitors for government funding; the Bush administration claimed the federal government had discriminated against faith-based organizations in the past. Since 2001, faith-based organizations have received $1.1 billion in federal and state funding with the mandate to focus their efforts on at-risk youth, ex-offenders and prisoners, homeless men and women, substance abusers, and welfare-to-work families.[38] The OFBCI chose Prison Fellowship as one of four national partners for a $22.5 million workplace reentry program for ex-offenders.[39] Former PF officials also lead Dare Mighty Things, which received a $2.2 million grant by the Department of Health and Human Services and now serves as a clearinghouse for faith-based and community groups applying for federal money.[40]

On February 5, 2009, President Obama signed Amendments to Executive Order 13199, establishing the White House Office and President's Advisory Council on Faith-Based and Neighborhood Partnerships. That office works across eleven government agencies as a resource for nonprofits and community organizations, both secular and religious, for financial resources and access to grants. In his 2009 inaugural speech, Obama struck a balance between the necessity for government intervention in a period of economic emergency and the power of individuals to effect change in their own lives: "But no matter how much money we invest or how sensibly we design our policies, the change that Americans are looking for will not come from government alone."[41]

The efficacy of these new religious and political coalitions around prisons is based on differing views of what has caused mass incarceration as we know it today. One misconception is that the prison system is a result of tough-on-crime policies supported only by conservative politicians. In fact, it was bipartisan dynamics that helped build the prison system, as Naomi Murakawa argues in *The First Civil Right*.[42] President Ronald Reagan may have kicked off the War on Drugs and pushed the Federal Sentencing Guidelines, but President Bill Clinton gave us the Violent Crime Control and Law Enforcement Act, providing nearly $10 billion for funding new prisons in the 1990s. Senator Joseph Biden led the Senate in amending the provisions of Clinton's 1994 omnibus crime bill: it expanded the death penalty and created new mandatory minimum sentences.

A constellation of economic, social, and political factors has fueled prison growth, and scholars have come to argue that crime is not the driver of incarceration.[43] Recently, scholars and others have begun to demonstrate that crime and incarceration are not causal. Some portion of the current decline in crime is attributable to tough sentencing and release policies, but crime is also affected by trends in employment and drug-abuse rates. To counteract the argument that more prisons lead to less crime, the Sentencing Project found that states that lagged behind the national average in rising incarceration rates during the 1990s actually experienced a steeper decline in crime rates than states above the national average.

Some scholars have taken the view that prisons are a response to social movements and a way for the state to manage and control surplus populations. Jonathan Simon, a University of California–Berkeley law professor, argues that mass imprisonment is a new approach not just to manage crime but manage society.[44] He outlines how an insular, risk-averse, and punitive social ethic has reshaped not only how the bottom half lives but how the top half does as well. Robert Perkinson, the author of *Texas Tough*, argues that the prison boom is a backlash against the civil rights movement: "It was states'-rights conservatives, inspired by George Wallace, who first seized on crime as a polarizing issue in national politics; the Republican Right thereafter picked up the baton and used it as a cudgel against liberalism for almost half a century."[45] Perkinson shows that just as convict leasing, lynching, and segregation developed in the turbulent wake of the emancipation of slaves, mass imprisonment took hold in reaction to the first African American freedom movement, the civil rights movement. In the latter, as white conservatives surrendered on integration, they insisted on getting much tougher on crime, to which they symbolically chained a host of developments they found troubling, from civil disobedience to urban rebellions. In 1960, the US prison population was 60 percent white. By 2005, it was 70 percent nonwhite. In the same Southern jurisdictions that avidly resisted integration, prison populations first started to grow (in the late 1960s versus the mid-1970s nationally) and experienced intense expansion.

In *The New Jim Crow*, Michelle Alexander traces the rise of the carceral system to the drug wars and their disproportionate effect on African American communities.[46] Beginning in the 1970s, police, prosecutors, judges, and parole boards also began to exert their enormous discretionary power in a more punitive way, which included stiffer punishments for drug offenses, the proliferation of mandatory minimums, three-strikes laws, truth-in-sentencing legislation, draconian sex-offender measures, mandatory sentencing guidelines, and life sentences.[47] The War on Drugs also conjured the specter of "the super-predator," a pathological and violent inner-city youth whose moral sense is so degraded that rehabilitation is not a possibility.[48] Ironically, John DiIulio, who went on to direct the White House Office of Faith-Based and Community Initiatives and support many studies about faith-based programs under George Bush's presidency, coined the phrase "super-predator" and ushered in the laws that enabled juveniles to be sentenced as adults and placed in adult prisons, often without the possibility of parole.

Law-and-order candidates for political office have consistently performed better at election time in the United States. Americans' collective reactions to violent crime—especially homicide, which rocketed upward in the 1960s, leveled off in the 1980s, and fell in the 1990s—are so pervasive, Jonathan Simon contends, that crime fighting has become a paradigmatic means of governing, a pathway to authority and legitimacy for policymakers.[49] Governors and presidents, even more so after 9/11, have increasingly posed as lawmen on the campaign trail, while crime victims have become an idealized class of citizens deemed especially worthy of government intervention.

The strides made by Right on Crime to make prisons a national issue cannot be discounted. In 2015, President Obama visited a maximum-security prison in Maryland. In the 2016 election, unlike in previous election cycles, presidential candidates have actively debated mass incarceration.

Right on Crime has made an impact on policy, but it has also performed the ideological work of shifting perceptions of prisons and punishment. Faith-based ministries, with their emphasis on the potential for change, are a crucial piece of this ideological shift in how the public views people in prison. While Levin focuses on fiscal responsibility and safety, the ministries in prison highlight the individual's potential for change. American attitudes about punishment derive from underlying cultural norms in American identity, according to law professor Robert Ferguson, who elaborates a typology of cultural traits and their implications for why we punish so severely in America. These traits are proportionality, mercy, forgiveness, toleration, individualism, freedom.[50] When we think of proportionality, we tend to think the punishment must increase with the severity of the crime. With mercy, the impulse is to think that criminals take advantage of it. With forgiveness, we don't grant it until the sin has been paid for in some way. Toleration is withdrawn if someone is convicted. Individualism translates to a need for strict accountability. Freedom can be taken away if necessary. All these beliefs contribute in various ways to how Americans conceive of prisons. In arguing that prisoners are not incorrigible and capable of transformation, the faith-based ministries contribute to a broader conversation about why we punish for longer and longer periods and what is the purpose of the prison itself.

Even though faith-based groups helped shift the public debate about the potential for people to change, scholars like Marie Gottschalk, a professor at the University of Pennsylvania, have argued that we still need to address violent crimes and the people who commit them. If we released everyone now serving time in state prisons whose primary charge is a drug offense, we would reduce the state prison population by only 20 percent.[51] In 2012, the Bureau of Justice Statistics reported a decline in the US prison population for the second consecutive year due to reported decreases in twenty-six state departments of corrections.[52] Advocacy groups and policy analysts across the political spectrum celebrated, but they neglected the "slight" increase in US prisoners housed in private prison facilities and the increase in federal prisoners, as Kay Whitlock and Nancy Heitzeg have noted in their series on the bipartisan coalition.[53] New reform efforts make three faulty assumptions according to Whitlock and Heitzeg: we can dismantle the prison system without addressing policing practices and biases that determine who is funneled into the criminal legal system; the existing system is basically fair, and people caught up in it deserve to be there; and we don't need to challenge or critique the structural inequalities of a capitalist system.

As the United States has dismantled the welfare state, it has simultaneously created the carceral state. "Prisons are partial geographical solutions to political economic crises, organized by the state, which is itself in crisis," geographer Ruth Gilmore argues. She claims that California's prison boom is a "prison fix" to a problem of fourfold surplus: capital, land, labor, and state capacity. If you want to know why so many prisons were built, Gilmore argues, don't look to crime rates. "Look instead to economic depression in the agricultural regions of the state, and the search for new jobs and new ways of attracting state dollars in these areas. Look at the collapse of social services in urban areas of southern California."[54] The US states that have experienced a *decrease* in spending per capita on welfare have tended to experience an *increase* in spending on prisons. Countries that have gaping income inequalities generally have higher violent crime rates and often higher incarceration rates.

The recent prison-reform coalitions rarely discuss what to do about violent criminals and extremely long sentences, or what should happen to people once they are in prison. As Gilmore writes, "Most campaigns to decrease sentences for nonviolent convictions simultaneously decrease pressure to revise—indeed often explicitly promise never to change—sentences for serious, violent or sexual felonies."[55] Questions about the distinction between somebody who's done something horrible and somebody who is a horrible person are central to how faith-based ministries conceive of their work, even if they focus exclusively on the individual. Right on Crime doesn't attend to these distinctions. Grover Norquist, a Right on Crime signatory, argued, "You're seeing a lot of people are sent to prison who perhaps ought not to be in prison, in terms of some cost-benefit analysis. And, again, we're conservatives. I think there are a bunch of people who deserve to be in prison forever. I think there are some people that deserve to be in prison for a long time. I don't get weepy about the whole idea."[56]

The Right on Crime perspective lacks an analysis of the root causes for why we imprison, because it is rooted in the conservative fiscal assumption that privatization, rather than the expansion of social services, is a solution to mass incarceration. In an interview about her book *Caught*, Gottschalk discusses the structural shifts that need to happen so that people don't end up in prison initially; she claims she'll believe that people like Norquist, Gingrich, and other leaders on the Right are truly ready to make significant dents in the carceral state the day they begin supporting Medicaid expansion under the Affordable Care Act. Gottschalk writes, "If you care about reentry and about keeping people out of prison in the first place, there's no public policy that you should support more strongly now than Medicaid expansion. Medicaid expansion gives states huge infusions of federal money to expand mental health services, substance abuse treatment, and medical care for many of the people who are most likely to end up in prison. It also allows states and localities to shift a significant portion of their correctional health care costs to the federal tab."[57]

In 2008, the federal Second Chance Act was signed into law with the intention of improving outcomes for people returning to communities from prisons and jails. The legislation authorizes federal grants to government agencies and nonprofit organizations to provide employment assistance, substance abuse treatment, housing, family programming, mentoring, victim support, and other services that can help reduce recidivism.[58] Texas and other states have chased after federal Second Chance and justice reinvestment dollars, which are a relative pittance. Meanwhile, according to Gottschalk, they have been eschewing the billions of dollars in Medicaid funding that could provide real second chances to people released from prison, many of whom, truth be told, never had a first chance.

In fiscal 2012, Congress allocated just $63 million for the Second Chance Act, which works out to less than $100 for each person released from prison and jail that year. Compare that to the estimated $100 billion Texas will forfeit in federal dollars over the next decade because of its decision to opt out of Medicaid expansion. The NAACP issued a report about prison spending versus education spending that points to the difference between trying to change the social factors that affect the rate of imprisonment and what Gottschalk calls "tinkering with the carceral state" and Wilbert Rideau terms "trimming the fat" but leaving the rest intact. Over the past three decades, state and local government expenditures on prisons and jails have increased about three times as fast as spending on elementary and secondary education.[59] When asked to discuss this disparity with Benjamin Jealous, former NAACP president, Norquist refused to talk about redirecting money toward public education. "That's a separate discussion," he said.[60]

# CAPTIVITY AND FREEDOM

OVER TWO HUNDRED YEARS AGO, in many of the same states where faith-based prisons seek to transform men and women in prison, millions of African Americans were enslaved by landowners who professed to be Christians. Christians justified their ownership of slaves by referencing the Bible. Jefferson Davis, president of the Confederate States of America, wrote, "[Slavery] was established by decree of Almighty God. . . . It is sanctioned in the Bible, in both Testaments, from Genesis to Revelation. . . . It has existed in all ages, has been found among the people of the highest civilization, and in nations of the highest proficiency in the arts." The Reverend R. Furman of South Carolina, a Baptist, argued, "The right of holding slaves is clearly established in the Holy Scriptures, both by precept and example." In a contrasting view, William Wells Brown, a prominent abolitionist who was born into slavery, wrote of slaveholders and their religion in the antebellum South:

Slaveholders hide themselves behind the church. A more praying, preaching, psalm-singing people cannot be found than the slaveholders at the south. The religion of the south is referred to every day, to prove that slaveholders are good, pious men. But with all their pretensions, and all the aid which they get from the northern church, they cannot succeed in deceiving the Christian portion of the world. Their child-robbing, man-stealing, woman-whipping, chain-forging, marriage-destroying,

slave-manufacturing, man-slaying religion, will not be received as genuine; and the people of the free states cannot expect to live in union
with slaveholders, without becoming contaminated with slavery.[1]

By 1833, England had outlawed the slave trade due to a vociferous group
of religious reformers who decried the practice as anti-Christian and anti-
democratic. In England, devoted Anglican evangelicals joined forces with
pious Quakers and railed against slave owners through sermons, writings,
and meetings. The Society for the Abolition of the Slave Trade, founded
in 1787, set a standard of religious involvement in politics as a pressing
moral issue that would be imitated across the Atlantic many years later.[2]

Eventually, thousands of religious people in the South moved toward
the conviction that God abhorred slavery. It was a momentous theological, ideological, and social upheaval. Quakers imagined more just forms
of punishment, which would become the penitentiary, and they were the
first religious denomination to adamantly oppose human bondage by as-
serting the love of God for every human being, regardless of color, sex,
or station in life. During the 1830s, the majority of abolitionists were
Northern white churchgoers, and their clergy and antislavery activism
relied on the conviction that all people were made in God's image. Abolitionists worked to convert naysayers to their point of view. One repented
of slaveholding and pledged to follow God's command that all people were
created equal.

In 1829, David Walker, a free black man in the North, wrote, "Are we
MEN!!—I ask you, O my brethren, are we MEN? Did our Creator make
us to be slaves to dust and ashes like ourselves?" Abolitionists drew on the
significance of Exodus in the Bible to argue that it revealed divine opposition to human systems of oppression and bondage.[3] In their eyes, God's
concern for the poor, the oppressed, and the enslaved was found throughout scripture. Antislavery advocates often quoted the mission statement
of Jesus himself, taking it as the text for their sermons: "The Spirit of
the Lord is upon me, because he hath anointed me to preach the Gospel
to the poor . . . to preach deliverance to the captives . . . to set at liberty
them that are bruised" (Luke 4:18). The emancipation of slaves, they argued, was on the agenda of Jesus and an extenstion of his Gospel of the

kingdom. Redemption for abolitionists signified the soul and the body, a physical and a spiritual transformation. "O burst thou all their chains in sunder," prayed John Wesley, the founder of Methodism, "more especially the chains of their sins; Thou Saviour of all, make them free, that they may be free indeed."[4]

The Christian origins of slavery and abolitionism provide a striking analogy for mass incarceration today because Christians revised their most fundamental and cherished beliefs about an entrenched institution. It demonstrates that gargantuan shifts in thinking are possible through theological and ethical lenses, and it is all the more important because mass incarceration still bears an uncanny resemblance to slavery in its racial disproportion and brutality.

Today, in many faith-based prison ministries, social justice as a driving force of religious belief is absent. Proclaiming the Gospel is the means and the end. However, just as Christian slave owners were converted to anti-slavery efforts, so might conservative churches involved in prison ministry begin to conceptualize their role in the prison as one of spreading faith *and* justice. For most abolitionist Christians, ending the slave trade and evangelizing non-Christians were complementary activities. Equiano's *Interesting Narrative*, for example, was both an antislavery tract and an evangelical conversion story.[5] Dynamic evangelical movements, like Methodism and Baptism, were at the forefront of the British antislavery movement from the 1780s to the 1830s.[6] They bore eloquent testimony to the transforming power of the Gospel to alter injustice in the world.

Faith-based ministries that have intimate and daily contact with people behind bars could contribute to a revitalized Christianity that forges new avenues and possibilities for forgiveness and redemption, instead of retribution and endless punishment. Faith-based ministries might ask what the purpose of a prison is and what the role of a faith-based organization inside it is. As to the purpose of the American system of mass incarceration, Michel Foucault, writing in the 1980s, pessimistically characterized it as indefinitely replicating itself:

At the time of the creation of Auburn and the Philadelphia prison, which served as models (with very little change until now) for the great machines of incarceration, it was believed that something indeed was produced: "virtuous" men. Now we know, and the administration is perfectly aware, that no such thing is produced. That nothing at all is produced. That it is a question simply of a great sleight of hand, a curious mechanism of circular elimination: society eliminates by sending to prison people whom prison breaks up, crushes, physically eliminates. . . . The prison eliminates them by "freeing" them and sending them back to society; the state in which they come out insures that society will eliminate them once again, sending them to prison. . . . Attica is a machine for elimination, a form of prodigious stomach, a kidney that consumes, destroys, breaks up and then rejects, and that consumes in order to eliminate what it has already eliminated.[7]

One clear way to end mass incarceration is to close prisons and lay off the people who work in them. Even though some states have enacted new legislation to reduce prison populations, there are still powerful interests that profit politically and economically from mass imprisonment. Prisons are part of an economic complex that generates significant amounts of money for people, from phone companies that overcharge to private businesses that utilize cheap prison labor.

Concepts like captivity and redemption also become lost in the procedures of the criminal legal system in the United States, with its prosecutors, juries, lawyers, judges, and police officers. In many cases, procedural issues take precedence over issues of justice and fairness. Herman Wallace, who spent forty-one years in a six-by-nine-foot cell in Angola, was released from solitary because the judge ruled that the jury composition at his trial violated the Fourteenth Amendment. It wasn't because he had existed in a room the size of some bathrooms for forty years, or was dying of cancer, or that the judge ruled solitary is a form of torture.

Many people leaving prison now describe themselves as "returning citizens." If we consider people in and outside prisons as citizens, can we justify the way we warehouse and treat them? If prisoners' lives truly mattered, would we send them to places where youth barter sex for food; where people go blind and die of medical neglect; where someone will be raped; where women are separated from their children forever;

where a woman is shackled during childbirth; where a transgender, gay, or gender-nonconforming person is subject to unthinkable abuse; where people are moved hundreds of miles from their families; and where they are driven mad in solitary confinement cells for years? To recognize that prisoners' lives matter means that we force ourselves to look at the purpose of prisons and the purpose of faith-based and other groups within them.

The language of theology and morality, central to faith-based work, is often absent from discussions of mass incarceration. In focusing on individual conversion, many faith-based prison ministries neglect the broader issues of how people came to prison and end up fortifying the prison's rationale of control, surveillance, governance, and vengeance. One way to begin would be for faith-based groups to consider how to contend with violence, both that committed by those in prison and the violence of the prison system itself. This would mean rethinking the connection between individual salvation and collective forms of responsibility. As political philosopher Judith Butler writes of the tension between acts and the conditions that shape them,

> Those who commit acts of violence are surely responsible for them; they are not dupes or mechanisms of an impersonal social force, but agents with responsibility. On the other hand, these individuals are formed, and we would be making a mistake if we reduced their actions to purely self-generated acts of will or symptoms of individual pathology or "evil." To ask these questions is not to say that the conditions are at fault rather than the individual. It is, rather, to *rethink the relation between conditions and acts.*[8]

As Monica from the women's prison in Louisiana said about herself, the crime is always going to be there. But people also evolve and transform. If we believe that, whether through religious or secular means, when are we going to forgive her for it?

Some religious groups have claimed the mantle of social justice and articulated redemptive alternatives to retribution. The American Friends Service Committee, a Quaker organization, works against incarceration.[9] The ACLU has engaged faith-based organizations and churches as part of the Coalition for Public Safety to lobby against mandatory minimum sentencing laws and life sentences for juveniles. Catholics have been at the forefront of efforts to defeat the death penalty.[10] Congregations in churches like Riverside in New York City and the Unitarian Universalist Association have chosen to read Michelle Alexander's *The New Jim Crow.* The Samuel DeWitt Proctor Conference, a network of thousands of progressive black churches, has chosen mass incarceration as one of its main priorities for the coming years. Few of these groups, however, are regularly inside American prisons in the same numbers as nondenominational and conservative evangelical organizations.

Another tactic for the churches would be to embolden and support those who have experienced incarceration in leading movements to dismantle it. The hunger strikes in Georgia and protests against solitary confinement organized by prisoners demonstrate the ways organizing can occur in even the most restrictive spaces. Groups like Nation Inside, JustLeadership, VOTE, and All of Us or None create community-based strategies against mass incarceration driven by people who have been in prison and live in the communities most affected by mass incarceration. (The first conference for formerly incarcerated people was held in Oakland, California, in September 2016 with more than five hundred attendees.) Part of the necessary work of a social movement led by formerly incarcerated people is to stop stigmatizing returning citizens with voting restrictions, housing discrimination, and parole conditions that prohibit travel or owning a cell phone.

Higher education programs in prison present possibilities for collective mobilization and intellectual autonomy. The prison uprisings throughout the 1970s—from Pontiac to Attica—pushed for greater access to relevant and quality education for people behind bars. These movements linked educational access to broader aims of self-determination, racial justice, and prison abolition, and were connected to larger radical freedom struggles of the period. Unlike some faith-based ministries such as the seminary programs, education programs can have explicit political goals: educational access for those living on the inside is a human right, and education programming in prison is one tactic among others seeking redistributive justice.

Those who spend time with prisoners in seminaries, Bible studies, trauma counseling, and religious services could also raise issues to their congregations and communities, such as abolishing a sentence of life without the possibility of parole. This would force them to ask what kind of redemption is possible when a person cannot leave prison. Life without parole is a nearly unheard-of sentence in Europe. In the closed prisons of Norway, which more closely resemble the American system, individuals have their own cells and are allowed out of them most of the day while they work or study toward college.[11] In Norway, the maximum possible prison sentence is twenty-one years. In the other Scandinavian countries, life sentences are allowable in theory, but in practice, it is extremely rare for a person to serve over twenty years. Even Anders Behring Breivik, who massacred sixty-nine people, many of them youths, on Norway's Utoya Island in 2011, received twenty-one years in prison with the option to extend every five after that.

Years ago, American governors and presidents used executive clemency to express mercy or to make a broader political statement. On Christmas Day 1912, at the height of Jim Crow, Governor George Donaghey of Arkansas, a fierce opponent of the brutal convict-leasing system in the South, commuted the sentences of hundreds of state prisoners in a gesture that made national headlines. There are examples and precedents for other ways of imagining punishment.

For years, the United States has been exceptional not only because it holds so many people under lock and key but also because the conditions in many of its prisons and jails are so degrading and dehumanizing, compared to those in many other Western countries. In Norway, people live in open prisons in wooden bungalows, where they cook communal meals. They work jobs such as growing vegetables in the prison farm, repairing bicycles, and caring for the horses in the prison stables, and enjoy recreations including swimming, sunbathing, horseback riding, and tennis. They can work outside the prison and visit their families over the holidays while monitored by electronic bracelets. American exceptionalism is usually the justification that the moderate punishment regimes of Europe don't apply here.

While there are significant differences between the United States and Norway, this doesn't mean the Norwegian example is an impossibility or should be ignored. Scandinavian correctional officers are trained for two years and go through a selective process, unlike officers in the United States, who sometimes spend only four weeks in a course. Norwegian prisons are more expensive to maintain, but Norway has one-tenth the incarceration rate of the United States due to more lenient sentencing policies. Scandinavian countries have the lowest murder rates in the world, partially due to their historic homogeneity but also to their robust welfare state, which makes crime less an incentive for the poor. Their prison policies are determined by experts rather than politicians.[12] Many would say that the United States could never accomplish what Scandinavians (or the Europeans generally) have because we are a large and highly diverse nation, but this myth and reliance on our own exceptionalism, even as a negative, prohibits us from imagining other possibilities.

Part of the necessary work to prevent people from ending up in prison is to do precisely what Right on Crime would oppose: expand the welfare state so that people have access to child care, affordable housing, mental health and addiction services, trauma counseling for women and veterans, health care, universal preschool, and high-quality public schools that disrupt the school-to-prison pipeline. Elderly people who no longer pose a threat to society could be released and provided with robust services to aid their transition back to the free world. Faith-based groups could address the hidden system of detention centers, where private companies like the GEO Group and Corrections Corporation of America are now profiting through immigrant detention.

Faith-based ministries may have a stated commitment to redemption, but for them, redemption occurs within prison walls. Like Jonathan Burnside, many have faith in mass incarceration. Many faith-based ministries believe that prisons are necessary for religious awakening to occur; prisons are where punishment is just and necessary to encounter God and oneself. Instead of focusing on individual transformation through relationships with God, Christian ministries in prison must address our collective responsibility to create and support a just society.[13]

Perhaps punishment is unjustifiable until we have brought about deep social, political, legal, and moral changes in ourselves and our society, by which time, there might be no need for punishment. The church has the potential to attack the related ideologies of neoliberal economics and retribution based on what the Bible says about being our sister's or brother's keeper. "At the heart of this attack lies a conception of human life grounded not on violence, and the logic of an eye for an eye, but on forgiveness," Timothy Gorringe writes in *God's Just Vengeance*.[14]

Abolition of the slave trade seemed inconceivable in the early 1800s, but it did eventually occur. Angela Davis, a professor and prison activist, argues that abolition is a horizon, just as it was when slavery appeared to be the only possible way of life.[15] The carceral state was built, and it can be dismantled. When we imagine other possibilities, we inch closer to making them a reality. Davis argues that we can imagine not so much the abolition of prisons, but "the abolition of a society that could have prisons, that could have slavery, that could have the wage, and therefore not abolition as the elimination of anything but abolition as the founding of a new society."[16] José Muñoz wrote of "the warm illumination of a horizon imbued with potentiality . . . an ideality that can be distilled from the past and used to imagine a future," in his book *Cruising Utopia*. He was talking about queerness, but his vision applies also to our current prison system.

> The here and now is a prison house. We must strive, in the face of the here and now's totalizing rendering of reality, to think and feel a *then and there*. Some will say that all we have are the pleasures of this moment, but we must never settle for that minimal transport; we must dream and enact . . . other ways of being in the world, and ultimately new worlds.[17]

Faith-based groups seem uniquely situated to join and lead this work, wherever it may lead.

Monica's story begs the question of what is our responsibility to the people who spend their lives in captivity. The legal system, as it stands, does not have the capacity for redemption and forgiveness, especially in states where men and women go to prison for life without any possibility of parole. Although faith-based groups' concept of redemption is limited by their belief in the conversion of the individual, there is a possibility for a more capacious understanding of redemption that addresses the question of autonomy and freedom outside the prison. First, ministries, the state, the prison, and all of us need to ask the question Norris Henderson poses, "Are you giving people the help they need or the help you think they need?"

# ACKNOWLEDGMENTS

PRISONS ARE PLACES OF DESOLATION, suffering, and concealment, but I have also found them filled with hopeful, curious, flawed, and generous people—prisoners, staff, and volunteers, who extended themselves to me in person and in writing. This book is only possible because of those conversations, the hours in classes and groups with them, and their patience with my continual barrage of questions. The men and women I have come to know in prisons around the country evince a courageous form of self-making.

I finished a draft of this book at the marvelous Hedgebrook residency for women writers. Thank you to the conviviality of my fellow writers in residence and to staff members Vito Zingarelli and Amy Wheeler. This project was also supported by a National Endowment for the Humanities fellowship, the Institute for Advanced Study at Princeton, a research grant from Ohio State University, and an Open Society Foundation Soros Justice fellowship, overseen by Adam Culbreath and Christina Voight. Papers related to this project were presented at the American Academy of Religion and the American Studies Association, as well as before audiences at the University of Florida, New York University, Washington University in St. Louis, Princeton University, California State University at Chico, the University of California at Davis, the University of Puget Sound, the University of Washington, and Saint Martin's University who commented on this work and asked questions that ultimately made it stronger. Kathy Woodward and Miriam Bartha at the Simpson Center for the Humanities and the Department of Gender, Women, and Sexuality Studies at the University of Washington hosted me and connected me with many colleagues. Dr. Ben Phillips, Brandon Warren, Dr. John Robson, and Dr. Kristi Miller provided Southern hospitality and, more importantly, time to meet their students and listen. For their comments and ideas in so many venues, thank you to Tom O'Connor, Jodi Schorb, Amy Abugo Ongiri, Marie Gottschalk, Dylan Rodriguez, Ann Pellegrini, Bethany Moreton, Marie Griffith, Melani McAlister, Diane Winston, Katie Lofton, Kevin Lewis O'Neill, Daromir Rudoy, Rebecca Wanzo, Brendan Kiley, Trysh Travis, Tim Aubry, Sarah Pike, Julie Sze, Elizabeth Castelli, Jack Hawley, Laura McTighe, Hakim Ali, Robin McGinty, Ann Neumann, and the editors at *Guernica* magazine. Amy Caldwell has been an astute reader and editor of my work for many years, and Susan Lumenello and Jane Gebhart caught many things I didn't see.

I am fortunate to be a part of many sustaining and overlapping intellectual communities. My former colleagues at Ohio State University were early advocates of this project, particularly Hugh Urban and Julia Watson. My colleagues at the University of Puget Sound are models of conviviality: Greta Austin, Kristin Bartanen, Robin Jacobson, Seth Weinberger, Priti Joshi, Jonathon Stockdale, and Suzanne Holland. Students in my Crime and Punishment and Utopia classes embraced and debated the ideas here, particularly Logan Miller. My compatriots in the world of prisons keep me sane, particularly Jody Lewen, Daniel Karpowitz, Stacey Reeh, Sean Pica, Kim Bogucki, Kyes Stevens, and Mary Gould. I am grateful to Brendan Kiley and Smoke Farm comrades for making a place for me and to the audiences at the Smoke Farm Symposium. Mary Weir, Kailin Mooney, Chanel Rhymes, Mary Dewine, Melanie Maltry, and Holly Johnson at the Freedom Education Project at Puget Sound (FEPPS) rose to the occasion so I could finish this project. Everyone should be so fortunate as to be a part of the committed and generous network of Soros Justice fellows, who rooted for this book from the beginning: Liam Johnston, Calvin Duncan, Mujahid Farid, Jackie Sumell, Luis Trelles, Amanda Alexander, Marbre Stahly-Butts, Olga Tomchin, Mark Obbie, Alisa Roth, Heather Thompson, Jean Casella, James Ridgeway, Lisa Riordan Seville, and Renee Feltz. I hold the deepest respect and admiration for Wilbert

Rideau, who changed and clarified my thinking in conversations and correspondence, and to Norris Henderson, who first asked me the question that animates this book.

Several people have been interlocutors over the years for this project. Angela Zito first asked whether I wanted to teach a class in Bayview Correctional Facility and has continually pushed and challenged me. That prison is now a building that hosts organizations dedicated to gender equality. My intellectual friendship with Stuart Smithers has provided me with a sense of pessimistic utopianism. Megan Sweeney collaborated with me in the early stages on a panel and was a close reader of some of the early versions of chapter 6. Gillian Harkins and Alys Weinbaum waded through many drafts with rigor, humor, and insight. Mary Thomas has been a conversation partner, critic, and stalwart friend for many years, and this book only exists because of her and long walks on Whidbey. Kim Gilmore, Cathy Harris, Mary Thomas, Abby Crain, Sujung Kim, Maisie Weissman, Maria Riley, Andrea L'Tainen, Kate Grossman, Becca Graves, Rena Rosenwasser, and Shireen Deboo remind me continually of the pleasures of long and daily friendships.

My family propelled this book through the birth of two children, a cross-country move, and a new job. Sue and Bob Erzen, Alex Erzen and Angela Wallis, George and Amy Marsh, Bill Quigley, and the wondrous Tilda and Clive allow me to step into the fray each day.

And, finally, thank you to the FEPPS students at the Washington Corrections Center for Women, whose bravery and brilliance have taught me so much about what it means to build a life in captivity.

# NOTES

Many quotes and much information come from my interviews with men and women in prisons in Louisiana, Ohio, Texas, California, and New York, both in person and through correspondence, from 2005 to 2015.

**INTRODUCTION**

1. Prison Policy Project, "States of Incarceration: The Global Context, http://www.prisonpolicy.org/global/, accessed July 18, 2016.
2. Pat Nolan, "Supreme Court Demands End to Prison Overcrowding," *Inside Out,* June 2011, http://www.prisonfellowship.org/inside-out/io-issue/june-2011/entry/20/15421.
3. For a vivid and trenchant analysis of how prisoners interact in the many religious groups active in contemporary prisons, see Joshua Dubler's ethnography of Graterford Prison, *Down in the Chapel: Religious Life in an American Prison* (New York: Farrar, Straus and Giroux, 2013). The classic text on life inside a maximum penitentiary is James B. Jacobs, *Stateville: The Penitentiary in Mass Society* (Chicago: University of Chicago Press, 1977).
4. "Faith-Based Programs," OJP Fact Sheet, Office of Justice Programs, November 2011, http://www.ojp.usdoj.gov/newsroom/factsheets/ojpfs_faith-basedprog.html. See also Alexander Volokh, "Do Faith-Based Prisons Work?" *Alabama Law Review* 63, no. 1 (2001): 43–95; US Department of Justice, National Institute of Corrections, "Residential Faith-Based Programs in State Corrections," September 2005, http://nicic.gov/Library/020820, accessed March 16, 2014; and "Faith-Based and Community Initiatives in Corrections," n.d., http://nicic.gov/FaithBasedInitiatives, accessed March 16, 2014.
5. "Fact Sheet: Prison Fellowship," DeMoss, 2016, http://demoss.com/newsrooms/pf/background/prison-fellowship-fact-sheet.
6. Jonathan Simon, "Beyond the Panopticon: Mass Imprisonment and the Humanities," *Law, Culture and the Humanities* 6, no. 327 (2010): 329.
7. Ruth Wilson Gilmore, *Golden Gulag: Prisons, Surplus, Crisis, and Opposition in Globalizing California* (Berkeley: University of California Press, 2007), 54.
8. M. E. Torre et al., "A Space for Co-construction Counter Stories Under Surveillance," *International Journal of Critical Psychology* 3 (2001): 149–66.

9. Peter Wagner, Leah Sakala, and Josh Begley, "States of Incarceration: The Global Context," Prison Policy Initiative, 2016, http://www.prisonpolicy.org /global/.

10. Ibid.

11. Eduardo Porter, "In the US, Punishment Comes Before the Crimes," *New York Times*, April 29, 2014, http://www.nytimes.com/2014/04/30/business/economy /in-the-us-punishment-comes-before-the-crimes.html?_r=1.

12. These books present the successes and failures of the faith-based offices under Bush by people who worked there: John J. DiIulio Jr., *Godly Republic: A Centrist Blueprint for America's Faith-Based Future* (Berkeley: University of California Press, 2007); David Kuo, *Tempting Faith: An Inside Story of Political Seduction* (New York: Free Press, 2006); and Rebecca Sager, *Faith, Politics, and Power: The Politics of Faith-Based Initiatives* (New York: Oxford University Press, 2010), 107–9. Sager writes that states require documentation for faith-based groups' claims of superior service. In 1999, the state of Louisiana enacted a law to measure recidivism rates, increase the number of volunteers working in prisons, and develop relationships with churches, synagogues, mosques, and other religious institutions to facilitate transfer back to the community.

13. Timothy Gorringe, *God's Just Vengeance: Crime, Violence and the Rhetoric of Salvation* (Cambridge, UK: Cambridge University Press, 1996), 252.

14. Beth E. Richie, *Arrested Justice: Black Women, Violence and America's Prison Nation* (New York: New York University Press, 2012).

15. Caleb Smith, *The Prison and the American Imagination* (New Haven, CT: Yale University Press, 2009), 10, 20, 173.

16. Mary Rowlandson, *The Sovereignty and Goodness of God* (1682; Boston: Bedford, 1997).

17. Toni Morrison, *Playing in the Dark: Whiteness and the Literary Imagination* (Cambridge, MA: Harvard University Press, 1992).

18. T. M. Osborne, *Within Prison Walls* (New York: Appleton, 1913), 324.

19. See Prison Policy Initiatives, *Breaking Down Mass Incarceration in the 2010 Census: State-by-State Incarceration Rates by Race/Ethnicity*, for a detailed look at all fifty states. Jeremy Travis, Bruce Western, and Steve Redburn, eds., *The Growth of Incarceration in the United States: Exploring Causes and Consequences* (Washington, DC: National Academies Press, 2014).

20. Jonathan Burnside, with Nancy Loucks, Joanna R. Adler, and Gerry Rose, *My Brother's Keeper: Faith-Based Units in Prison* (London: Willan Publishing, 2005), 354.

21. Nicole Hahn Rafter, *Partial Justice: Women, Prisons and Social Control*, second ed. (New Brunswick, NJ: Transaction Publishers, 2004).

22. Gorringe, *God's Just Vengeance*, 143.

23. Ibid., 142.

## CHAPTER 1: THE CONVERT'S HEART

1. Pat Nolan, "Mass Incarceration in the United States: At What Cost?," testimony of Pat Nolan, vice president of Prison Fellowship, to the Joint Economic Committee of the US Congress in Support of the Second Chance Act, October 4, 2007.

2. Bill Glass, "Recidivism Cure: Change Inmates' Hearts, Inside Out," *The Slammer,* January 16, 2010, accessed July 11, 2016, http://www.the-slammer.org /carousel/recidivism-cure-change-inmates%E2%80%99-hearts-inside-out.

3. Steve McCoy, personal interview.

4. Karen Katz, *Devilz Dollz: The Secret World of Women in the Outlaw Biker Subculture* (Indianapolis: Dog Ear Publishing, 2011); and Catherine Roster, "'Girl Power' and Participation in Macho Recreation: The Case of Female Harley Riders," *Leisure Sciences* 29, no. 5 (October–December 2007): 443–61.

5. C. J. Forsyth and J. F. Quinn, "Leathers and Rolexes: The Symbolism and Values of the Motorcycle Club," *Deviant Behaviour: An Interdisciplinary Journal* 30, no. 3 (2009): 235–65.

6. See Randy Balmer, *Blessed Assurance: A History of Evangelicalism in America* (Boston: Beacon Press, 1999).

7. James Bielo, *Words upon the Word: An Ethnography of Evangelical Bible Study* (New York: New York University Press, 2009), 137.

8. See Nathan Hatch, *The Democratization of American Religion* (New Haven, CT: Yale University Press, 1989); Christine Heyrman, *Southern Cross: The Beginnings of the Bible Belt* (New York: Alfred A. Knopf, 1997); Laurence Moore, *Religious Outsiders and the Making of America* (New York: Oxford University Press, 1986); Whitney Cross, *The Burned-Over District: The Social and Intellectual History of Enthusiastic Religion in Western New York, 1800–1850* (Ithaca, NY: Cornell University Press, 1950).

9. State of Louisiana, Court of Appeal, Third Circuit, 04–30 consolidated with 04–57, State of Louisiana v. Patricia Anderson, Appeal from the Thirteenth Judicial District Court, Parish of Evangeline, No. 66–513FA, Honorable John Larry Vidrine, District Judge, Ulysses Gene Thibodeaux, Chief Judge; State of Louisiana, Court of Appeal, Third Circuit, 05–1406, State of Louisiana v. Larry Surratt and Patricia Anderson, Appeal from the Thirteenth Judicial District Court, Parish of Evangeline, No. 66–513FA, Honorable John Larry Vidrine, District Judge, Glen Gremillion, Judge.

10. This is detailed in the appeal above and in newspaper articles. Mandy M. Goodnight, "Murder Suspect Arrested in Texas," *Town Talk*, April 24, 2003.

11. Robyn R. Warhol and Helena Michie, "Twelve-Step Teleology: Narratives of Recovery/Recovery as Narrative," in *Getting a Life: Everyday Uses of Autobiography,* ed. Sidonie Smith and Julia Watson (Ann Arbor: University of Michigan Press, 2002), 329.

12. Shadd Maruna, *Making Good: How Ex-Convicts Reform and Rebuild Their Lives* (Washington, DC: American Psychological Association, 2001), 87.

13. Steve W. Lemke, "Evangelical Theology in the Twenty-First Century," presidential address, 2000 Southwest Regional meeting, Evangelical Theological Society, Southwestern Baptist Theological Seminary, http://www.nobts.edu/ faculty/itor/lemkesw/personal/Evangelical%20Theology.html.

14. Susan Harding, *The Book of Jerry Falwell: Fundamentalist Language and Politics* (Princeton, NJ: Princeton University Press, 2001), 37.

15. Bella Brodski, "Testimony," in *The Encyclopedia of Life Writing,* ed. Margaretta Jolly (Chicago: Fitzroy-Dearborn, 2001).

16. Todd Clear, "The Value of Religion in Prisons: An Inmate Perspective," *Journal of Contemporary Criminal Justice* 16, no. 1 (February 2000): 58.

17. In *Criminal Intimacy: Prison and the Uneven History of Modern American Sexuality* (Chicago: University of Chicago Press, 2008), Regina Kunzel writes the history of the sexual worlds of prisoners in the nineteenth and twentieth centuries, and looks at film to analyze the representation of sex in women's prisons.

## CHAPTER 2: THE PENITENTIARY AND THE FARM

1. Matthew W. Meskell, "An American Resolution: The History of Prisons in the United States from 1777–1877," *Stanford Law Review* 51, no. 4 (April 1999): 839; and W. David Lewis, *From Newgate to Dannemora: The Rise of the Penitentiary in New York, 1796–1848* (Ithaca, NY: Cornell University Press, 1965), 19.

2. Andrew Skotnicki, *Religion and the Development of the American Penal System* (Lanham, MD: University Press of America, 2000), 30.

3. Ibid., 145.

4. Ibid., 17.

5. David J. Rothman, "Perfecting the Prison: United States, 1789–1865," in *The Oxford History of the Prison: The Practice of Punishment in Western Society*, ed. Norval Morris and David J. Rothman (New York: Oxford University Press, 2007).

6. Skotnicki, *Religion and the Development of the American Penal System*, 12–13.

7. Lewis, *From Newgate to Dannemora*, 9.

8. Rothman, "Perfecting the Prison," 102.

9. Skotnicki, *Religion and the Development of the American Penal System*, 30. In 1790, spurred by the democratic republican experiment of the new nation, the Pennsylvania legislature established the legal foundation for the prison system as we know it today.

10. Jennifer Graber, *The Furnace of Affliction: Prisons in Antebellum America* (Chapel Hill: University of North Carolina Press, 2011).

11. Ibid., 12.

12. Michel Foucault, *Discipline and Punish: The Birth of the Prison* (New York: Random House, 1977), 138.

13. Graber, *The Furnace of Affliction*, 236–37.

14. Skotnicki, *Religion and the Development of the American Penal System*, 57.

15. Harry Elmer Barnes, *The Evolution of Penology in Pennsylvania* (Indianapolis: Bobbs-Merrill Company, 1927), quoted in ibid., 67.

16. Alexis de Tocqueville and Gustave de Beaumont, *On the Penitentiary System in the United States and Its Application in France* (orig. 1833; Carbondale: Southern Illinois University Press, 1964), 65.

17. Ibid., 122.

18. Skotnicki, *Religion and the Development of the American Penal System*, 40.

19. Edgardo Rotman, "The Failure of Reform: United States 1865–1965," in Morris and Rothman, *The Oxford History of the Prison*.

20. Skotnicki, *Religion and the Development of the American Penal System*, 52.

21. Ibid., 57.

22. Graber, *The Furnace of Affliction*, 99. This history is recounted in Ted Conover, *New Jack: Guarding Sing Sing* (New York: Vintage, 2001).

23. Tocqueville and Beaumont, *On the Penitentiary System in the United States and Its Application in France*, 163–64.
24. Graber, *The Furnace of Affliction*, 82.
25. Tocqueville and Beaumont, *On the Penitentiary System in the United States and Its Application in France*, 60.
26. Graber, *The Furnace of Affliction*, 86.
27. Ibid.
28. Rothman, "Perfecting the Prison: United States 1789–1865."
29. Graber, *The Furnace of Affliction*, 129.
30. Rothman, "Perfecting the Prison," 107.
31. Robert Perkinson, *Texas Tough: The Rise of America's Prison Empire* (New York: Metropolitan Books, 2010), 8.
32. The definitive history of this period is Eric Foner, *Reconstruction: America's Unfinished Revolution, 1863–1877* (New York: Harper Perennial Classics, 2002).
33. Perkinson, *Texas Tough*, 86–87.
34. W. E. B. Du Bois, *Black Reconstruction in America: An Essay Toward a History of the Part Which Black Folk Played in the Attempt to Reconstruct Democracy in America, 1860–1880* (1935; repr. New York: Free Press, 1998), 26.
35. Perkinson, *Texas Tough*, 149.
36. Ibid., 128.
37. David M. Oshinsky, *Worse than Slavery: Parchman Farm and the Ordeal of Jim Crow Justice* (New York: Free Press, 1996), 70.
38. Skotnicki, *Religion and the Development of the American Penal System*, 138.
39. Rothman, "Perfecting the Prison," 144–45.
40. Rotman, "The Failure of Reform," 151.
41. Jonathan Simon, "Sanctioning Government: Explaining America's Severity Revolution," *University of Miami Law Review* 56 (2001): 217.
42. Kendrick Oliver, "Attica, Watergate, and the Origin of Evangelical Prison Ministry, 1969–1975," in *American Evangelicals and the 1960s*, ed. Axel R. Schäfer (Madison: University of Wisconsin Press, 2013), 121–38.
43. "Watergate Revisited: The Key Players," *Washington Post*, June 2005, http://www.washingtonpost.com/wp-srv/onpolitics/watergate/charles.html, accessed August 31, 2006.
44. Charles Colson, *Born Again* (London: Hodder and Stoughton, 1976), 62. See also John Perry, *God Behind Bars: The Amazing Story of Prison Fellowship* (Nashville: Thomas Nelson, 2006).
45. See Mario Ottoboni, *Transforming Criminals: An Introduction to the APAC Methodology* (Washington, DC: Prison Fellowship International, 2003); and Ottoboni, *Kill the Criminal, Save the Person: The APAC Methodology* (Washington, DC: Prison Fellowship International, 2000).
46. Ottoboni, *Kill the Criminal, Save the Person.*
47. Ibid.
48. Jonathan Burnside, with Nancy Loucks, Joanna R. Adler, and Gerry Rose, *My Brother's Keeper: Faith-Based Units in Prison* (London: Willan Publishing, 2005), 7.
49. Ibid., 22.
50. Ibid., 27.
51. Ibid., 17.

52. IFI Freedom Initiative, Program Details, https://www.prisonfellowship.org /about/in-prison/, accessed July 11, 2016. See also Tanya Erzen, "Testimonial Politics: The Christian Right's Faith-Based Approach to Marriage and Imprisonment," *American Quarterly* 59, no. 3 (September 2006): 991–1015.

53. Jeanette Hercik, *Navigating a New Horizon: Promising Pathways to Prisoner Reintegration* (Fairfax, VA: Caliber Associates, March 2004); Jeanette Hercik, *Rediscovering Compassion: An Evaluation of Kairos Horizon Communities in Prison* (Fairfax, VA: Caliber Associates, March 2004).

54. Burnside, *My Brother's Keeper*, 35.

55. Ibid., 52–3.

56. Ibid., 53.

57. Ibid., 54.

58. Ibid., 41.

59. Graber, *The Furnace of Affliction*, 125.

60. Skotnicki, *Religion and the Development of the American Penal System*, 57. Quote is on p. 71 in George W. Smith, *A Defense of the System of Solitary Confinement of Prisoners Adopted by the State of Pennsylvania* (Philadelphia: E. G. Dorsey, 1833).

## CHAPTER 3: THE MISSIONARIES

1. *Cast the First Stone*, directed by Jonathan Stack and Nicolas Cuellar, 93 min. (Highest Common Denominator Media Group, 2014). See also Zachary Lazar, "We Forgive Those Who Trespass Against Us," *Brick*, Summer 2014, http://brickmag.com/we-forgive-those-who-trespass-against-us, accessed July 14, 2016.

2. Joe Allen, "Free Gary Tyler: Thirty Years of Injustice," http://www.freegary tyler.com/writings/isr.html, accessed July 11, 2016. Also see Bob Herbert, "A Death in Destrehan," *New York Times* February 1, 2007; Herbert, "Gary Tyler's Lost Decades," *New York Times*, February 5, 2007; and Herbert, "They Beat Gary So Bad," *New York Times*, February 8, 2007.

3. Wilbert Rideau, *In the Place of Justice: A Story of Punishment and Deliverance* (New York: Vintage Books, 2010), provides a comprehensive account of how Angola changed during the forty-four years he was incarcerated there and an insider's account of life inside the prison. Daniel Bergner, *God of the Rodeo: The Quest for Redemption in Louisiana's Angola Prison* (New York: Ballantine Books, 1998), also discusses the history of the prison and the individuals who live there and compete in the yearly rodeo. When I met Burl Cain, he referenced the Bergner book many times as untrue.

4. Tocqueville and Beaumont, *On the Penitentiary System in the United States and Its Application in France*, 87.

5. Foucault, *Discipline and Punish*, 294–95.

6. Russell Nestor, *Ministry from the Inside: How to Have a Successful, Effective Ministry While You Are in Prison or Elsewhere, Christian Inmate Manual* (Baton Rouge, LA: Free at Last Ministries, 2013), 20.

7. Ibid., 117–18.

8. Ibid., 92.

9. Ibid., 194.

10. Ibid., 47.

11. Katy Reckdahl, "Two Inmates Commit Suicide Saturday at Angola; No Connection Seen Between Deaths," *Advocate* (Baton Rouge, LA), April 6, 2016, http://www.theadvocate.com/new_orleans/news/article_7302a4b6–972b–5b13 –9f5d–1010e0d13aa8.html, accessed July 13, 2016.

12. See Prison Policy Initiatives, *Breaking Down Mass Incarceration in the 2010 Census: State-by-State Incarceration Rates by Race/Ethnicity*, May 28, 2014, for a detailed look at all fifty states.

13. Elizabeth Crisp and David Mitchell, "See the List: Jindal Grants Clemency to Personal Butler—a Convicted Killer—Plus 20 Other People," *Advocate*, January 13, 2016, http://www.theadvocate.com/baton_rouge/news/politics/article _fac55ac5–4692–5dc5–bff7–8ca12b75947f.html, accessed September 14, 2016.

14. Sheila Byrd, "Inmates Earn Seminary Degrees While in Prison," Associated Press, May 29, 2009, http://www.dailylocal.com/article/DL/20090529/LIFE01 /305299985; Paul F. South, "Seminary's Georgia Prison Program to Be Dedicated April 17," April 15, 2008, http://d1109452-7815.site.myhosting.com /Publications/News/GAPrison08.html, accessed July 11, 2016; and Massarah Mikati, "The Success of Prison Seminary Programs," *Deseret News* (UT), July 11, 2015.

15. Gordon Russell and Maya Lau, "Fall of Burl Cain: How 1 Last Side Deal Led to Angola Warden Undoing," *Advocate*, December 15, 2015, http://www .theadvocate.com/new_orleans/news/politics/article_b3f58cfe–8d69–57c3–bd53 –2ab81682ab19.html; James Gill, "For Ex-Angola Warden Burl Cain: It Was His Buddies Assessing His Job Performance," *Advocate*, April 3, 2016, http://www .theadvocate.com/new_orleans/opinion/james_gill/article_befabb01–9e4c–5071 –9dce–79d4694c819a.html, accessed July 13, 2016; and Steve Hardy, "No Charges but Eye-Opening Findings from State Police Probe into Angola Payroll Fraud," *Advocate*, April 11, 2016, http://www.theadvocate.com/baton_rouge/news /article_87392451-5bc7-5baf-b7d3-76a734a6e712.html, accessed July 13, 2016.

16. Nestor, *Ministry from the Inside*, 128.

17. Ibid.

## CHAPTER 4: THE CHAPEL

1. Rick Hohl, "Faith and Character Based Initiatives in Corrections: Do They Work?," Florida Department of Law Enforcement website, http://www.fdle .state.fl.us/cms/FCJEI/Programs1/SLP/Documents/Full-Text/Hohl-Rick -paper.aspx, accessed July 14, 2016.

2. Siobhan Morrissey, "Good-Faith Efforts: Despite Their Promise, Faith-Based Prisons in Florida Raise Constitutional Concerns," e-report, *ABA Journal* 3 (2004): 20; Lynn S. Branham, "Go and Sin No More: The Constitutionality of Governmentally Funded Faith-Based Prison Units," *University of Michigan Journal of Law Reform* 37 (2004): 291; and Douglas Roy, "Doin' Time in God's House: Why Faith-Based Rehabilitation Programs Violate the Establishment Clause," *Southern California Law Review* 78 (2005): 795.

3. Frank Cerabino, "Praise the Lawtey Correctional Institution," *Palm Beach Post*, December 25, 2003.

4. Janet Jakobsen and Ann Pellegrini, *Love the Sin: Sexual Regulation and the Limits of Tolerance* (New York: New York University Press, 2003).

5. For information about the rise of mega-churches, see Donald Miller, *Reinventing American Protestantism: Christianity in the New Millennium* (Berkeley: University of California Press, 1997); Steve Ellington, *The Megachurch and the Mainline: Remaking Religious Tradition in the Twenty-First Century* (Chicago: University of Chicago Press, 2007); Jeff Sharlet, "Soldiers of Christ: Inside America's Most Powerful Megachurch," *Harper's Magazine*, May 26, 2005; Jonathon Mahler, "The Soul of the New Exurb," *New York Times Magazine*, March 27, 2005; Malcolm Gladwell, "The Cellular Church," *New Yorker*, September 12, 2005; and Scott Thumma, Dave Travis, and Warren Bird, *Megachurches Today 2005: Summary of Research Findings*, Hartford Institute for Religion Research, Hartford Seminary, February 2006, http://hirr.hartsem.edu/megachurch/megasto-day2005_summaryreport.html.

6. Jack Miles, "Prisoners and Other Strangers," *Beliefnet*, an excerpt from "Ethics of the Neighbor," speech given at the First Natalie Limonick Symposium on Jewish Civilization, UCLA Center for Jewish Studies, May 16, 2004, http://www.beliefnet.com/news/2004/05/prisoners-and-other-strangers.aspx, accessed July 14, 2016.

7. Miles, "Prisoners and Other Strangers."

8. More information about the development of the FBCIs is available on the Department of Corrections website, http://www.dc.state.fl.us/oth/faith/index.html, under the heading "Faith and Character Based Correctional Initiative," accessed August 24, 2007.

9. Java Ahmed, "Governor Champions Faith-Based Prison Initiative PLUS Program Hopes to Stop Repeat Offenders," Louisiana Department of Corrections, September 7, 2005; "Faith Behind Bars Programs Aim to Uplift but Foes Say State Oversteps Bounds," *Atlanta Journal Constitution*, August 22, 2004; David Dishneau, "Prisoners' Rights of Passage," *Washington Times*, January 9, 2005.

10. Rob Boston, "Iowa Inmate Indoctrination Program on Trial," *Americans United for the Separation of Church and State*, December 2005, https://www.au.org/church-state/december-2005-church-state/featured/iowa-inmate-indoctrination-on-trial, accessed September 14, 2016.

11. Burnside, *My Brother's Keeper*, 198.

12. Florida Department of Corrections, *1999-2000 Annual Report: This Year's Highlights and Accomplishments*, http://www.dc.state.fl.us/pub/annual/9900/accomplishments.html, accessed September 16, 2016.

13. Burnside, *My Brother's Keeper*, 204–5.

14. Ibid., 232.

15. Alan Cooperman, "An Infusion of Religious Funds in Florida Prisons: Church Outreach Seeks to Rehabilitate Inmates," *Washington Post*, April 25, 2004.

16. The two articles that referenced this were Laurie Goodstein, "Prisons Purging Books on Faith from Libraries," *New York Times*, September 10, 2007; and Neela Banerjee, "Prisons to Restore Purged Religious Books," *New York Times*, September 27, 2007.

17. Pew Research Center, *Religion in Prisons: A 50-State Survey of Prison Chaplains* (Washington, DC: Pew Forum on Religion and Public Life, March 22, 2012), http://www.pewforum.org/Social-Welfare/prison-chaplains-exec.aspx, accessed July 14, 2016.

18. Winnifred Sullivan, *A Ministry of Presence: Chaplaincy, Spiritual Care, and the Law* (Chicago: University of Chicago Press, 2014).

19. Ibid.

20. Ibid.

21. Tom O'Connor and Jeff B. Duncan, "Religion and Prison Programming: The Role, Impact and Future Direction of Faith in Correctional Systems," *Offender Programs Report* 11, no. 6 (March–April 2008): 86.

22. Ibid., 87.

23. Dusty Hoesly, "Religion, Secularism, and the Chaplaincy," Religious Studies Project, University of California, Santa Barbara, April 24, 2013, published in response to the Religious Studies Project's interview "Ministries of Presence: Chaplains as Priests of the Secular," http://www.religiousstudiesproject.com /2013/04/24/religion-secularism-and-the-chaplaincy-by-dusty-hoesly/.

24. James A. Beckford and Sophie Gilliat, *Religion in Prison: Equal Rites in a Multi-Faith Society* (Cambridge, UK: Cambridge University Press, 1998).

25. Ibid., 6.

26. Jody Sundt and Francis T. Cullen, "The Role of the Contemporary Prison Chaplain," *Prison Journal* 78, no. 3 (August 1998): 271–98.

27. Historian Anne C. Loveland attributes the shift to mainly Protestant conservative chaplains as occurring during the Vietnam War, when many liberal churches opposed to the war supplied fewer chaplains, creating a vacuum filled by conservative churches. This imbalance was exacerbated by regulation revisions in the 1980s that helped create hundreds of new "endorsing agencies" that brought a flood of evangelical chaplains into the military and by the simple fact that evangelical and Pentecostal churches are the fastest growing in the United States. See Anne Loveland, *Change and Conflict in the US Army Chaplain Corps Since 1945*, Legacies of War (Nashville: University of Tennessee Press, 2014).

28. Melissa Phillip, "Justice for All: Federal Ruling Confirms Religious Rights of Muslims in Texas Prisons," *Houston Chronicle*, May 21, 2014.

29. Dane Schiller, "Federal Ruling: Texas Prisons Violating Rights of Muslims," *Houston Chronicle*, May 1, 2014. According to the article: "In states like California, there is no limit on the number of prisoners who can gather for religious matters. The state also has a team of religious professionals at each of its 34 prisons. We have staff in every prison to accommodate five religious denominations," said Bill Sessa, a spokesman for the California Department of Corrections and Rehabilitation, "a Catholic priest, a Protestant chaplain, a Jewish rabbi, a Native American healer and a Muslim imam."

30. Nestor, *Ministry from the Inside*.

31. Sarah Barringer Gordon, *The Spirit of the Law: Religious Voices and the Constitution in Modern America* (Cambridge, MA: Harvard University Press, 2010), chapter 4.

32. Gordon argues in *The Spirit of the Law* that Jim Crow might not have been law in the North, but the racial restrictions on union jobs, neighborhood redlining, and poor schools were only variations on the same racism that had plagued African Americans in the South. W. D. Fard, founder of the Nation of Islam and a mysterious figure who intentionally obscured his origins, taught those he met in Detroit a nobler version of African American history: they were members of the

lost tribe of Shabazz and had been stolen from Mecca by slave traders, and their true scripture was the Qur'an. Fard created a history for them outside of Christianity, the religion of the oppressor, the blue-eyed devil. To those living in the slums of Detroit, his assurance that Allah would return them to paradise was deeply compelling. Not only did the Nation provide a sacred history for struggling people, but its rules differentiated them from the majority and provided a strong and proud identity. Fard's teachings drew upon earlier religious traditions like the Moorish Science Temple of America and Marcus Garvey's movement, which emphasized community solidarity and pride.

33. Gordon writes that Fard disappeared, again, under mysterious circumstances. Elijah Muhammad, born Robert Poole, believed Fard was Allah calling him to lead the black nation back to its authentic faith, Islam. Muhammad had been raised as a Southern Baptist, and he assimilated some of that theology into the Nation's beliefs. He placed human history into dispensations and claimed the world had been under the rule of Satan for six thousand years, and now separation must come between God's people and the devil. He urged his followers to resist integration.

34. Malcolm X with Alex Haley, *The Autobiography of Malcolm X* (New York: Grove Press, 1965), 193.

35. Gordon, *The Spirit of the Law*, 96.

36. Ibid., 98.

37. Malcolm X, *The Autobiography of Malcolm X*, 195.

38. Gordon, *The Spirit of the Law*, 119.

39. Ruffin v. Commonwealth, 62 Va 790, 793 1871, in ibid., 113.

40. Gordon, *The Spirit of the Law*, 122.

41. Heather Thompson, *Blood in the Water: The Attica Prison Uprising of 1971 and Its Legacy* (New York: Pantheon, 2016).

42. Clear, "The Value of Religion in Prisons," 66.

43. Ibid., 70.

44. Chuck Colson, "Allah Blues: The Wrong Kind of Prison Fellowship," *Breakpoint Commentary*, October 18, 2005.

45. Pew Research Center, *Religion in Prisons*.

46. Winnifred Sullivan, *Prison Religion: Faith-Based Reform and the Constitution* (Princeton, NJ: Princeton University Press, 2009).

47. Nathaniel Odle, "Privilege Through Prayer: Examining Bible-Based Prison Rehabilitation Programs Under the Establishment Clause," *Texas Journal on Civil Liberties and Civil Rights* (Spring 2007).

48. Rob Boston, "Victory in Iowa," Americans United for the Separation of Church and State, http://www.au.org/site/News2?page=NewsArticle&id=8313&abbr=cs_, accessed August 23, 2006.

49. Sullivan, *Prison Religion*.

50. Mark Early, "A Troubling Verdict," *Breakpoint Commentaries*, June 6, 2006, http://www.breakpoint.org/bpcommentaries/entry/13/13519, accessed September 14, 2016.

51. Jenny Phillips, dir., *The Dhamma Brothers*, documentary film, 2009, http://www.dhammabrothers.com/Project.htm.

52. Emily Chiang, "The *Turner* Standard: Balancing Constitutional Rights & Governmental Interests in Prison," *University of California Irvine Law Forum Journal* 5 (Fall 2007): 1–25.

53. Enrique Armijo, "Belief Behind Bars: Religious Freedom in Prison, RLUIPA, and the Establishment Clause," *New England Journal on Crime and Civil Confinement* 31 (2005): 297.

54. See Winnifred Fallers Sullivan, *The Impossibility of Religious Freedom* (Princeton, NJ: Princeton University Press, 2007).

55. "Florida Prisons Are in a State of Perpetual Crisis," editorial, *Times Union* (Jacksonville), March 30, 2015, http://jacksonville.com/opinion/editorials/2015–03 –30/story/florida-prisons-are-state-perpetual-crisis.

## CHAPTER 5: THE FATHER AND SON AND THE LIMITED POWER OF FORGIVENESS

1. Gorringe, *God's Just Vengeance*, 7.

2. Ibid., 12.

3. Mark Lewis Taylor, *The Executed God: The Way of the Cross in Lockdown America* (Minneapolis: Fortress Press, 2001), 97–98.

4. Ted Grimsrud, "The Logic of Retribution and Its Consequences," *Peace Theology*, https://peacetheology.net/restorative-justice/3-the-logic-of-retribution -and-its-consequences/, accessed July 17, 2016.

5. Gorringe, *God's Just Vengeance*, 27.

6. Ibid., 240.

7. Taylor, *The Executed God*, 97–98.

8. Rene Girard, *Violence and the Sacred* (Baltimore: Johns Hopkins University Press, 1979); and Gorringe, *God's Just Vengeance*, 26.

9. Gorringe, *God's Just Vengeance*, 214.

10. Christopher Marshall, *Beyond Retribution: A New Testament Vision for Justice, Crime and Punishment* (Grand Rapids, MI: William B. Eerdmans, 2001), 264.

11. Ibid., 267. See also James Samuel Logan, *Good Punishment? Christian Moral Practice and US Imprisonment* (Grand Rapids, MI: William B. Eerdmans, 2008).

12. Dennis Pierce, *Prison Ministry: Hope Behind the Wall* (New York: Haworth Pastoral Press, 2006).

13. Ibid., 77.

14. Ibid., 88.

15. Ibid., 125.

16. Ibid., 127.

17. Ibid., 134.

18. Laura McTighe, *"Why Are You Here?" Challenging the Prison System, Challenging Ourselves*, pamphlet, Books Through Bars, Contexts Collection.

19. Bridges to Life was inspired by the Prison Fellowship Ministry's Sycamore Tree Project, which offers a biblical model of transformation to deal with sin and its consequences, offenders, and victims.

20. Robert A. Ferguson, *Inferno: An Anatomy of American Punishment* (Cambridge, MA: Harvard University Press, 2014), 82.

21. Ibid., 84.

22. Mark Obbie, "These People Need to Know What We Have Gone Through," *Slate*, July 19, 2015.

23. Sujatha Baliga spoke about how restorative justice was used in this homicide case in a pre-plea context on *Talk of the Nation*, NPR, July 28, 2011, www.npr .org/2011/07/28/138791912/victims-confront-offenders-face-to-face; Howard Zehr, *The Little Book of Restorative Justice* (Intercourse, PA: Good Books,

2002); Howard Zehr, *Changing Lenses: A New Focus for Crime and Justice*, 3rd ed. (Scottdale, PA: Herald Press, 2005).

24. Lorraine S. Amstutz, *The Little Book of Victim Offender Conferencing: Bringing Victims and Offenders Together in Dialogue* (Intercourse, PA: Good Books, 2009); and Carolyn Boyes-Watson, *Peacemaking Circles & Urban Youth: Bringing Justice Home* (St. Paul, MN: Living Justice Press, 2008).

25. Susan Herman, *Parallel Justice for Victims of Crime* (Washington, DC: National Center for Victims of Crime, 2010); Gerry Johnstone, ed., *A Restorative Justice Reader: Texts, Sources, Context* (London: Willan Publishing, 2003).

26. Mark Yantzi, *Sexual Offending and Restoration* (Scottdale, PA: Herald Press, 2008).

27. Some data about the effectiveness of restorative processes can be found in Lawrence W. Sherman and Heather Strang, *Restorative Justice: The Evidence* (London: Smith Institute, 2007), http://www.iirp.edu/pdf/RJ_full_report.pdf.

28. Barb Toews, *The Little Book of Restorative Justice for People in Prison: Rebuilding the Web of Relationships* (Intercourse, PA: Good Books, 2006).

29. Mark Obbie, "Why Victims Face the Criminals Who Hurt Them," *Pacific Standard*, December 20, 2010.

30. M. Gunderson and S. Pessinguia, "Undefinable Relationship," TEDx, Washington Corrections Center for Women, posted April 8, 2015, https://www.youtube.com/watch?v=2ZtjkE0-5tA&index=11&list=PLUOQSTnnJJfusA_-uTT6l-zE6xqTbf7uw.

31. This article takes a look at the role restorative justice can play in homicide cases as a part of the plea negotiation process: Paul Tullis, "Can Forgiveness Play a Role in Restorative Justice?," *New York Times Magazine*, January 4, 2013. This *Today* episode discusses how the family in the above-mentioned case chose restorative justice: www.today.com/video/today/50384919%20-%2050384919%2350384919.January 7, 2013.

32. Tullis, "Can Forgiveness Play a Role in Restorative Justice?"

## CHAPTER 6: MOTHERS AND SERVANTS IN THE SAVIOR PRISON

1. Julie Ajinkya, "Rethinking How to Address the Growing Female Prison Population," Center for American Progress, Friday, March 8, 2013, https://www.americanprogress.org/issues/women/news/2013/03/08/55787/rethinking-how-to-address-the-growing-female-prison-population/, accessed September 14, 2016.

2. Beth E. Richie, *Arrested Justice: Black Women, Violence and America's Prison Nation* (New York: New York University Press, 2012), 51–52; and Kathryn Watterson, *Women in Prison: Inside the Concrete Womb*, rev. ed. (Boston: Northeastern University Press, 1996).

3. Lawrence A. Greenfeld and Tracy L. Snell, *Women Offenders: Bureau of Justice Statistics Special Report* (Washington, DC: US Department of Justice, 1999), http://www.ojp.usdoj.gov/bjs/pub//wo.pdf, accessed June 12, 2008.

4. There are several books that include essays by and perspectives of women from inside prison. Megan Sweeney, ed., *The Story Within Us: Women Prisoners Reflect on Reading* (Urbana: University of Illinois Press, 2012), has long narratives that address many of these issues. Other examples include Robin Levi and Ayelet

Waldman, eds., *Inside This Place, Not of It: Narratives from Women's Prisons* (San Francisco: McSweeney's Books, 2011), and Rickie Solinger, Paula C. Johnson, Martha L. Raimon, Tina Reynolds, and Ruby Tapia, eds., *Interrupted Life: Experiences of Incarcerated Women in the United States* (Berkeley: University of California Press, 2010). Other memoirs of life in prison include Piper Kerman, *Orange Is the New Black: My Year in a Women's Prison* (New York: Spiegel and Grau, 2011), and Erin George, *A Woman Doing Life: Notes from a Prison for Women* (New York: Oxford University Press, 2010). George is serving a life sentence in Virginia. For issues about conducting ethnography with women, see Beth Richie, "Feminist Ethnographies of Women in Prison," *Feminist Studies* 30, no. 2 (Summer 2004): 438–50, and Jennifer Gonnerman, *Life on the Outside: The Prison Odyssey of Elaine Bartlett* (New York: Farrar, Straus and Giroux, 2004).

5. Arlene F. Lee, Philip M. Genty, and Mimi Laver, "The Impact of the Adoption and Safe Families Act on Children of Incarcerated Parents," in Solinger et al., *Interrupted Life*.

6. In *Breaking Women: Gender, Race and the New Politics of Imprisonment* (New York: New York University Press, 2013), Jill McCorkel, although not talking about faith-based groups, writes that with private groups doing the work of the state, there is a profit logic to habilation, as offenders cannot be cured and, thus, they are always needed in the prison. Lynne A. Haney, *Offending Women: Power, Punishment and the Regulation of Desire* (Berkeley: University of California Press, 2010).

7. Nicole Hahn Rafter, *Partial Justice: Women, Prisons and Social Control*, 2nd ed. (New Brunswick, NJ: Transaction Publishers, 2004), 149.

8. McCorkel, *Breaking Women*, 43.

9. Cristina Rathbone, *A World Apart: Women, Prison, and Life Behind Bars* (New York: Random House, 2005).

10. McCorkel, *Breaking Women*, 42.

11. See Kathy Peiss, *Cheap Amusements: Working Women and Leisure in Turn-of-the-Century New York* (Philadelphia: Temple University Press, 1986).

12. Angela Davis, *Are Prisons Obsolete?* (New York: Seven Stories Press, 2003).

13. McCorkel, *Breaking Women*, 78–80.

14. Victoria Law, *Resistance Behind Bars: The Struggles of Incarcerated Women* (Oakland, CA: PM Press, 2009), 45. Law discusses how a 2000 Bureau of Justice report found that 54 percent of mothers in state prisons had never been visited by their children.

15. Marie Griffith, *God's Daughters: Evangelical Women and the Power of Submission* (Berkeley: University of California Press, 1997), and Brenda Brasher, *Godly Women: Fundamentalism and Female Power* (New Brunswick, NJ: Rutgers University Press, 1998).

16. Christopher J. Mumola, *Bureau of Justice Statistics Special Report: Incarcerated Parents and Their Children* (Washington, DC: US Department of Justice, August 2000).

17. Brandy Bauer, Jamie Hart, Anne Hopewell, and Naomi Tein, *Research and Practice Symposium on Marriage and Incarceration: A Meeting Summary* (Washington, DC: US Department of Health and Human Services, Office of the Assistant Secretary for Planning and Evaluation, January 2007).

18. Sandra Enos, *Mothering from the Inside: Parenting in a Women's Prison* (Albany, New York: State University of New York Press, 2001). For a global perspective on this issue, see Gordana Elijdupovic and Rebecca Jaremko Bromwich, *Incarcerated Mothers: Oppression and Resistance* (Ontario: Demeter Press, 2013).

19. Burnside, *My Brother's Keeper,* 198.

20. Pat Nolan, "Fathering from Prison," *Justice Fellowship Newsletter,* http://www .justicefellowship.org/news-and-events/15961-fathering-from-prison, accessed June 20, 2011.

21. Barack Obama, "Obama's Speech on Fatherhood," *RealClearPolitics,* June 2008, http://www.realclearpolitics.com/articles/2008/06/obamas_speech_on _fatherhood.html.

22. "Spotlight on Dads Back in Touch: Reconnecting with Your Children," National Responsible Fatherhood Clearinghouse (NRFC), October 2009.

23. Anna Gavanas, "Domesticating Masculinity and Masculinizing Domesticity in Contemporary U.S. Fatherhood Politics," *Social Politics: International Studies in Gender, State and Society* 11, no. 2 (Summer 2004): 247–66.

24. Anne M. Nurse, *Fatherhood Arrested: Parenting from Within the Juvenile Justice System* (Nashville, TN: Vanderbilt University Press, 2002).

25. Melanie Heath "State of Our Unions: Marriage Promotion and the Contested Power of Heterosexuality," *Gender & Society* 23 (2009): 27.

26. Jacinta Bronte-Tinkew, Mary Burkhauser, Kassim Mbwana, Allison Metz, and Ashleigh Collins, *Elements of Promising Practice in Programs Serving Fathers Involved in the Criminal Justice System* (Washington, DC: US Department of Health and Human Services, May 2008); Jacinta Bronte-Tinkew, Mary Burkhauser, Sara Ericson, and Allison Metz, "What Works in Programs Serving Fathers Involved in the Criminal Justice System? Lessons from Evidence-Based Evaluations," NRFC Practice Brief, September 2008.

27. Kevin Lewis O'Neill, *City of God* (Oakland: University of California Press, 2010).

28. Megan Sweeney, *Reading Is My Window: Books and the Art of Reading in Women's Prisons* (Chapel Hill: University of North Carolina, 2010), 209.

29. Jennifer Sullivan, "$1M Awarded to 5 Washington Inmates in Sex-Assault Lawsuit," *Seattle Times,* June 12, 2009, http://www.seattletimes.com/seattle-news /1m-awarded-to-5-washington-inmates-in-sex-assault-lawsuit/.

30. "Organizational Charter of 'The Women's Village,'" Washington Corrections Center for Women, September 2010.

## CHAPTER 7: THE REFORMERS

1. Jim Liske, "The Heart of the Matter," *Prison Fellowship Ministries Newsletter,* August 30, 2012.

2. Byron R. Johnson with R. B. Tompkins and D. Webb, *Objective Hope: Assessing the Effectiveness of Faith-Based Organizations: A Review of the Literature* (Philadelphia: University of Pennsylvania Center for Research on Religion and Urban Civil Society, 2002; Byron R. Johnson and D. B. Larson, *The InnerChange Freedom Initiative: A Preliminary Evaluation of a Faith-Based Prison Program* (Philadelphia: University of Pennsylvania Center for Research on Religion and Urban Civil Society, 2003).

3. Byron Johnson, *More God, Less Crime: Why Faith Matters and How It Could Matter More* (West Conshohocken, PA: Templeton, 2011), 158–59.

4. Ibid., 164.

5. Johnson recently completed a new study on Angola's seminary claiming that the seminary creates identity change and positive benefits for men in the program. Michael Hallett, Joshua Hays, Byron R. Johnson, Sung Joon Jang, Grant Duwe, *The Angola Prison Seminary: Effects of Faith-Based Ministry on Identity Transformation, Desistance, and Rehabilitation* (New York: Routledge, 2016).

6. Mark A. R. Kleiman discredited the Pennsylvania study on InnerChange, claiming that it used faulty methodology. See "Faith-Based Fudging: How a Bush-Promoted Conservative Prison Program Fakes Success by Massaging Data," *Slate*, August 5, 2003, http://www.slate.com/id/2086617/.

7. Ibid.

8. "Study Hints at Efficacy of Florida's Faith-Based Prisons," Urban Institute, October 19, 2007, http://www.urban.org/publications/901122.html, accessed July 17, 2016.

9. Alexander Volokh, "Do Faith-Based Prisons Work?," *Alabama Law Review* 63 (2011): 1–43. See also his 2014 series in the *Washington Post* based on this article: "What If Faith-Based Prisons Just Attract Better Prisoners?," *Washington Post*, February 11, 2014; "Faith-Based Prisons: Ideas for More Valid Evaluations," *Washington Post*, February 12, 2014; "Faith-Based Prisons: The Valid Studies," *Washington Post*, February 13, 2014; and "Is There Any Way Forward for Faith-Based Prisons?," *Washington Post*, February 14, 2014.

10. Volokh, "Is There Any Way Forward for Faith-Based Prisons?"

11. Kent R. Kerley, Todd L. Matthews, and Troy C. Blanchard, "Religiosity, Religious Participation and Negative Prison Behaviors," *Journal for the Scientific Study of Religion* 44 (November 11, 2005).

12. Center for Research on Religion and Civil Society (CRRUCS), *Objective Hope: Assessing the Effectiveness of Faith-Based Organizations: A Review of the Literature*, 2002.

13. Volokh, "Is There Any Way Forward for Faith-Based Prisons?"

14. Loïc Wacquant, "The Curious Eclipse of Prison Ethnography in the Age of Mass Incarceration," *Ethnography* 3, no. 4 (2002): 371–97, 381. See also Wacquant, *Punishing the Poor: The Neoliberal Government of Social Insecurity* (Durham, NC: Duke University Press, 2009).

15. Pat Nolan, "Supreme Court Demands End to Prison Overcrowding," *Prison Fellowship*, June 9, 2011, https://www.prisonfellowship.org/2011/06/supreme-court-demands-end-to-prison-overcrowding/, accessed July 17, 2016.

16. Ibid.

17. Samantha M. Shapiro, "Charles Colson's Jails for Jesus," *Mother Jones*, November/December 2003.

18. Right on Crime, "The Conservative Approach to Criminal Justice, Fighting Crime, Supporting Victims, and Protecting Taxpayers," http://rightoncrime.com/.

19. Newt Gingrich and Pat Nolan, "Prison Reform: A Smart Way for States to Save Money and Lives," *Washington Post*, January 7, 2011.

20. Public Safety Performance Project, *Public Opinion on Sentencing and Corrections Policy in America* (Washington, DC: Pew Charitable Trusts, March 30, 2012),

http://www.pewtrusts.org/en/research-and-analysis/analysis/2012/03/30
/public-opinion-on-sentencing-and-corrections-policy-in-america.

21. Christian Henrichson and Ruth Delaney, *The Price of Prisons: What Incarceration Costs Taxpayers* (New York: Vera Institute of Justice, 2012), https://www.vera .org/publications/the-price-of-prisons-what-incarceration-costs-taxpayers.

22. Carl Hulse, "Unlikely Cause Unites the Left and the Right: Justice Reform," *New York Times*, February 18, 2015, http://www.nytimes.com/2015/02/19 /us/politics/unlikely-cause-unites-the-left-and-the-right-justice-reform .html?_r=0.

23. "About the Coalition for Public Safety," Coalition for Public Safety website, http://www.coalitionforpublicsafety.org/about/, accessed July 17, 2016.

24. Leon Neyfakh, "A Koch and a Smile," *Slate*, February 19, 2015, http://www .slate.com/articles/news_and_politics/crime/2015/02/coalition_for_public _safety_do_republicans_and_democrats_really_see_eye.html.

25. Alex Altman, "Will Congress Reform the Criminal Justice System?," NPR, March 26, 2015.

26. Jesse McKinley, "Pat Robertson Says Marijuana Use Should Be Legal," *New York Times*, March 7, 2012.

27. Shapiro, "Jails for Jesus."

28. Reid Wilson, "Tough Texas Gets Results by Going Softer on Crime," *Washington Post*, November 27, 2014; and Marc Levin, "Texas No Longer a Repeat Offender on Prisons," *Washington Post*, February 21, 2008.

29. Wilson, "Tough Texas Gets Results by Going Softer on Crime."

30. James Ridgeway, "Pat Nolan's Evangelical Prison Reform," *Solitary Watch*, August 8, 2013, http://solitarywatch.com/2013/08/08/draft-pat-nolans-evangelical -prison-reform/.

31. David Dagan and Steven Teles, "The Conservative War on Prisons," *Washington Monthly*, November/December 2012.

32. Lisa Guenther, *Solitary Confinement: Social Death and Its Afterlives* (Minneapolis: Minnesota University Press, 2013).

33. David Dagan and Steven Teles, "Locked In? Conservative Reform and the Future of Mass Incarceration," *Annals of the American Academy of Political and Social Science* 651 (January 2014): 1266–76; and Steven Teles and David Dagan, *Prison Break: Why Conservatives Turned Against Mass Incarceration* (New York: Oxford University Press, 2016).

34. McCorkel, *Breaking Women*.

35. Mark A. R. Kleiman, Angela Hawken, and Ross Halperin, "We Don't Need to Keep Criminals in Prison to Punish Them," *Vox*, March 18, 2015, http://www.vox .com/2015/3/18/8226957/prison-reform-graduated-reentry, accessed July 17, 2016.

36. Ibid.

37. Governor's Advisory Task Force on Faith-Based Community Service Groups, *Faith in Action: A New Vision for Church-State Cooperation in Texas*, State of Texas, December 1996, http://www.scribd.com/doc/249455442/Texas-Faith-in -Action-1996-pdf, accessed July 17, 2016.

38. As governor of Texas, George W. Bush signed into law the ability for faith-based organizations to provide services for the state, which included Prison Fellowship. See also Jo Renee Formicola, Mary C. Segers, and Paul Weber,

*Faith-Based Initiatives and the Bush Administration: The Good, the Bad and the Ugly* (Lanham, MD: Rowman & Littlefield, 2003).

39. Esther Kaplan, "Follow the Money," *Nation*, November 1, 2004, 1.

40. Ibid.

41. Barack Obama, First Inaugural Address, January 2009.

42. Naomi Murakawa, *The First Civil Right: How Liberals Built Prison America* (New York: Oxford University Press, 2014), 260.

43. National Research Council of the National Academies, *The Growth of Incarceration in the United States: Exploring Causes and Consequences* (Washington, DC: National Academies Press, 2014).

44. Jonathan Simon, *Governing Through Crime: How the War on Crime Transformed American Democracy and Created a Culture of Fear* (New York: Oxford University Press, 2007). In de-unionized workplaces, Simon finds that blue- and white-collar employees alike are subject to more surveillance, more restrictions on behavior (both on and off the clock), and more legalistic discipline than in the past. He regrets that, in schools, music and art classes have given way to metal detectors and locker searches. Even the family, he argues, has become "a nexus of crime." On one hand, family members are regarded as potential criminals, a partial consequence of feminist campaigns against domestic violence. On the other, well-heeled parents spend heavily to fortify their homes against external threats, purchasing intruder-alert systems, nanny cams, and, if their teens stray, home drug-testing kits. As much as the five thousand prisons that now punctuate the American landscape, gated communities and battleship SUVs symbolize the birth of a fearful nation. As white conservatives surrendered on integration, they insisted on getting much tougher on crime. Simon argues, "Governing through crime does not, and I believe, cannot make us more secure."

45. Robert Perkinson, "Guarded Hope: Lessons from the History of the Prison Boom," *Boston Review*, July 14, 2008.

46. Michelle Alexander, *The New Jim Crow: Mass Incarceration in the Age of Colorblindness* (New York: New Press, 2012).

47. Marie Gottschalk, *Caught: The Prison State and the Lockdown of American Politics* (Princeton, NJ: Princeton University Press, 2015); and Gottschalk, "It's Not Just the Drug War," *Jacobin*, March 3, 2015, https://www.jacobinmag.com/2015/03/mass-incarceration-war-on-drugs/, accessed July 16, 2016.

48. See Anne Hendrixson, "Super-Predator Meets Teenage Mom: Exploding the Myth of the Out-of-Control Youth," in *Policing the National Body: Race, Gender, and Criminalization*, ed. Jael Silliman and Anannya Bhattacharjee (Boston: South End Press, 2002); Khalil Gibran Muhammad, *The Condemnation of Blackness: Race, Crime, and the Making of Modern Urban America* (Cambridge, MA: Harvard University Press, 2010); and Bruce Western, *Punishment and Inequality in America* (New York: Russell Sage Foundation, 2007).

49. Simon, *Governing Through Crime*.

50. Ferguson, *Inferno*, 175.

51. Gottschalk, "It's Not Just the Drug War."

52. Bureau of Justice Statistics, "Prison Population Declined in 26 States During 2011," press release, December 17, 2012, http://www.bjs.gov/content/pub/press/p11pr.cfm, accessed July 17, 2016.

53. Kay Whitlock and Nancy A. Heitzeg, "'Bipartisan' Criminal Justice Reform: A Misguided Merger," *Truthout*, February 24, 2015, http://www.truth-out.org /news/item/29272-bipartisan-criminal-justice-reform-pushes-privatization -erases-root-causes.

54. Ruth Wilson Gilmore, *Golden Gulag: Prisons, Surplus, Crisis, and Opposition in Globalizing California* (Berkeley: University of California Press, 2007), 26.

55. Ruth Wilson Gilmore, "The Worrying State of the Anti-Prison Movement," in *Social Justice: A Journal of Crime, Conflict, and World Order* (February 23, 2015).

56. Interview with Benjamin Jealous and Grover Norquist, *NewsHour*, PBS, April 7, 2011, http://www.pbs.org/newshour/bb/social_issues-jan-june11-incarceration _04–07/.

57. Gottschalk, "It's Not Just the Drug War."

58. "Second Chance Act," Bureau of Justice Affairs and the Council of State Governments, http://csgjusticecenter.org/nrrc/projects/second-chance-act/.

59. Christopher Ingraham, "The States That Spend More Money on Prisoners Than College Students," *Washington Post*, *Wonk* blog, July 7, 2016; "State and Local Expenditures on Corrections and Education: A Brief from the US Department of Education," Policy and Program Studies Service, July 2016, http:// www2.ed.gov/rschstat/eval/other/expenditures-corrections-education/brief .pdf, accessed July 17, 2016.

60. Interview with Jealous and Norquist.

## EPILOGUE

1. William Wells Brown, *Narrative of William W. Brown, a Fugitive Slave*, 2nd ed. (Boston: Anti-Slavery Office, 1848).

2. Christopher Leslie Brown, *Moral Capital: Foundations of British Abolitionism* (Chapel Hill: University of North Carolina Press, 2006).

3. A. Raboteau, "African Americans, Exodus and the New Israel," in *Religion and American Culture*, ed. D. G. Hackett (New York: Routledge, 1995), 81.

4. John Wesley, *Thoughts Upon Slavery: A Collection of Religious Tracts* (Philadelphia: Joseph Crukshank, 1778), 28, https://archive.org/details/thoughtsuponslav00wesl.

5. Olaudah Equiano, *The Interesting Narrative of the Life of Olaudah Equiano, or Gustavus Vassa, the African. Written by Himself* (London: Privately printed by the author, 1789), available at *Documenting the American South*.

6. Christine Bolt and Seymour Drescher, eds., *Anti-Slavery, Religion, and Reform: Essays in Memory of Roger Anstey* (Folkestone, UK: W. Dawson, 1980), 47.

7. Foucault, *Discipline and Punish*, 120–21.

8. Judith Butler, *Precarious Life: The Powers of Mourning and Violence* (New York: Verso, 2004). Emphasis in the original.

9. American Friends Service Committee, "Addressing Prisons," http://www.afsc .org/key-issues/issue/addressing-prisons, accessed July 16, 2016.

10. Alfredo Garcia, "The New Jim Crow: Churches Respond to Mass Incarceration," *Religion and Politics*, August 13, 2013.

11. Benjamin Geselowitz, "The US Prison System in Comparative Perspective: The Scandinavian Cases," https://www.incarceratedvoices.com/the-u-s-prison -system-in-comparative-perspective-the-scandinavian-cases/, accessed July 16, 2016.

12. Doran Larson, "Why Scandinavian Prisons Are Superior," *Atlantic*, September 14, 2013, http://www.theatlantic.com/international/archive/2013/09/why-scandinavian-prisons-are-superior/279949/.

13. Gorringe, *God's Just Vengeance*, 259.

14. Ibid., 270.

15. Angela Y. Davis, *Are Prisons Obsolete?* (New York: Seven Stories Press, 2003). Other groups have been making this argument, such as Critical Resistance, INCITE!, Prison Culture Blog, Project NIA, Detention Watch Network, Streetwise and Safe, Center for Constitutional Rights, Prison Policy Initiative, Prison Legal News, The Real Cost of Prisons Project, Juvenile Justice Project of Louisiana, Transformative Justice Law Project of Illinois, Solitary Watch, Sylvia Rivera Law Project, and American Friends Service Committee (AFSC).

16. Stefano Harney and Fred Moten, *The Undercommons: Fugitive Planning & Black Study* (Wivenhoe, UK: Autonomedia/Minor Compositions, 2013).

17. José Muñoz, *Cruising Utopia: The Then and There of Queer Futurity* (New York: New York University Press, 2009), 1.

# INDEX